SENATOR JOSIAH WILLIAM BAILEY
OF NORTH CAROLINA

Compliments of
B. Stenberg
Staff Photographer
Worcester Evening Post

SENATOR JOSIAH WILLIAM BAILEY
OF NORTH CAROLINA

A political biography

John Robert Moore

Duke University Press
Durham, N.C.
1968

PRINTED IN THE UNITED STATES OF
AMERICA BY KINGSPORT PRESS, INC.

PREFACE

THIS BOOK represents an attempt to understand and define the political career of Josiah William Bailey (1873–1946). Bailey was an influential spokesman of liberal reforms in North Carolina between 1895 and 1930 and an outstanding leader of southern conservatives in the United States Senate from 1931 to 1946. In his half-century of public service to his state and nation, he was subsequently labeled a dangerous radical, a progressive liberal, a constitutional conservative, and a reactionary obstructionist. The labels were nurtured by friend and foe as each viewed Bailey's course through partisan eyes. He was in fact a Wilsonian liberal in the Roosevelt era. He brought to consideration of state and national problems an eighteenth- and nineteenth-century liberal theory of economics and politics that served well during the prosperous first three decades of the twentieth century but which limited his vision and response during the successive crises of the Great Depression and the Second World War.

In analyzing Bailey's career, the most meaningful results are derived from probing the relationship between his political philosophy and his practice of politics. Hopefully, this effort to understand conservative political leadership in a democratic society will illuminate current as well as past difficulties in solving social and economic problems. Bailey represented a significant group in the Congress and the nation whose sincerity, diligence, and intelligence (then and today) are unquestioned, but whose recognition of and approach to national issues often prove inadequate. This study attempts to separate the Bailey legend from the fact in the perspective of history and to determine, by applying the test of consistency to his thought and record, whether there was any pattern in Bailey's leadership. Readers of this book in manuscript have invariably observed either in praise or criticism that it is a "sympathetic" biography. This was not my intention. Yet it is sympathetic in that I have not found it necessary to disparage Bailey's ideals, motivations, and actions in the process of criticizing them.

This biography is based almost exclusively upon research in the sources, particularly the vast and heretofore largely unexplored Josiah William Bailey Papers in the Duke University Library. The half-million pieces in this unedited collection were heavily relied on in order that Bailey's career might be portrayed as far as possible in his own words. Secondary sources are cited only where there is special indebtedness.

I acknowledge with pleasure the assistance received from many individuals in the completion of this study. I am especially grateful to Professor Richard L. Watson, Jr., of Duke University, whose unfailing counsel has benefited me at every point. My colleagues at the University of Southwestern Louisiana, Professors Amos E. Simpson, W. Magruder Drake, and Paul T. Nolan, offered advice and encouragement that hastened completion. I am also deeply indebted to the Bailey family, especially Mrs. Josiah W. Bailey and Mr. James H. Pou Bailey, for their frank and unrestrained comments. Bailey's secretaries, Mr. A. Hand James and Mr. Thad S. Page, assisted by permitting me to use manuscripts in their personal collections as well as by revealing many intimate details concerning Bailey which were not a matter of public record. Also to Miss Mattie Russell of the Duke Manuscript Department and Miss Florence Blakely of the Duke Reference Department I extend appreciation for their most willing aid.

J. R. M.

CONTENTS

ILLUSTRATIONS

SENATOR JOSIAH WILLIAM BAILEY
OF NORTH CAROLINA

CHAPTER ONE

POLITICAL APPRENTICESHIP

"I KNOW very well that I shall be in Washington just about what I have been in North Carolina," confided Josiah William Bailey on beginning his fifteen years of service as United States senator in 1931.[1] At the age of fifty-eight he entered the Senate with many misgivings and few illusions that he would be changed by his new environment. He described himself correctly as a veteran politician with a propensity for battle that thrust him, unwisely perhaps, into repeated struggles. A man of studied dignity, he seemed proud and haughty to many of his contemporaries. Grave in expression, his angular features displayed a prominent nose, a lantern jaw, and greying temples. He dressed with austere, almost Edwardian, taste that favored dark, carefully buttoned suits, somber ties, and high, starched collars at which he often tugged when speaking. Seemingly cold and aloof, his manner and appearance hinted at the Baptist minister he once had considered becoming. Deeply religious but not strait-laced, he enjoyed a before-dinner drink, smoked two packs of cigarettes a day for forty years, and frequently played poker with friends. He seldom smiled or revealed personal emotion, but recounted stories incorrigibly and dearly loved a good pun. His speeches nearly always included biblical phrases expressing an abiding sense of moral indignation, which quickly earned him in the Senate the not so affectionate sobriquet of "Holy Joe" Bailey.

Recognized as North Carolina's finest orator, Bailey found his element on the Senate floor. His artfully couched language, thoughtful argumentation, and fine dramatic sense invariably drew appreciative attention even from word-weary colleagues. Describing him as the characteristic southerner, William S. White captured the mood created by Bailey:

1. Bailey to George W. Connor, November 16, 1931, *Josiah William Bailey Papers*, Manuscript Department, Duke University Library, Durham, N.C.

He will begin softly, with wry self-deprecation, almost with an embarrassment of humility. He will say that he has, of course, only a very few words; all too well is he aware that it is not for *him* to intrude long upon the deliberations of his betters here. He will find to have been very sound, indeed, nearly all that has been said before, by foe and friend.

And then, as he goes along and the clock hands slip by, the tone, at first imperceptibly, will change. The voice toward which men had been leaning more or less intently, so low and calm was it, will begin to rise in volume and to fall in tone. And at the end it has become a commanding pipe organ, rolling and thundering out before the wicked, the foolish, and the insensitive.[2]

His oratorical power coupled with a sharp, incisive intellect led his enemies to suspect him of demagogic inclinations, but he rarely sought applause through his speaking abilities. Although he could exchange pleasantries and shake hands when necessary with the typical politician's facility, he possessed a native antipathy to effusive men and to the custom of "backslapping." So strongly did he dislike the press of crowds that he instructed his secretaries always to direct him to a back exit after public speaking engagements. The contrast between his commanding presence on the speaker's platform and his reclusive social personality sprang in part from early self-discipline. During his twenties, he taught for seven years at a Monday night Baptist Young People's Union, benefiting from continuous presentation of serious topics. He "walked every afternoon in the woods, trying to learn to speak in public, meditating on my themes and practicing my voice and expressions." Such exercise took its toll, however, for Bailey admitted that "a fellow who develops the speaking faculty under these conditions is not likely to get over it. My friends sometimes say I am unduly solemn."[3]

Although generous and warmhearted, Bailey seldom overcame an innate reluctance to convey emotional feeling. At the age of forty-two he married Edith Pou, some twenty years his junior and daughter of one of the most influential lawyers in North Carolina. They had five children: James Hinton Pou, Annie Elizabeth, Josiah William, Jr.,

2. William S. White, Citadel, *The Story of the U.S. Senate* (New York, 1956), p. 73. White refers specifically to Senators Josiah W. Bailey of North Carolina and Walter F. George of Georgia.
3. Bailey to R. F. Beasley, December 11, 1936, *Bailey Papers.*

Edith Pou, and Sallie. Bailey and his wife, whom he addressed in courtly fashion as "Miss Edith," had a delightful relationship with few serious disagreements, although each would occasionally exasperate the other. Since Bailey never learned to drive a car, he often attempted to persuade "Miss Edith" to drive him and the children around the countryside on Sunday afternoons, while she could think of nothing less preferred. Nevertheless, about once each month Bailey would finally badger her into compliance. Bailey, who never seemed to make allowances for people and often insulted his best political friends, depended upon "Miss Edith" to supply the charm in the family—an undertaking which she accomplished with such natural ability that she became an invaluable aid to the Senator in political affairs. Even with members of his family Bailey rarely showed overt affection, but his children realized that he held a rich devotion to them. He frequently took them for long walks in the woods, identifying all the trees, birds, and animals they encountered. He often spent Sunday afternoons at "Billy Taylor's farm" watching a squirrel build its nest or catching crawfish or constructing tiny bamboo water wheels in a little stream. He seemed to his children completely content to pass the hours watching the wheel turn. His family suspected that he wrote magazine stories, probably children's adventure tales, but Bailey would never discuss it and they could not discover where or under what name the tales appeared. Bailey's deep and abiding love for nature did find public expression in numerous poems and essays, a not uncommon endeavor for a gentleman of his generation.[4]

An inveterate fisherman, Bailey anticipated his next excursion literally months in advance, collecting the latest lures and newest techniques. He once spent several summer months devising sinkers weighing from six ounces to two pounds to use in deep-trolling. Fishing for Spanish mackerel in the Gulf Stream off Morehead City, he baited his lines with the thick, hard, hollow legs of loons, although wildlife preservation laws forbade even possession of these. He would polish the loon-legs for months by rubbing them together in his pockets. Visitors and friends became perplexed, if not disconcerted, as they watched him fooling with something in his pockets, but few ever summoned courage to ask him just what he was doing. Bailey always used a battered copper tackle box given him by his good friend,

4. See, for example, Josiah W. Bailey, "The Call of the Cardinal," *Progressive Farmer*, LXII (March, 1947).

former Senator Harry Hawes. The weak catch on the box spilt its contents into the boat at least once during every trip, but Bailey refused to acquire another, protesting with unassailable logic that Hawes was a born fisherman and should know what was best.

Often in poor health, Bailey suffered from migraine headaches which sometimes incapacitated him for days. His eldest son remembered him best lying on a couch with an ice pack to his head. Bailey took "B.C. Powders" for relief and became so dependent upon them that his first secretary, Thad S. Page, kept a packet in his desk in case Bailey exhausted his own supply. Years later when Bailey's doctors explained that excessive use of the powders had contributed to his high blood pressure, Bailey, thinking that Page had also been addicted, worriedly instructed his former secretary to cut down. During his years in the Senate, he usually retired for several weeks each year to the Duke University Hospital for a checkup and rest, returning from these periods of quiet and seclusion with renewed vigor. He believed that he lived on borrowed time after his sixtieth birthday, since his family had all been short-lived, his father dying at the age of fifty-nine following a cerebral stroke. This by no means limited his senatorial activities, for he threw himself without restraint into any controversy that aroused him, but it increased his conscious determination to look beyond temporary panaceas to the permanent welfare of future generations.

A first generation North Carolinian, Josiah William Bailey was born the third child and second son of Christopher Thomas and Annie Sarah Bailey on September 14, 1873, at Warrenton, North Carolina. Three years later, his father, who had served as pastor of Baptist churches in Edenton, Hertford, and Warrenton, relocated the family in Raleigh, assuming editorship of the *Biblical Recorder*, the official weekly newspaper of the North Carolina Baptist Convention. Young Josiah grew up in Raleigh, where he received his early education in the Raleigh Township Graded Schools (1880–87) and at the Raleigh Male Academy (1887–89).[5] His boyhood years knew the peaceful and untroubled existence that sprang from a modest but assured economic foundation and from an atmosphere of family har-

5. Archibald Henderson, *The Old North State and the New* (Chicago, 1941), p. 19; *The National Cyclopedia of American Biography* (New York, 1934), Vol. D, p. 440; *History of North Carolina: Family and Personal History* (New York, 1956), IV, 676–677; *Encyclopedia of Southern Baptists* (Nashville, 1958), I, 103; "Josiah William Bailey—North Carolina" [1931?], anonymous sketch in *Bailey Papers*.

mony. Domestic simplicity, quiet affection, and mutual respect characterized the Bailey household. "As a child in that home," Bailey fondly recalled, "it seems to me that we were as well off as the most wealthy. . . . There was no thought of poverty; there was no privation; there was no complaining. Our mother knew how to save and how to work. . . . It was a home of constant cheer, of newspapers, magazines, and books; of no little home talk and blessing; and of constant care of children." The enjoyment that accompanies a healthy body, a lively mind, games of sport, and high marks at school filled these early years. Long walks and fishing trips with his father, who possessed an ironical sense of humor and a broad general knowledge of woodcraft, made a lasting impression.[6]

At the age of fifteen Bailey entered Wake Forest College, where he displayed such marked ability as a writer that fellow students elected him editor of the college newspaper. His course of study adhered only loosely to the recommended schedule. He read extensively in the English classics and avidly studied Greek. He seriously considered pursuing graduate studies in Greek under a scholarship from Johns Hopkins University, but circumstances turned him from academe. He was graduated from Wake Forest College with the Bachelor of Arts degree in June, 1893, and immediately assumed the editorial duties of his father, who had been largely incapacitated by a cerebral stroke. Young Bailey had not reached his twentieth birthday, but he fulfilled his new responsibilities so competently that following his father's death in June, 1895, the Baptist State Convention officially elected him editor of the *Biblical Recorder*. His early editorial obligations forced him to acquire a dignity unusual for his age, which gave to all but close friends an impression of aloofness, aristocracy, and occasionally snobbishness. He later asserted that the bane of his existence was the constant stream of visitors. "When I was editor of the Recorder," he recalled, "the Baptist preachers, waiting for trains mainly, would spend their time in my office utterly oblivious of the fact that I was business manager, editor, bookkeeper, collector, and office boy. They had plenty of time and I had none. . . . They would get comfortable in their chairs and settle down like a steady rain, a three or four day rain, and there I was perfectly helpless."[7]

Bailey gave able expression to his views on religious, moral, and

6. *Biblical Recorder*, January 2, 1935, p. 12.
7. Bailey to Thad S. Page, Alexandria, Va., December 29, 1941, in Page's personal collection.

social topics in the first two columns of the *Biblical Recorder*, which boasted the second largest circulation of all periodicals in North Carolina. He soon gained the respect and admiration of many members of the secular press and a large following among North Carolina's Baptists. A contemporary, George W. Paschal, recalled that "his ability and talent at once gained him recognition and while only a youth he attained a position of influence almost unequalled in the Baptist annals of the State." The editorship steadied and channeled Bailey's youthful enthusiasm. While adopting a generally constructive policy, he never hesitated to expose wrongs observed in church and state affairs. Most notable was his dynamic and sustained demand for direct legislative appropriation of funds for North Carolina's public schools.[8]

The April 10, 1895, issue of the *Recorder* established Bailey's editorial policy. "Next to Baptist churches," he pledged, "the Recorder takes it as its peculiar aim to hasten the day when the State will be dotted with school houses, public schools, academies, boarding schools, and institutions of general education."[9] Five years of editorials urging North Carolina to educate its children, revealing distressed school conditions, and demanding legislative aid for their improvement, proved that he had made no idle pledge. The plight of the public schools had aroused great concern for over two decades and had stimulated educational reformers such as Charles D. McIver, Edwin A. Alderman, Charles B. Aycock, and many others, whose contributions can scarcely be overestimated.[10] Arriving late on the educational battleground, Bailey's fight for free schools was particularly fortunate since political developments had largely obscured needed reforms. In 1892 the recently formed Populist party joined with Republicans to oust Democrats from office and precipitated a six-year power struggle between the parties that subordinated educa-

8. George W. Paschal, "The Truth as to the Public School Advancement in North Carolina" (November, 1929), pp. 20–21, *Bailey Papers*.
9. *Biblical Recorder*, April 10, 1895, p. 2.
10. See: Rose Howell Holder, *McIver of North Carolina* (Chapel Hill, 1957); Dumas Malone, *Edwin A. Alderman* (New York, 1940); Oliver H. Orr, Jr., *Charles Brantley Aycock* (Chapel Hill, 1961); Edgar Wallace Knight, *Public School Education in North Carolina* (Boston, 1916); Samuel Hunter Thompson, "The Legislative Development of Public School Support in North Carolina" (unpublished doctoral dissertation, University of North Carolina, 1936); Edward Jennings Carter, "The Educational Awakening in the South" (unpublished doctoral dissertation, University of North Carolina, 1943).

tional problems to the exigencies of partisan politics.[11] Bailey's campaign to reawaken the sentiment and to recreate the unity necessary for progress toward improved schools could not have begun at a better time.

Bailey published an article in February, 1897, summarizing his arguments for state aid to public schools. He alleged that only 62 per cent of the 635,000 children of school age were actually enrolled in public schools, and that of this 62 per cent only 1 per cent attended regularly. The average school term amounted to sixty days, instead of the four month term required by the Constitution of North Carolina. While 7,500 school districts existed, at least 600 had no public schools. The remedy would be found in a special legislative appropriation of $100,000 from the general fund for the public schools and in an increase in the regular school tax from eighteen to twenty cents. This would make possible the four-month term, better teachers' salaries, and closer supervision of schools.[12] When the Fusionist (Populist and Republican) Legislature convened in 1897, Bailey stood at its doors personally handing out his views in pamphlet form to members. He repeatedly demanded a hearing before the House Committee on Education until his sixth request met success. Then, with State Superintendent of Public Instruction Charles H. Mebane and Corresponding Secretary of the North Carolina Baptist Convention John E. White, Bailey led in advocating direct appropriations by the General Assembly.[13] Opposition came from Edwin A. Alderman and Charles D. McIver, the recognized leaders of education reform, who favored local taxation. Alderman as president of the State University and McIver as president of the State Normal College probably feared that direct appropriations for elementary and secondary schools might reduce already inadequate funds alloted to their own institutions. Fusionist opponents of direct state aid joined with advocates of local taxation to enact a law requiring a referendum in every township on whether a special tax of ten cents on property and thirty cents on the poll should be levied to prolong the school term.[14]

11. See Helen Gray Edmonds, *The Negro and Fusion Politics in North Carolina, 1894–1901* (Chapel Hill, 1951).

12. *Biblical Recorder*, February 3, 1897, p. 1.

13. John Ellington White, "When the Tide Began to Turn for Popular Education in North Carolina, 1890–1900," *Proceedings of the State Literary and Historical Association of North Carolina* (Raleigh, 1922), pp. 33–44.

14. Josiah W. Bailey, "Popular Education and the Race Problem in North Carolina," *Outlook*, LXVIII (May 11, 1901), 114–117.

Bailey's sincere concern for the public school cause was revealed by his willingness to forget temporarily the opposition of McIver and Alderman and to join with them in the campaign for local tax assessments. Bailey distributed literature and spoke for the special tax along with many prominent educational leaders who freely gave themselves to the cause. Less than fifteen townships out of more than fifteen hundred approved the special tax. Bailey later explained that the campaign failed in part because some people did not understand the proposal, while others opposed increased taxation on general principles, and still others, particularly among Democrats, withheld support because the initiative came from the Fusionist Legislature. The universal reason for opposition, however, was belief that Negroes would benefit as much as whites. "I may cite this instance of one man with six children to educate, whose extra tax would not have amounted to fifty cents, who refused for this reason to vote for it," Bailey commented.[15]

In his appeals for direct appropriation, Bailey contended with an awkward relation to state institutions of higher learning. He undertook as editor of the *Biblical Recorder* to promote and protect the interests of the Baptist denominational college, while he actively sponsored measures for improvement of public education on elementary and secondary levels, seemingly at the expense of the state-supported university and college. This dual role led many observers, then and more recently, to disparage his efforts and to obscure his real contributions. The Charlotte *Daily Observer* pointedly noted in 1895 that "the North Carolina Baptist 'Association' (Convention) was more zealous for the success of its Baptist college than for the betterment of the public school system in the State."[16] A recent, if not less biased, student concluded that since Baptists feared that state-supported universities and colleges would compete too successfully with the Baptist college at Wake Forest, "it is perhaps fair to say that their extensive arguments in behalf of public-schools were largely smoke-screens" for their determined attempts to cripple state institutions of higher learning.[17]

15. *Ibid.*

16. Charlotte *Observer*, quoted in Pashal, "Public School Advancement," p. 24, *Bailey Papers*.

17. Herbert Lee Swain, "Editorial Views of the Religious Press on Education in North Carolina" (unpublished master's thesis, University of North Carolina, 1942), p. 187.

Since interpretation of Bailey's role rests so thoroughly upon assumptions concerning his motives, the truth of the matter is difficult to determine. Bailey's attitude as expressed in editorials revealed great favoritism toward denominational colleges as sources of Christian education and some hostility toward state institutions because of their entirely secular outlook. He chiefly complained, however, that since the services of the state colleges reached only a favored few of the people, common taxes could better be expended for public schools benefiting the great majority. Yet if Bailey's apparent bias bears recognition, the tendency of state-supported colleges to guard jealously their own appropriations from the legislature should also be noted. "Neither of the Presidents of the State institutions," Bailey caustically observed on March 17, 1897, "worked for the public school appropriations until appropriations for their own institutions had been secured."[18] Although the presidents would have been remiss in their own responsibilities had they done otherwise, Bailey believed that the deficiency of funds for public schools resulted from constantly increasing appropriations to the University of North Carolina and the State Normal and Industrial College. He actively opposed enlarged assistance to those institutions, which seemingly aggrandized themselves at the expense of general education. The key would seem to be that sufficient revenues were not available to support both higher and lower educational systems adequately. Bailey's campaign was motivated by sincere concern over educational conditions, but his leadership among Baptists encouraged detractors to point solely to denominational bias against state colleges. In later years, Bailey could never understand why his contributions were unrecognized and, in turn, undervalued contributions of other leaders.[19]

Although a Democrat, Bailey accepted appointment in 1895 to the State Board of Agriculture under the Republican governor, Daniel L. Russell, who had been elected by the fusion of Populists, Negroes, and Republicans. Bailey and Benjamin F. Aycock, brother of Charles B. Aycock who would be elected Democratic governor in 1900, were appointed by Russell as representing the minority. Bailey's service under a Republican administration and with the Negro politician James H. Young on the Board would return to haunt him several decades later. Indeed, this appointment proved politically embarrass-

18. *Biblical Recorder*, March 17, 1897, p. 2.
19. Bailey to Livingston Johnson, December 12, 1922, *Bailey Papers*.

ing late in 1897, when Democratic party leaders began to organize the "white supremacy" campaign that would break the Fusionists' control in 1898. Bailey resigned from the Board of Agriculture to join Democratic leaders. During the subsequent campaign he made his first political speech at Thomasville, denouncing Russell's administration and supporting "white supremacy." Significantly, the victorious white supremacy legislature restored Bailey to the Board of Agriculture in 1899.[20]

According to Josephus Daniels, editor of the Raleigh *News and Observer*, Democrats heralded Bailey's Thomasville speech as "a statement of a man who, seeking to serve the Agricultural Department of the State, had accepted a position as a member of the State Board of Agriculture under Russell, and had felt impelled to resign his position because of the rottenness of the Russell administration." Daniels himself did not accept the general view of Bailey's motives. He wrote in 1941:

> When the white supremacy campaign, in the early stages seemed critical and the leaders were doubtful of the result and were seeking to bring to their aid every possible influence, Bailey, White, and others held a conference with State Chairman Simmons and Governor Jarvis, one of the elder statesmen whose influence was great. As a result of this secret conference, Jarvis and Simmons agreed that if the opponents of increased appropriations [for state institutions of higher learning] would throw their influence toward victory for white supremacy, they would guarantee that the Legislature would make no increases.
> . . . This agreement being secured, Bailey, White, and others fought the Fusionists.[21]

In 1901 the *Standard*, a Presbyterian journal, made essentially the same accusation of a secret agreement, but Bailey protested to a friend at the time that "to argue over such a charge would be weakness. To ignore it would be confession. There was nothing to be done but deny it."[22] Although the charge was substantially true, it told only half the story.

Allying himself with Furnifold M. Simmons, the state Democratic

20. N. Y. Gulley, *Josiah W. Bailey: A Brief Sketch* (Raleigh, 1924), p. 2; Bailey to F. S. Worthy, April 23, 1930, *Bailey Papers*.
21. Josephus Daniels, *Editor in Politics* (Chapel Hill, 1941), p. 319.
22. Bailey to Charles E. Taylor, August 20, 1901, *Bailey Papers*.

party chairman, and Charles B. Aycock, the prospective Democratic nominee for governor, Bailey reasoned that the Negro vote needed to be displaced before progress could resume. He determined, however, to secure definite commitments from major political leaders for needed reforms before lending aid to the campaign. Bailey made a bargain with Simmons "that I would support the white supremacy campaign if he would agree that the first appropriation made by a Democratic legislature should not be less than $100,000 and should be for the public schools, and further that he should give an opportunity to church people and the better type of men and women with respect to the liquor traffic."[23] Public school appropriations became thoroughly entwined with the proposed constitutional amendment which provided that prospective voters who came of age after 1908 must read and write to be eligible to vote. To meet possible objections, the General Assembly approved a law in 1899 securing a four-month school term and supporting the principle of direct appropriations to public schools with a grant of $100,000 annually. Superintendant of Public Instruction Charles Mebane drew up the bill, and Bailey spoke in its support before the Joint Committee on Education of the legislature.[24] Since the public school appropriation made up a large part of the budget, appropriations for state colleges were not raised. The bargain between Bailey and Simmons had been kept, and the state's responsibility for public education had been firmly established. While Bailey rejoiced, the reaction of advocates of local taxation and higher learning was typified by McIver's remark to Simmons that "you have sold us out."[25]

In the 1900 election Bailey supported the constitutional amendment to disfranchise Negroes in the *Biblical Recorder* and campaigned for Simmons, the senatorial candidate, and Aycock, the gubernatorial candidate. In January, 1901, Aycock was inaugurated governor, and the General Assembly convened with an overwhelmingly Democratic majority. Aycock put the Democratic campaign pledge of four-month schools and of state financial aid squarely before the legislature. In the difficult fight that followed, the *Biblical Recorder* steadfastly backed the Governor, while Bailey himself penned

23. Bailey to Walter Montgomery, June 12, 1943, *Bailey Papers.*
24. Charles H. Mebane to editor of the Catawba *News-Enterprise*, July 24, 1923, *Bailey Papers.*
25. J. Fred Rippy (ed.), *F. M. Simmons, Statesman of the New South, Memoirs and Addresses* (Durham, 1936), p. 15.

an article entitled "Popular Education and the Race Problem in North Carolina," which had wide circulation in the *Outlook*. He traced the difficulties in securing direct state aid for public education to reluctance by many whites to use common taxes to maintain Negro schools. Opposition rested only partly on unwillingness to educate Negroes to pass literacy tests for voting. Some whites believed that educating a Negro would "ruin a good farm hand." Others contended that school funds which were already inadequate for white needs should not be spent on Negro children, who would not be deterred from attending school because of poor clothes and would, thus, acquire reading and writing skills more rapidly. Race prejudice arising from antipathy of poor whites who competed with Negroes in the labor market was obviously a large factor. Bailey applauded Aycock's determined resistance to legislative proposals that would apportion school funds to the races on the basis of property ownership or that would permit either race to vote a tax exclusively on itself for the schools of its children. "There are many of us," he observed, "who believe that not a few people in North Carolina would be indifferent to the education of the white children if they should be assured that the negroes should not be educated. It is against these that the Governor now declares that he stands, as he has stood, for 'universal education.' "[26]

Bailey also defended North Carolina's disfranchisement of the Negro in an essay entitled "The Case for the South," published in the *Forum*. His defense avoided the dark emotionalism and reminders of threats to southern womanhood that typified the white supremacy campaign, but his assumption of inherent Anglo-Saxon superiority was clearly discernible. He declared that the Civil War's most deplorable effect had been creation of "a mass of freed Negroes, unversed in government, susceptible to every kind of darkness, yet invested with the high prerogatives of Anglo-Saxon self-sovereignty and cooperative government." Northern adventurers had filled the hearts of the freedmen "with a bitterness and a suspicion of their former masters that had not been known before." Enfranchisement of a "host of ignorant men of a lower race" had forced southern white people either to stand together in politics no matter what might be the corruption in their party or to yield large areas of North Carolina to Negro rule. "Reforms and more timely laws have come tardily, lest

26. Bailey, "Popular Education and the Race Problem," pp. 114–117.

their suddenness might divide the white vote. . . . [T]he one insurmountable obstacle to progress politically has been the presence of a large body of negro voters, ignorant and irretrievably prejudiced." He argued that the disfranchising amendment had been ratified to save the state from moral prostration rather than in prejudice against the Negro or in favor of any party. In proof he noted that since ratification "there is a demand for a fair election law, for better schools, and for progressive legislation; and there is good earnest that this demand will be heard."[27]

Between 1903 and 1907 Bailey took up leadership of the temperance movement. Elected chairman of the executive committee of the Anti-Saloon League, he exerted the full influence of the *Biblical Recorder* to arouse public opinion. He organized 174 local temperance leagues and led subsequent campaigns to prohibit manufacture and sale of intoxicants. He successfully lobbied sixty days in the General Assembly of 1903 for the Watts Bill to exclude saloons and distilleries from rural districts and to establish the principle of "local option." In 1904 and 1905 he conducted local-option elections in which thirty out of thirty-one established local prohibition. Under his forceful leadership, Charlotte, Greensboro, Durham, Goldsboro, New Bern, Elizabeth City, and Raleigh voted out the open saloon. Only 162 saloons remained at the end of his campaign with these limited to thirteen out of one hundred counties. In the General Assembly of 1905 he fought for the Ward Bill to exclude saloons from towns of one thousand population and less. Enactment of the Ward Bill constituted a major victory for the temperance movement.[28]

Throughout Bailey's tenure as Anti-Saloon League chairman, he advocated local option and refused to ally with the national league. When late in 1907 other temperance leaders agitated for state prohibition and leaned toward national prohibition, Bailey countered with an article on "The Political Treatment of the Drink Evil." After indicating the extent and gravity of the problem and the history of temperance organizations, he argued for regulation of liquor traffic by local option and against broader efforts. Dismissing national prohibition as unfeasible, he suggested that "our national power is not

27. Josiah W. Bailey, "The Case for the South," *Forum* (April, 1901), pp. 226–230.

28. J. M. Broughton, *Bailey's Record on Liquor and the Liquor Traffic* (Raleigh, 1930), *North Carolina Collection*, University of North Carolina. See also Daniel J. Whitener, *Prohibition in North Carolina* (Chapel Hill, 1945).

sufficient to control in local affairs. . . . To cope with a situation of this kind would require a centralization of authority contrary to all the American precedents and really subversive of the spirit of American institutions. . . . [S]elf-government does not proceed from the national head downward; it proceeds from the local community upward." As for state prohibition, he recorded that of twenty-three states adopting it in the preceding fifty years, only three in 1907 still maintained it. The overwhelming conclusion was that *"liquor traffic regulations can be no stronger than the local opinion will bear."* Local option automatically obtained majority support and placed on the people themselves responsibility for enforcement. "It ought to be a fixed rule of American politics," he asserted, "never to accept a responsibility which may be discharged by the electorate. This is self-government."[29] Bailey held to this rule for forty years.

When the Anti-Saloon League declared for state prohibition in late 1907, Bailey resigned as chairman, informing the league that local option would best rid North Carolina of remaining saloons. He later admitted that this break with prevailing sentiment required some courage, but he fully supported the prohibition campaign in 1908. With the advent of national prohibition in 1920, Bailey was called to Washington to participate on the committee established to devise a plan of national enforcement. The majority recommended appropriation of two million dollars for enforcement, but Bailey, recognizing the proportions of the task, filed a minority report calling for ten million dollars the first year alone.[30] The subsequent history of that "noble experiment" demonstrated both the wisdom of his arguments for local option and the realism of his enforcement suggestions.

At the age of thirty-two Bailey began the study of law under tutelage of S. F. Mordecai of Trinity College and N. Y. Gulley of Wake Forest College. He resigned editorship of the *Biblical Recorder* in 1907 and secured admittance to the state bar in February, 1908, setting up legal practice in Raleigh with his brother-in-law, W. N. Jones.[31] Bailey left few clues to his reasons for abandoning a well-established editorial career. He had, however, never been entirely happy with his editorship, having taken that responsibility to assist

29. Josiah W. Bailey, "The Political Treatment of the Drink Evil," *South Atlantic Quarterly*, V (April, 1907), 109–124.

30. Broughton, *Bailey's Record on Liquor*, p. 5.

31. L. P. McLendon, *For U.S. Senator: Josiah W. Bailey* (Raleigh, 1930), p. 2, *North Carolina Collection*; *Biblical Recorder*, January 2, 1935, p. 4.

his ailing father. Even after his resignation, he asserted that "over a long period, I would dream that I was still editor and the dream was never a happy dream."[32] The editorship did not provide great financial security, since his salary derived entirely from funds remaining from subscriptions and advertisements after meeting the paper's expenses. Ten years after entering the law, Bailey was numbered among the twenty best-paid attorneys in North Carolina.[33] Probably the most cogent reason for the career change was that editorship of a denominational newspaper restricted the scope of his political activities, whereas legal practice opened wide opportunities for political endeavor and preferment.

Only a few months after being admitted to the state bar, Bailey plunged into the bitter factional strife within the Democratic party. He vigorously supported for governor Locke Craig of Asheville, who had also the backing of Senator Simmons and former Governor Aycock, against the insurgent and successful candidate, William W. Kitchin, a popular congressman from Roxboro. Although Kitchin won the gubernatorial nomination at the Democratic State Convention on the sixty-first ballot, Bailey's support for Craig and his record on prohibition prompted the convention to nominate him for elector-at-large by unanimous vote. The Republican administration of Theodore Roosevelt had reached its highest popularity in North Carolina, and the Republican presidential nominee, William Howard Taft, was Roosevelt's personal choice. The Democratic candidate, William Jennings Bryan, had lost his two previous campaigns in 1896 and 1900, and the party's nominee in 1904, Alton B. Parker, had won fewer votes than Bryan. Bailey's victory in the November balloting over the Republican nominee for elector-at-large was by no means assured.[34]

Canvassing for Bryan, Bailey attacked abuse of power by trusts, special privileges derived from high protective tariffs, private control of public service cooperations, and corrupting influences of political bossism, but soft-pedaled Bryan's advocacy of free silver and criticism of imperialism. Elected in November after an arduous campaign, Bailey delivered the Elector's Speech in the Electoral College of North Carolina on January 11, 1909. Although Bryan lost the

32. Bailey to John Calvin Slemp, October 20, 1929, *Bailey Papers*.
33. "Josiah William Bailey," anonymous sketch (1916), *Bailey Papers*.
34. Raleigh *News and Observer*, June 28, 1908, p. 1; Charlotte *Observer*, February 3, 1924, p. 8.

national election to Taft and the Democratic party suffered its fourth presidential defeat since Grover Cleveland's second administration, Bailey spoke optimistically of the party's future. Viewing "The Grounds of Democratic Hope," he stressed the party's progressive character and lauded Bryan as "the Knight Errant of mankind." "The last campaign will be notable in our American history," he affirmed, "because it has defined the issue about which vaguely now for the years past and very clearly for years to come the battle for the life of the American Republic must be fought. . . . It is the struggle for the people against the privileged—the predatory."[35]

Bailey concentrated on building his law practice and on participating in Wake County politics. As early as 1903, he had urged adoption of such progressive measures as the initiative and referendum, and in 1905 he had campaigned for ballot reform. Creating a "progressive" image, Bailey drafted and introduced the legalized primary law for Wake County which provided for the secret ballot and incorporated many features of the Australian ballot system. The law was superseded in 1915, however, by the statewide primary law, which he also advocated. As a member of Raleigh's Good Government Association, he fought for revision of the city charter in order to adopt the commission form of government, which was approved in 1913 by a two-to-one majority. He successfully campaigned to transfer the Raleigh Water Works from a private corporation to a city enterprise. He worked to abolish the officers' fee system in Wake County by placing officers on salaries and giving the fees to schools and roads and later estimated that the change saved the county about ten thousand dollars annually. Between 1909 and 1911 he served as a member of the Board of Education for Wake County, and from 1911 to 1913 as chairman of the State Child Labor Committee, which greatly improved the act limiting employment of children in industries.[36]

The year 1912 found Bailey in mild disagreement with Senator Simmons over the Democratic presidential nomination. He supported Woodrow Wilson, the outstanding progressive candidate, while Sim-

35. Josiah W. Bailey, *The Grounds of Democratic Hope* (Raleigh, 1909), p. 8, *North Carolina Collection*.

36. *Biblical Recorder*, February 11, 1903–April 26, 1905; Bailey to editor of the Madison *Herald*, March 25, 1914; anonymous sketch of Bailey (1936), *Bailey Papers*; Elizabeth H. Davidson, *Child Labor Legislation in the Southern Textile States* (Chapel Hill, 1939), pp. 110–111, 157–160.

mons backed Oscar W. Underwood, a conservative senator from Alabama. The disagreement did not carry over into state politics, for Bailey led in defending Simmons against opponents Governor William W. Kitchin, Chief Justice Walter Clark of the North Carolina Supreme Court, and former Governor Charles B. Aycock. Aycock died early in the senatorial race, but both Kitchin and Clark made dramatic and forceful campaigns. Since Simmons remained in Washington, D.C., the brunt of his campaign fell upon the powerful "machine" which he had built since 1900. Bailey, as one of Simmons' right-hand men, masterminded campaign strategy, defended the Senator against charges of machine politics, emphasized his constructive achievements, and praised Simmons as the "Organizer of Victory" in the 1898 white supremacy campaign.[37] Simmons won renomination in the Democratic senatorial primary by a landslide majority.

Bailey's fortunate support of the victorious Democratic presidential candidate and the triumphant senior senator of North Carolina placed him near the top of the state's patronage list. President Wilson appointed Bailey to the office of collector of internal revenue for the eastern district of North Carolina in 1913. Bailey later explained that "Mr. Simmons told me at the time that he was actuated by personal considerations. I think he was moved largely by appreciation of the campaign I made for him."[38] As collector for eastern North Carolina from 1913 to 1919, Bailey worked with Alston D. Watts, collector for the western district and Simmons' private secretary for the preceding twelve years. In respect to Watts's appointment, one scholar recorded that "he voted against a legalized primary and corrupt practices legislation; he was known to have been out of sympathy with anti-trust legislation, and was branded as the worst type of 'machine' politician. . . . The question that intrigued onlookers was whether Wilsonian progressivism could accommodate a reactionary of the Watts stripe."[39] Certainly Bailey could not accommodate himself to Watts, for an implacable enmity developed between the two men.

Governor Locke Craig appointed Bailey in 1913 to the North

---

37. Josiah W. Bailey, *Simmons—Organizer of Victory* (Raleigh, 1912), pp. 1–16, *North Carolina Collection*.

38. Bailey to Stacy Brewer, February 9, 1924, *Bailey Papers*.

39. Joseph Flake Steelman, "The Progressive Era in North Carolina, 1884–1917" (unpublished doctoral dissertation, University of North Carolina, 1955), pp. 367–368.

Carolina Constitutional Commission to recommend changes that would bring the state abreast of progressive ideas. After several months of discussion, the commission presented in July fourteen recommendations. The most important were (1) adoption of the initiative and referendum to facilitate direct democracy, (2) prevention of delays in trials through provision of emergency judges, (3) creation of intermediate appellate courts to speed administration of justice and to lighten burdens on the North Carolina Supreme Court, (4) reform of the revenue and taxation system to provide just and equal participation, and (5) requirement of a six-month public school term. Meeting in special session in September, 1913, the General Assembly approved ten of the fourteen amendments for submission to voters in the November, 1914, election, but dropped recommendations for initiative and referendum and for intermediate appellate courts.[40]

"I am a progressive Democrat," Bailey asserted unequivocally in March, 1914, as he took leadership of the liberal faction within the Democratic party in North Carolina.[41] He advanced a seven-point program for progressives: a statewide primary and corrupt-practices act, tax revision, an elastic judicial circuit system, enlarged state aid to public health and education, just freight and insurance rates, rural credit facilities for farmers, and an improved child labor law. Along with his good friends, Clarence Poe, editor of the *Progressive Farmer*, and H. Q. Alexander, president of the Farmers' Union, Bailey summoned progressive Democrats to Raleigh on April 8, 1914, to consider the proposals. The assembly, with seven hundred delegates attending, indorsed a broad reform platform for presentation to the Democratic State Convention in July.[42] Enthusiasm for progressive reform reached a peak in the ensuing campaign, but could not overcome either the conservative control of the Democratic party machinery or the apathetic indifference of most North Carolinians. The Democratic State Convention indorsed neither the constitutional amendments approved by the legislature nor the recommendations of the progressives. The proposed amendments were defeated in the

40. *Ibid.*, 374–375; Raleigh *News and Observer*, July 13, 1913, p. 1.
41. Bailey to editor of the Madison *Herald*, March 25, 1914, *Bailey Papers*.
42. Clarence Poe, *My First Eighty Years* (Chapel Hill, 1963), p. 212; Steelman, "The Progressive Era in North Carolina," pp. 375–376; Raleigh *News and Observer*, January 4, 1914, p. 1; Josiah W. Bailey, "Ruling Ideas in Politics in North Carolina," unpublished manuscript (1914), *Bailey Papers*.

November referendum. One student of progressivism in North Carolina observed that "the decision of the state Democratic convention to ignore the proposed amendments was perhaps the key factor behind the negative vote. Thus ended in failure a movement aimed toward revitalizing progressive democracy. The state turned down a course that was in keeping with the trend toward liberalism evidenced in other states and at the national level in Wilson."[43]

Defeated but not disheartened, Bailey battled for progressive reforms throughout the next fifteen years and based his campaign for the Democratic gubernatorial nomination in 1924 squarely on the platform he had enunciated in 1914. He supported the statewide primary approved in 1915, spoke before the General Assemby on behalf of woman's suffrage in 1917, and during the World War campaigned on the home front for the Red Cross and Liberty Bond drives. In 1919 and 1920 he represented the Farmers' Union before the General Assembly in opposition to increased property taxes and for an equitable distribution of tax burdens. Grudging acceptance of even the most moderate reforms by the dominant conservative faction of the Democratic party gradually alienated Bailey.

As collector of internal revenue for eastern North Carolina from 1913 to 1919 and as collector for the state after consolidation of districts in 1919, Bailey displayed vision and initiative. He reorganized the collecting and accounting systems and made an impressive record in performance of his duties. When he entered office the cost of collecting $100 came to seventy-five cents, but in 1921 after eight years of his administration the cost had dropped to twenty-five cents. Over the same period his responsibilities had greatly increased, since less than $5,000,000 was collected in 1913, while in 1921 collections amounted to $160,000,000.[44] His tenure ended abruptly in 1921 with defeat of the Democratic party in the 1920 presidential election and ascension of President Warren G. Harding. Relinquishing his office to the Republican appointee on October 24, 1921, Bailey returned to full-time legal practice with his father-in-law James Hinton Pou.

With the close of his eight-year tenure in office, Bailey's career entered a new phase. His career to 1921, as editor of a denominational newspaper, as crusader for various reforms, as sometime law-

43. Steelman, "The Progressive Era in North Carolina," pp. 385–386.
44. Gulley, *Josiah W. Bailey: A Brief Sketch*, p. 2.

yer, as holder of a federal office, and as political lieutenant for Senator Simmons, had been subordinate in nature. Had the Democratic party been victorious in 1920, Bailey might have continued in his lucrative federal position, but the vacuum created by his dismissal stimulated his political aspirations. His marked ability, knowledge of public affairs, and deep interest in political questions placed him in the front line of candidates for elective office. An ambitious man, Bailey had the fortune or misfortune of being a reliable and effective cog in the machinery of Simmons' organization. Yet he undoubtedly realized that continued lieutenancy under Simmons would not further his political career. He recognized that in view of his advancing years he could not wait patiently for the organization to draft him for high office, but that he must strike out on his own. He realized also the necessity of the state's adopting certain reforms without which it could make little progress.

CHAPTER TWO

GUBERNATORIAL CAMPAIGNER[1]

"I SUSPECT I shall have a fight to the finish with the machine, but I am ready for it. I have stood with the machine for the sake of Senator Simmons many years, but there are certain elements of it that will never harmonize with me."[2] Such were Bailey's thoughts early in 1922, although his activities gave little indication of his political ambition. Rumors had circulated for several months that he might campaign for governor in 1924, but the Raleigh *News and Observer* speculated that "A. Wilton McLean, W. B. Cooper, and John H. Kerr are apparently in the running in earnest with still a doubt as to the intention of J. W. Bailey."[3] Bailey neither confirmed nor denied the rumors, but apparently awaited only a dramatic moment to announce candidacy. That opportunity arrived during the Wake County primary election of county officers in June, 1922. A bitter contest had developed between John Hinsdale, W. F. Evans, and John Mills for the Democratic nomination for solicitor in the Seventh Judicial District. With the ballot split three ways, no candidate received a majority, and a second primary was held between Hinsdale and Evans. John Mills, the third contender, cast his lot with Hinsdale. With the battle intensified, Bailey stepped into the fray as a private citizen to support Evans.

Speaking to Evans' supporters, Bailey charged that a coalition of lawyers, bankers, and others sought to railroad Hinsdale into office. "I do not know," he vowed, "whether or not I shall lose votes for Governor tonight or not. I do not care. I know I am going to do my duty and let the future take care of itself."[4] As the second primary approached, he further alleged that certain lawless elements distrib-

---

1. This chapter was published in substantially this form by the *North Carolina Historical Review*, XLI (April, 1964), 190–213. © 1964 by the *North Carolina Historical Review*. Reprinted by permission of the Managing Editor.

2. Bailey to J. H. Weathers, April 28, 1922, *Bailey Papers*.

3. Raleigh *News and Observer*, January 2, 1922, p. 8.

4. *Ibid.*, June 13, 1922, p. 16.

uted large sums of money to corrupt votes in Wake and Franklin counties.[5] Raleigh's leading newspaper aptly reported that "in the latter days of the campaign less was heard of Bailey, but he had already centered the attention of the entire State on himself through the medium of a local fight. Many of his friends see in the overwhelming victory of the Bailey candidate, a measure of the strength that will come to Bailey two years hence when he goes out to battle with A. Wilton McLean for Governor."[6] The bountiful publicity harvest attested that Bailey had shrewdly chosen time and method of revealing his political intentions. His charges that certain members of Governor Cameron Morrison's administration, principally A. D. Watts as commissioner of revenue, used money to subvert the primary election system won for Bailey the guise of both a reformer and of an antimachine candidate.[7] The latter move held peculiar significance, since not only had he benefited from the political organization headed by Senator Simmons, but he had vigorously defended it against W. W. Kitchin's attacks in the 1912 senatorial campaign.

The subject of irregular election practices faded from the headlines in midsummer, while Bailey tended political fences. His willingness to put aside supposed discoveries of voting frauds was unusual for he normally held tenaciously to any needed reform. "Loyalty to the Party," he later explained, "required that I should hold my peace until after the November election."[8] As for fence-mending, in August he visited Senator Simmons in Washington to discuss both election irregularities and his possible candidacy.[9] Two decades later he observed:

> In 1918 I became aware of the cheating in our Primaries and Elections. I discovered that Watts had arranged to have thousands of absentee soldiers votes cast in the election. I took the matter up with Simmons and told him I would not stand for it, and in 1921 I demanded the Australian Ballot and a fair election system. He did not like my attitude as he said it would make trouble between him and Watts. I told him I was going ahead and would undertake to whip Watts and expected Simmons to lay off. He gave me a lecture on politics then and said he thought

5. *Ibid.*, June 26, 1922, p. 10.   6. *Ibid.*, July 3, 1922, p. 1.
7. *Ibid.*, June 26, 1922, p. 10.
8. Bailey to W. O. Saunders, March 18, 1924, *Bailey Papers.*
9. Bailey to J. Crawford Biggs, March 1, 1924, *Bailey Papers.*

I wished to be Governor, and he would assure me I would be Governor and might be Senator, but he wished me to be quiet and go along with him and the others. I told him I was unwilling to be quiet and I did not care to run for any office, but I was concerned about an election reform and would go ahead. I asked him if he would fight me if I ran for Governor and he said no he would take a neutral position.[10]

Reminding Simmons in 1924 of that August conference, Bailey recalled: "I mentioned to you that there was a possibility of my running for Governor; and you immediately said that as between me and any of your other friends, you would not take sides; and I said that I would expect no more of you than this."[11]

Following the general elections of November, 1922, Bailey more than compensated for his relative silence during the previous four months. In a lengthy public letter delivered to the Associated Press and published throughout North Carolina on November 22, he called on the Democratic party and the recently elected General Assembly for an extensive reform program. He specifically set forth four services for the state and party: (1) to safeguard and check the issuing of long-term bonds, (2) to reduce the volume of taxes for state, county, city, and town, (3) to rescue primary and election systems from corrupting use of money, and (4) to rehabilitate the office and curb the power of the state tax commissioner.[12]

On the issue of long-term bonds, Bailey argued straightforwardly that North Carolina must curb the tendency to tap the credit of the state at the expense of future generations. In urging reduction of taxes, he did not merely echo the politician's habitual cry for economy in government. He built his case solidly upon the almost threefold increase in taxes between 1912 and 1922. Proper efforts to secure business-like economy and elimination of sinecures, graft, and supernumeraries would, he estimated, save hundreds of thousands, if not millions, of dollars. His chief complaint about taxes, however, was that the burden fell heaviest upon farmers and owners of small homes.[13]

The first two issues of Bailey's reform program took precendence

10. Bailey to Walter Montgomery, June 12, 1943, *Bailey Papers.*
11. Bailey to Furnifold M. Simmons, March 20, 1924, *Bailey Papers.*
12. Raleigh *News and Observer*, November 22, 1922, p. 1.
13. *Ibid.*

in his own view, but neither carried the impact of his third and fourth points. He harshly denounced those persons who corrupted the primary and election system by purchasing votes and tampering with election officials and returns. Although he mentioned no names, he insisted that he knew "the man who boasts that he is 'the greatest fat-fry since Aaron,' and will name him when necessary." He bluntly asserted that "for the man who solicits . . . the man who pays . . . the man who takes the money the doors of the penitentiary should open." His demand for rehabilitation of the office of state tax commissioner, held by A. D. Watts, created great furor. Bailey intemperately asserted that "it ought to be made a penitentiary offense for him to solicit, receive, or distribute campaign contributions in primaries or elections. He ought to be utterly divorced from politics. . . . Otherwise, we stand guilty of having given to a tax-gatherer the power to raise unlimited funds for political purposes and return them with interest in favors at the public expense." If he had suggested such reforms prior to November's elections, he would have given aid and comfort to Republicans. He now urged reform in hope that the General Assembly might apply necessary remedies before the next election.[14]

Whatever Bailey's intentions may have been or the effect he desired to create with his sensational exposé, he quickly found himself embroiled in a conflict of personalities. The controversy stemmed from the immediate opposition of Governor Cameron Morrison, who justifiably considered Bailey's statements a direct attack on his administration. In the bitter exchange of accusations and recriminations, Bailey had difficulty in explaining support of Morrison in the 1920 primary and his dramatic break in 1922. He later asserted that "with regard to the machine, I did not consider the Simmons following in this state as a political machine; but when Governor Morrison came in, he converted his Administration into a machine."[15] Despite the blunting of the impact of his reform program, Bailey determined to impress deeply the need for reforms upon North Carolinians. He published his program in a pamphlet entitled *Four Services of Progress* and distributed it throughout the state. In the Preface he noted that his program had created wide interest, but that "I have seen but little discussion as to whether the policies proposed would serve or

14. *Ibid.*
15. Bailey to N.Y. Gulley, March 30, 1924, *Bailey Papers.*

disserve our Commonwealth. But much has been said upon the subject of how the expression of my views at this time might affect the contest for the Governorship in 1924! As if that were the question!"[16]

"The turning point in my political career was the discovery of what was going on in the 1922 primary," wrote Bailey on March 18, 1924.[17] His reasons for severing association with controlling elements of the Democratic party were not so simple or so idealistic as his public statements and letters indicated. Active in politics for more than fifteen years, he knew well the compromises involved in selecting candidates and in maintaining power. His name was connected in the public mind with the so-called Democratic machine, but this association was more the consequence of his support of Senator Simmons than the result of any control which he exerted upon that organization. Bailey himself protested, "I think the machine capitalized my support. I call your attention to the fact that from the day of my entrance into politics until now, I was fighting the political machine in Raleigh and Wake County."[18] Yet alongside the Bailey who rejected the excessive lengths to which he thought machine politics had been carried, there was the Bailey whose moderately successful political career had never included major elective office.

Through 1923 Bailey tested the measure of public support his candidacy might elicit. As an experienced politician he knew that he would need either influential backing of party leaders or a mighty ground swell of popular support. In relation to these hard political facts, his tactics in the 1922 primary and in his subsequent demand for legislative reforms had greater significance than superficial appearance warranted. Wade Harris, editor of the Charlotte *Observer* and never a Bailey sympathizer, correctly observed that "Mr. Bailey wants to be Governor and finding that about all the elements of the party were minded for another man—these elements consituting 'the machine' he is endeavoring to discredit the leaders of it to make capital for himself among the people."[19]

The problem of channeling public sentiment was manifold. Bailey's political activities had been limited largely to city and county levels, and his participation in state campaigns had always been as a

16. Josiah W. Bailey, *Four Services of Progress* (Raleigh, 1922), pp. 1–8, *Bailey Papers.*
17. Bailey to W. O. Saunders, March 18, 1924, *Bailey Papers.*
18. Bailey to Stacy Brewer, February 8, 1924, *Bailey Papers.*
19. Charlotte *Observer*, November 26, 1922, p. 6.

supporter rather than as a candidate. He now had to win recognition as a strong contender for the governorship. Since he would not receive backing from party leaders with whom he had formerly allied, his identification with the so-called Democratic machine could be only a liability in any attempt to arouse popular interest. Since his chances of success rested upon an informed and sympathetic public, his candidacy needed a firm base upon issues which would exploit public dissatisfaction with the existing order and stimulate the pulse of reform. In publishing *Four Services of Progress*, Bailey reconciled, perhaps unconsciously, his candidacy to these difficulties. He not only signaled his political availability, while bringing about statewide notice, but also showed his independence from the political machine, challenged the practices of Morrison's administration, and pointed the way to progressive reform.

Throughout the winter of 1923 Bailey maintained an attitude of inquiry. To urgings of supporters that he organize for the coming campaign, he remained quietly but firmly aloof. "While there is an extensive and increasing interest," he observed, "the people as a whole are not disposed to become intensely interested in a campaign that cannot really begin until 1924."[20] The public may have been indifferent, but not the supporters of Angus Wilton McLean, whose political career showed an impressive record of service to the Democratic party and the nation. From 1916 to 1924 McLean served as the North Carolina member of the National Executive Committee of the Democratic party. During the World War, he rendered conspicuous service as a director of the War Finance Corporation and as assistant secretary of the treasury.[21] The Charlotte *Observer* in a thinly disguised "news article" editorialized, "If reports that come into Raleigh from every district from the first to the tenth portray the actual political situation, and it is believed they do, McLean has the forces of influence active for him in four-fifths of the counties of the state. . . . Governor Morrison, O. Max Gardner, Robert N. Page, Senator F. M. Simmons, Senator Lee S. Overman, the entire North Carolina delegation to Congress."[22] This loose coalition of party leaders aiding McLean was only slightly exaggerated. Bailey had long

20. Raleigh *News and Observer*, July 8, 1923, p. 3.
21. See William H. Richardson, "Angus Wilton McLean," in David L. Corbitt (ed.), *Public Papers and Letters of Angus Wilton McLean, Governor of North Carolina, 1925–1929* (Raleigh, 1931), pp. vii–xvi.
22. Charlotte *Observer*, July 2, 1923, p. 1.

since recognized that his candidacy would not be indorsed by the party leaders, but he had hoped that his personal friendship with Simmons would at least prevent this recognized "boss" of the Democratic party organization from taking sides.

Hopes that Simmons would remain non-partisan collapsed on April 25, 1923, when Simmons announced in conversation with Bailey, "Now Mr. Bailey, you have been very candid with me; and I must tell you that I am going to support Mr. McLean for Governor."[23] Nine days later Simmons publicly announced that he would champion McLean's candidacy. Bailey formally responded that "my position is unchanged. I would not be fit to run for Governor, if my running depended upon the support of any man or set of men. . . . With all due respect, therefore, to any and all the powers, so far as I am concerned, the people must determine my course. 'The Machine' did not put me up; it can not pull me down."[24] If Bailey's statement showed disappointment, it also affirmed determination to carry his candidacy to the people of North Carolina. Simmons' support of McLean broke the last tie holding Bailey to the controlling elements of the party organization. Bailey precipitated the estrangement by his independent attitude and his denunciation of election irregularities, but Simmons made the final break. Looking back after twenty years, Bailey recalled, "But in 1923 before I had announced he sent for me and told me he must frankly tell me he would fight if I ran. This made a break between Simmons and myself. I told him I would fight back. Had he gone along with me in the matter of the election law I would have been his faithful supporter as long as he lived."[25] In 1923 he simply remarked: "He has tried to keep me from running; and, unfortunately for him, he tried in the wrong way—he really challenged me to run—and as I see it, made it almost necessary that I should run."[26] Almost at once he abandoned his former attitude of caution and his posture of quiet aloofness. His private letters and public speeches expressed a purposefulness of intent unknown before Simmons' announcement.

Bailey wrote of his campaign plans, "It will be no trouble to me to make a speech every night and, if necessary, I think I can make one

23. Bailey to Furnifold M. Simmons, March 30, 1924, *Bailey Papers*.
24. Raleigh *News and Observer*, July 8, 1923, p. 1.
25. Bailey to Walter Montgomery, June 12, 1943, *Bailey Papers*.
26. Bailey to Archibald Johnson, October 2, 1923, *Bailey Papers*.

every morning and every night. . . . My plans will be to travel and speak constantly for six months." He apparently considered his campaign experience and his oratorical ability among his chief advantages, but he was too astute to depend upon speeches alone. He understood that his chances rested upon psychological factors, for "no man can look abroad over the country at present, without being convinced that the people are tired of machines and bosses. A candidate must always depend upon psychological effect, rather than anything he may say or do. He must get the benefit of the mass movement, or lose out."[27] He realized also the necessity of cultivating a friendly press. He expected many city newspapers to be impartial, if not sympathetic, but he believed his major source of strength to be small county newspapers which could influence the farm vote.[28]

Friends and supporters continually urged Bailey to initiate county campaign organizations, but he refused to risk the danger of organizing precipitately. His campaign would need the appearance, if not the reality, of ever growing momentum as the June, 1924, primary approached. Intent on preventing his candidacy from bogging down, his plan called first upon an unrelenting speaking campaign and second on a thoroughgoing distribution of printed material. He hoped thereby to establish vital issues and arouse North Carolinians from their lethargy. "If I may judge from what I hear," he confided, "there is a tremendous revolt on against the machine, and its administration. Heaven knows, we have enough to arouse the last drop of red blood in the State."[29] His hopes had become dangerously high. By early October, 1923, he even toyed with the idea that Senator Simmons could be persuaded to abandon McLean and to join the Bailey camp.[30]

Former Governor Locke Craig, a political friend of both Bailey and Simmons, cautioned on November 24, "I would regret exceedingly for you to run for Governor. I feel sure that you cannot be nominated. . . . A great many people severely criticise our present governor and his policies, but there are influences that you can not overcome now."[31] This warning from a veteran politician for whom Bailey held high regard had a sobering effect, but did not dissuade him. Craig's

27. Bailey to Archibald Johnson, July 16, 1923, *Bailey Papers.*
28. Bailey to E. F. Watson, July 25, 1923, *Bailey Papers.*
29. Bailey to Walter Clark, August 2, 1923, A. L. Brooks and Hugh T. Lefler (eds.), *The Papers of Walter Clark* (Chapel Hill, 1950), II, 469–470.
30. Bailey to Archibald Johnson, October 2, 1923, *Bailey Papers.*
31. Locke Craig to Bailey, November 24, 1923, *Bailey Papers.*

counsel did evoke a response revealing a depth of feeling and a measure of idealism that his most eloquent speeches had seldom expressed. "I got into politics by accident," Bailey explained, "and my first venture in general politics was founded in my regard for you." Because so much in politics disgusted him, he had verged always on renouncing political activities. His only real satisfaction was "in my successful wars against a crowd of rascals in Wake County and Raleigh" and in his hopes that "whipping the same sort of rascals in the State" might prove equally gratifying. As for the gubernatorial race, he contended, "Suppose I refuse to do it; what will become of the Democratic Party and the State? This is the matter that is giving me concern." He perceived that the campaign would be arduous and admitted desire to quit politics altogether in order to enjoy more fully his home and legal practice. "On the other hand, I have a natural propensity for battle—a propensity that puzzles me, it seems so strange to my real nature. Nevertheless, it seizes me, and thrusts me into one political struggle after another."[32]

Bailey formally announced candidacy on January 17, 1924. "I am now a candidate," he attested, "because I believe there is a service to be rendered, a cause to represent. . . . I have not been thrust forward as the candidate of any group or faction." He advanced an eleven-point platform to (1) relieve land from unjust tax burdens, (2) foster progress with emphasis upon moral and spiritual factors, (3) secure a dollar's worth of public service for every tax dollar, (4) terminate the policy of special favors and privileges in the state's administration, (5) call the people to renewed devotion to law and order, (6) encourage farm ownership and make farm life attractive, (7) establish election and primary laws removing the power of money from politics, (8) strengthen local self-government, (9) renew the Democratic party's spirit by direct contact with constituents and by full and free discussion, (10) break down within the Democratic party a political machine seeking power only to serve itself, and (11) evoke the unrelenting assertion of the public will as the way to economy, just freight rates, justice in taxation, and agricultural relief.[33]

Every sign pointed to a fast-moving and hard-hitting contest. Bailey's recognized opponent Angus W. McLean had made no public

32. Bailey to Locke Craig, November 28, 1923, *Bailey Papers.*
33. Raleigh *News and Observer*, January 17, 1924, p. 1.

statements, but permitted his followers to push his candidacy. Between mid-January and mid-March, however, Bailey presented fewer than three speeches per week of which only six were avowedly political. If the press accurately reflected the situation, he engaged chiefly in a letter-writing rather than a speaking campaign. He had hardly announced before becoming embroiled in prolonged and indecisive editorial controversies. In the most outstanding instance, a total of thirteen letters and editorials were exchanged between Bailey and Wade H. Harris, editor of the Charlotte *Observer*, and its Raleigh correspondent, Brock Barkley. The controversy was personal and consequently bitter. Bailey's participation did little to enhance his image before the voters. He did succeed in forcing Harris and Barkley to reveal the offices they held under the Morrison administration and the salaries they received.[34]

Opening his speaking campaign at Raleigh on March 10, Bailey discussed *The Way of Progress in North Carolina*. Stressing the direct relation of politics to human welfare, he explained that there were "500,000 homes in North Carolina of which 450,000 were cottages wherein resided families on incomes of less than $2,000 per year and that at least 350,000 of these families were living on less than $900 per year." The state faced the three great tasks of securing just freight rates, equal taxation, and a political awakening that might restore representative government. Relief for farmers and homeowners was the immediate task, for "the average farmer pays 13 per cent of his income in taxes. The average for the rest of us is only 11 per cent." Adverse and unfair freight rates presented the greatest obstacle to progress. Railroads had conspired to exploit North Carolina's failure to secure a through line from the Middle West. So-called independent short lines, set up by the large railroads, lawfully charged higher freight rates.[35] During the following months he hammered at these points with little deviation, professing, "I may not be elected Governor; but one thing is certain; I am going to inform the people."[36]

Bailey's presentation of the problems confronting North Carolina

34. See, for example, Raleigh *News and Observer*, Durham *Morning Herald*, and Charlotte *Observer*, January 17, 1924, to March 10, 1924; Harris as president of the North Carolina Railroad Company received $95 a month, while Barkley as secretary to the North Carolina Water Transportation Commission received $150 a month (Charlotte *Observer*, January 23, 1924, p. 8).

35. Greensboro *Daily News*, March 11, 1924, p. 1.

36. Bailey to Walter Clark, March 22, 1924, *Bailey Papers*.

constituted an almost singlehanded endeavor, since his organization was woefully inadequate. He had not yet selected a statewide campaign manager, much less marshaled aid of possible county managers. His organizational difficulties compared with those of almost any insurgent candidate in his first state race. Although known throughout North Carolina, he had not previously worked to create ties of personal loyalty. Unable to command the regular party machinery for distributing publicity, advising on local issues, arranging rallies, and marshaling workers, he counted heavily on broadcasting ideas through speeches, letters, and newspapers. "Some votes are made by spending money, and a few by telling lies," he optimistically contended, "but the great body of our people vote in response to instinctive impulses—and these impulses are always derived from ideas spread abroad."[37] His theories may have been sound, but his lack of organization seriously hampered his efforts. Just two months before the primary, Judge Walter Clark advised, "Of course it has not escaped you that the campaign of the Opposition was to postpone and prevent any discussion as long as possible and after that to 'chill' any debate so that the news that there is opposition, and the ground of it, shall not reach the masses and from information I get, they are succeeding in this far more than you are doubtless aware."[38]

Bailey pursued a noteworthy course on campaign expenses. He not only abided by the law limiting political expenditures to $6,500, but also provided that amount from his own pocket. When a supporter contributed funds, Bailey returned it with the explanation, "I very greatly appreciate your letter and your kindness in sending the check. I made up my mind, however, when I announced my candidacy, that I would accept no contributions whatever. I think you see why."[39] In conscientiously keeping the law, he often had difficulty explaining his course to supporters who pointed out that a little money discreetly placed in the counties might sway the primary. Not only did he reject such suggestions, but he also refused requests that he pay potential campaign workers. His soft replies may have turned his supporters' wrath, but Bailey himself deeply resented such promptings. "I think that one of the most deplorable facts that I know of is that our candidates are disposed to spend more than the law allows," he complained, "and that in the many counties there are so-called 'work-

37. Bailey to J. M. Parrott, March 22, 1924, *Bailey Papers*.
38. Walter Clark to Bailey, April 5, 1924, *Bailey Papers*.
39. Bailey to D. L. Gore, February 15, 1924, *Bailey Papers*.

ers' who expect from $24 to $500 for their influence. . . . I am turning all of them down—flatly."[40]

In mid-April Bailey announced that Charles L. Shuping, a Greensboro attorney who had been the Guilford County manager for Robert N. Page in the 1920 gubernatorial primary, would manage his statewide campaign. Shuping immediately assumed charge of Bailey's headquarters in Raleigh and began the tedious and delicate task of recruiting county leaders. He worked with considerable success to perfect the county organizations. Difficulty still existed, of course, in recruiting able and determined workers, but in many communities the Bailey forces achieved surprising strength. In Greensboro 41 supporters met on the night of April 23 at the Guilford County Courthouse to form a "Bailey for Governor Club." They brought with them a roster containing names of 381 persons pledging support, and formulated plans for boosting Bailey's candidacy.[41] Although Shuping searched unsuccessfully in some counties, by mid-May he had set up some form of organization in almost every county.

Leaving problems of organization in Shuping's capable hands, Bailey embarked on a speaking tour which he confidently announced would continue until the June primary. Appealing directly to the voters, he drew large crowds in Wake, Nash, Durham, Johnson, Cleveland, Northampton, Edgecombe, and Franklin counties in the first two weeks. The subject of his speeches remained always the same—taxation, freight rates, and machine politics, but his single-mindedness caught the voters' attention. The Greensboro *Daily News* reported that "six weeks ago it was recorded that the Bailey tax speeches were getting next to the voters, so much so that easterners declared a party statement would be necessary. Since then the state convention has met. Its platform was admirably adapted to Bailey's speeches, but not purposely so. . . . It promises millennial peace to every discontented tax-payer and Bailey is discontenting a pile of them." The *Daily News* also recorded that when the State Bar Association met at Pinehurst on May 1, the lawyers favoring McLean admitted that "Bailey must be watched because he is making a strong appeal to the rural people."[42]

Moving into western North Carolina early in May, Bailey told a cheering throng at Thomasville that they faced four important issues.

40. Bailey to Tom P. Jimison, March 22, 1924, *Bailey Papers*.
41. Greensboro *Daily News*, April 24, 1924, p. 1.
42. *Ibid.*, April 28, 1924, p. 1.

The state must give back to the counties more of the burdens of government. Until that had been done, land taxes would continue to increase. Machine control of the Democratic party and the state could be corrected only by adoption of the Australian ballot and court review of election results. He promised not only to resist freight rate discrimination against the state, but also to fight the proposed increase of rates, pointing out that the Atlantic Coast Line and the Southern Railway paid large dividends to stockholders on watered common stock. He further pledged to institute a program of economy in the expenditure of public money, and noted that the Morrison administration notoriously and boastfully supported his opponent. "It looks to me," he caustically observed, "at any rate that they think I meant business when I said I would get a dollar's worth of service for a dollar's taxes."[43]

Bailey clearly hoped to encourage suspicions that certain vested interests used the state government to their own profit. He implied that these interests greatly feared election of a reform government. In mid-May an ardent Bailey supporter, N. Y. Gulley, went further in a political advertisement entitled: "What the Atlantic Coast Line has at Stake in the Gubernatorial Race." Gulley revealed that McLean had been president of the Virginia-Carolina Railroad Company, running to Lumberton, and connecting with the Atlantic Coast Line near Hope Mills, until January 2, 1924, when he had resigned to run for the governorship. According to Gulley, the Virginia-Carolina Railroad claimed the right to charge higher rates because of its independence, "Yet all this time, every dollar of the stock (while it stood on the books of the company in the name of Mr. A. W. McLean), was really owned by the Atlantic Coast Line Railroad company, and was held by that company endorsed in blank by Mr. McLean." This accusation implied that McLean himself had collaborated with the large railroads in exploiting North Carolina, and supported similar charges made by Bailey. Gulley also observed that considerable evidence indicated that the Atlantic Coast Line Railroad financed McLean's campaign to maintain a hold on the next state administration. "Mr. McLean," he impugned, "is an honorable man . . . but the men or interests that want Mr. McLean to be governor, are under no $6,500 limit, and they are spending lavishly on his behalf."[44]

In the final swing of his campaign before audiences in Lenoir,

43. Speech of Josiah W. Bailey at Thomasville, May 2, 1924, *Bailey Papers.*
44. Raleigh *News and Observer*, May 12, 1924, p. 10.

Greene, and Wayne counties on June 5, Bailey confessed, "The fight is yours, I have finished my part and I leave the rest to you. . . . But if I am not nominated I shall go right on, joining in the common battle against the Republicans in November, but not quitting my fight to reform the Democratic party."[45] The correspondent assigned by the Raleigh *News and Observer* caught the essential spirit of Bailey's campaign:

> His speeches today reflected the strange admixture of confidence and indifference which has made the Bailey campaign a marvel to everyone in the State except the candidate. All the way through . . . he has had his own idea about the way things were going and has not appeared surprised at developments. When the Bailey showing at the State convention was so small as to be pitiful, the candidate did not seem perturbed. . . . About two weeks ago when his dormant strength suddenly crystalized, Bailey took it just as calmly. Now on the eve of the primary, when his opponents and his friends alike seem confident of the result, he takes the situation in the same spirit.[46]

This insight hit upon the strangest aspect of Bailey's candidacy and campaign, for outside his public statements and occasional flashes of personal optimism, he never believed that he would win the nomination. He aimed first to inform the people and only second to win the nomination. Fully understanding that he would be a personal candidate, he appealed directly to the people, and there he rested his cause. Instead of hiring workers, he sought and received hundreds of volunteers. The response to his candidacy greatly encouraged him, but he faced tremendous opposition.

His campaign, although generally constructive, drew support from regions of North Carolina most rife with discontent. The conflict between rural-agrarian east and the urban-industrial west over taxation admirably suited his purposes. His repeated calls for readjustment of taxation probably appealed to the rampant sectional feelings of the west, while his pleas for agricultural redemption and just freight rates found favor chiefly in the east. The coupling of the two issues, however, had a canceling effect in centers of urban industry, for Bailey used both taxation and freight rate issues in his appeal to

45. *Ibid.*, June 6, 1924, p. 1 .   46. *Ibid.*

the farm vote and offered little, if any, concession to industrial and big business interests.

The nature of Bailey's campaign may have influenced the outcome of the primary for he received the most intense support from eastern counties and suffered his worst defeats in the west. On the other hand, the patch of northeastern counties in which he won easy victories were traditionally antiorganization. The Simmons machine was avowedly aligned with big business and industrial interests in the west, although Simmons himself had strong personal strength in the southeast around his home. Angus W. McLean, a native of Robeson County in southern North Carolina, drew large majorities as expected from neighboring counties. In the northwest and in the southwest Bailey met two centers of resistance. In Iredell County Bailey's archenemy A. D. Watts effectively controlled the political situation. From Cleveland County O. Max Gardner, the unsuccessful insurgent candidate against Morrison in the 1920 gubernatorial primary, had extended his influence throughout the State. In view of the loose coalition of high state officials and of the two factional organizations headed by Simmons and Gardner within the Democratic party supporting McLean, Bailey undoubtedly anticipated defeat.

Bailey's experience in politics had been considerable, but never before had he sought a high elective office. To rise above his position as a local bureaucrat, he needed to signal vividly his political availability, while simultaneously drawing about him a nucleus of loyal supporters and dependable organizers. As an individual and insurgent candidate he had no established party hierarchy of State and county chairmen and precinct committeemen to carry his message to the voters. Although he did have personal friends of varying political usefulness, his major task was to secure competent county managers and allied helpers. His refusal to hire campaign workers may be seen as a deliberate strategem calculated to build a personal organization dependent entirely on volunteers. Such a following, attracted without inducements, money, or hope of reward, might achieve no more than a nominal showing in the first statewide race, but would likely survive campaign after campaign no matter how overwhelming the victory or how crushing the defeat. Bailey, entering a contest he knew he could not win, created for himself an image of party regularity and of political and social reform, while simultaneously developing an organization based upon personal allegiance.

On Saturday, June 7, the people of North Carolina made known their choice for governor. Returns from the 100 counties, representing 1,719 precincts, moved McLean's majority steadily upward. The final majority was officially declared by the Election Board to be 67,624, with McLean carrying 83 of the 100 counties by majorities ranging from ten votes to 4,000. The total vote was 151,198 for McLean to 83,574 for Bailey.[47]

Bailey issued a formal statement on June 9, pledging continued support to the Democratic party. "Five months ago," he affirmed, "I set out upon an undertaking—being nothing less than to interpret the spirit of Progressive Democracy in our Commonwealth. . . . I stated as the principle of this undertaking that politics ought not to be regarded as the means of power or honors or office or privilege, but as the means of maintaining human rights and welfare and progress." The number of persons supporting his cause afforded substantial encouragement, for no good cause was ever defeated. "Let us press on," he urged, "with patience born of courage and confidence founded upon faith in the right. We are at the beginning, not the end of our struggle."[48]

Throughout Bailey's campaign a subtle sense of perspective extending far beyond the June primary had been evident. His comments on his defeat reinforced the supposition that his campaign had been more than a battle to win the Democratic gubernatorial nomination. Two days before the primary, John E. White, an old schoolmate and close personal friend of Bailey, remarked to a newspaper correspondent that "he has told me all along in letters and personally that he cannot carry the State . . . but Bailey has the long view. He has something else in his mind. He isn't done. He has just begun."[49] Although White let slip only a few public hints, he declared privately to Bailey that "you have vastly increased your political and moral prestige in North Carolina. . . . Max Gardner will fall into your footsteps, and when he runs for Governor it will be in the animus of his unforgotten defeat by Morrison and his resentment of the machine. If Simmons lives four years more and the field is open for a new deal in the U.S. Senatorship, no man in the field could defeat you."[50] Bailey replied cautiously: "Your estimate of the campaign is

---

47. *Ibid.*, June 19, 1924, p. 1.   48. *Ibid.*, June 10, 1924, p. 1.
49. Greensboro *Daily News*, June 9, 1924, p. 1.
50. John E. White to Bailey, June 10, 1924, *Bailey Papers.*

pleasing. Gardner and I are not likely to become political brothers. I think he wants to be Governor at any cost. He will probably offer an alliance with me. . . . Our cause has been pretty well advanced; and I have no question about our opportunity arriving in due season."[51]

If there could have been any doubt that Bailey looked to future triumphs, the tone of his letters following the primary dispelled the illusion. He wrote, "I think we have a very fine start. . . . The present situation will break down rapidly—there will be developments which none of us now anticipate."[52] On his campaign, he affirmed, "What we needed was a stronger organization; this we will obtain in due season. . . . We did probably as well as we could have hoped in the first campaign."[53] In his most definitive statement, however, he asserted that "events will develop quite rapidly. I do not hesitate to say to you that I am going to hold the trust committed to me. . . . I believe there are at least 83,600 people who will stand with me; and I think there will be many more. . . . This is quite an army. It will not go to pieces." He apparently evaluated the political situation with some goal in mind, for he concluded that "the present line-up cannot be maintained. The Simmons and Gardner coalition will not last. Whenever it breaks, I will be in a position to move—and I shall move."[54]

51. Bailey to John E. White, July 9, 1924, *Bailey Papers*. Later Bailey declared: "I supported Gardner in 1928 on a specific promise to stand for an Australian Ballot law. He gave me the promise in writing and he performed it." Bailey to Walter Montgomery, June 12, 1943, *Bailey Papers*.
52. Bailey to R. G. Grady, June 30, 1924, *Bailey Papers*.
53. Bailey to S. A. Adams, July 9, 1924, *Bailey Papers*.
54. Bailey to Santford Martin, July 5, 1924, *Bailey Papers*.

CHAPTER THREE

LIBERAL SPOKESMAN

"MAY THE Democratic Party Look to the South for National Restoration?" speculated Bailey late in 1925 in a critical examination and diagnosis of the ills of his party. He regretfully but unequivocally answered "No" for the immediate future. Two serious defects— factionalism and divided leadership—afflicted the Democratic party. Both Alfred E. Smith of New York and William G. McAdoo of California faced handicaps, since the South would not fight under Smith's banner and McAdoo could not command allegiance of northern Democrats. Hopes for appearance of national leadership from the South seemed groundless, for the South normally put forward only lesser leaders in politics, while men of greater stature devoted themselves to commerce and industry. Excepting Cleveland and Wilson, Democrats had produced only small politicians, rather than statesmen. Yet the Democratic party's chief difficulty was its failure "to present a coherent and constructive interpretation of National life and aspirations" by grasping at "one 'paramount issue' after another." The party led by catching the popular ear, rather than by offering causes founded in conviction. There had been the "holy cause" of free silver in 1896 and anti-imperialism in 1900, the tariff-for-revenue-only issue for many decades and the League of Nations in 1920. Hoping to benefit from Republican errors and becoming merely the spokesmen of the hour, Democratic leaders permitted the party to suffer immense loss of confidence in its capacity for sound policy and left it without causes that could outlast many campaigns. "What but defeat could have expected of a party that thus presents causes, as supreme issues in one campaign only to abandon them in the next," Bailey demanded.[1]

What then was the prospect for the Democratic party? How could

1. Josiah W. Bailey, "May the Democratic Party Look to the South for National Restoration?" *Reviewer*, V (October, 1925), 43–49.

it rediscover itself as an instrument of popular government rather than political opportunism? Some Republican blunder or some period of depression and reaction might offer opportunity for Democratic victory, but "its one need in this hour is a great liberal to lead. . . . Whenever the Democratic party shall convince the American people that it is the Party of Liberalism, it will return to power and service." It mattered little where this much-needed leadership originated if it was capable and in accord with the Democratic party's principle of equality and its character as a vehicle "whereby the people may preserve popular government in the interest of all under the Constitution." Until the party found leadership that could guide rather than appease the common man, Democrats would fail to serve their nation in or out of power.[2]

By the summer of 1927 Bailey still foresaw no bright prospects for Democrats nationally, although he himself undertook to repair personal political fences and to institute a new measure of harmony on the state level. In March he wrote a warmly conversational letter to his old political mentor and more recent antagonist Senator F. M. Simmons, who had just recovered from a long siege of illness. Bailey assured Simmons that he felt no impairment of his friendship and professed, "I have not seen the hour and never expect to see the hour when I would not vote for you for the Senate."[3] In reaffirming allegiance, Bailey may have had no ulterior motive, but he knew that Simmons' age and health militated against his retaining office for many more years. He knew also that many North Carolinians considered him a potential successor to Simmons, but that Simmons was so respected as an elder statesman that succession would be impossible for anyone thought to be an opponent of the Senator. Responding to Bailey's overtures, Simmons expressed pleasure in knowing their friendship continued, for "that is as it should be, and I would have wished it all along. In the future I hope that nothing will occur that will disturb this attitude of mutual interest, friendship and sympathy."[4] Adding the finishing touches to the reconciliation, Simmons' personal secretary, Frank A. Hampton, acknowledged, "I always thought that the Senator never had a friend, who in office, was so

2. *Ibid.*
3. Bailey to Furnifold M. Simmons, March 22, 1927, *Bailey Papers.*
4. Furnifold M. Simmons to Bailey, April 4, 1927, *Bailey Papers.*

loyal and regardful of his wishes and interests in every single thing as yourself, and there was none who loved him better, or whom he loved better, than yourself."[5]

Bailey fixed an ambitious eye on Simmons' senatorial seat should Simmons retire in 1930 or should a vacancy occur earlier. To admirers soliciting his candidacy, he always replied that he had pledged Simmons faithful support as long as he wished public office, but expressed appreciation for the writer's confidence and indicated willingness to serve. He disliked the recent revision of the North Carolina law on succession to the Senate in case of vacancy that provided only a brief period between calling of the primary and the election. This revision benefited persons controlling the party organization, since the campaign would necessarily be short. He advised friends that "work ought to be done in a decent and proper way in advance," while noting that "it now appears that I could hold the support that I received in the race for Governor and that a great many of Senator Simmons' strong supporters, who were not for me in that race, would be for me in the race for the Senate."[6]

He also followed with interest and concern the growing prospects of Alfred E. Smith for the Democratic presidential nomination in 1928. Smith appealed as a great humanitarian and as a friend of business interests, but in mid-1927 Bailey opposed Smith's nomination on grounds that he was a Catholic. This was a political rather than a religious objection. "Let us not oppose Mr. Smith just because he is a Catholic," he counseled, "but because just now the election of a Catholic President of the United States would be calculated to involve us in Mexico."[7] Bailey's concern was not unjustified. Since 1924 when Plutarcho Elias Calles became president of Mexico, relations between Mexico and the United States had deteriorated. Calles threatened to overturn the agreement made by former President Alvaro Obregon in 1923 to respect American oil holdings by requiring American owners to exchange their titles for fifty-year leases. He also greatly aroused Catholic opinion in the United States by opening a bloody campaign against the Catholic Church in Mexico. Early in 1927 a serious war scare developed when Secretary of State Frank B. Kellogg unwisely charged that the Calles government worked with

5. Frank A. Hampton to Bailey, April 23, 1927, *Bailey Papers.*
6. Bailey to C. H. Robertson, June 28, 1927, *Bailey Papers.*
7. Bailey to Livingston Johnson, June 8, 1927, *Bailey Papers.*

Russian agents to establish a "Mexican-fostered Bolshevik hegemony intervening between the United States and the Panama Canal." Relations did not materially improve until after September, 1927, when appointment of Dwight Morrow as ambassador to Mexico brought a man of extraordinary tact and ability into the dispute. Morrow won a compromise settlement of the oil lands problem and also aided in ending the anticlerical campaign.[8]

Bailey's opposition to Smith derived almost entirely from awareness of the delicate position in which a Catholic president might be placed by continuing controversy with Mexico, not from Smith's Catholicism per se. He had consistently and staunchly fought for religious liberty and against religious intolerance. Warning the editor of the *Biblical Recorder* that denominational papers should not interfer in affairs of political parties, he advised that "the advocacy or opposing of candidates for office—no matter on what grounds—by denominational or ecclesiastical papers is in fact the first step in the union of Church and State."[9] Unfortunately for the national Democratic party in North Carolina, neither the *Recorder* nor other denominational papers followed Bailey's counsel. Bailey himself confessed growing impatience with denominational pettiness, observing that "my indifference to that relationship [church membership] has grown on me very steadily, and I think I am utterly hopeless. I do not like the Baptist mold or the church form of religion and have no affinity for either."[10]

Fear of Democratic party leaders that the Smith-McAdoo rivalry might precipitate a convention deadlock similar to the 1924 fiasco vanished in mid-September when McAdoo withdrew in interest of party harmony. Smith's commanding position gained further strength on September 23 when Democratic leaders from eight Pacific Coast and Rocky Mountain states indorsed the New Yorker's candidacy.[11] Although personally opposed, Bailey took no public stand for or against Smith, since he took pride in his thirty-four years as a faithful Democrat and intended to maintain loyalty regardless of the nominee. He saw the futility of attempting to block Smith's nomination, but realized that Smith's candidacy would give North Carolina Democrats considerable difficulty. With this in mind, he sent renewed

8. Harold Nicolson, *Dwight Morrow* (New York, 1935), pp. 294–347.
9. Bailey to Livingston Johnson, June 8, 1927, *Bailey Papers.*
10. Bailey to John E. White, January 8, 1927, *Bailey Papers.*
11. Roy V. Peel and Thomas C. Donnelly, *The 1928 Campaign* (New York, 1931), pp. 10–12.

assurances of support to O. Max Gardner, slated for the 1928 gubernatorial nomination.[12] Gardner promptly replied that he welcomed
Bailey's support, but feared the danger to the party that would result
from Smith's nomination. "I do not know how our people would
receive it," Gardner admitted, "but, as you know, one of the powerful
sources of the strength of the democratic party in North Carolina has
been the support of the moral forces of the state. . . . Smith's
nomination would upset this situation seriously."[13] Bailey responded
that despite the "hue and cry" that would be raised by these elements,
he foresaw no insurmountable difficulty in carrying North Carolina
for Smith and Gardner. Taking a purely practical view, he suggested
that "if we should not nominate Smith, the party would probably be
hopelessly divided four years hence. If we do nominate him he will in
all probability be beaten and eliminated."[14]

Smith's candidacy posed a dilemma for southern Democratic leaders. In late November, Bailey himself summed up this problem in
terms of the inner conflict which he felt. In the first place, although he
could consider not voting for Smith, he was a Democrat and not
inclined to any course affecting his party allegiance. Smith as governor of New York obviously met all tests of that great office and
enjoyed great political sagacity, the gift of popularity, and a fine
personal life. Secondly, he acknowledged a Roman Catholic's right to
run for president, despite Catholic approval of establishment of their
Church by the State. He would oppose Smith if he believed in such
establishment, "but I understand he draws a distinction—he speaks of
American Catholicism as Catholicism committed to United States
standards." He dismissed this aspect of Smith's candidacy from his
considerations. In the third place, he noted that failure to nominate
Smith would lead to temporary dissolution of the national Democratic
party, but "if we nominate and elect him, the Democratic party will
become the anti-Prohibition party, and the Solid South will break up
forever." Neither alternative seemed desirable, but dissolution would
at least present opportunity for sound reorganization. "A party so
dependent," he pointed out, "upon the Solid South, Tammany Hall
and the Irish Catholics is neither coherent nor substantial." If Smith
were nominated but beaten in the election, present uncongenial alli-

12. Bailey to O. Max Gardner, November 7, 1927, *Bailey Papers.*
13. O. Max Gardner to Bailey, November 8, 1927, *Bailey Papers.*
14. Bailey to O. Max Gardner, November 11, 1927, *Bailey Papers.*

ances would be maintained and reorganization would be deferred. Nevertheless, he could not escape his conviction that Smith deserved the nomination and would make a splendid president. Unable to resolve his dilemma he decided that "I shall take no part in the North Carolina campaign in the matter of delegates. . . . I am resolved to keep out of politics for a season."[15]

Democrats in North Carolina divided rapidly into pro-Smith and anti-Smith camps during the first quarter of 1928, although their rivalry still remained friendly. Senator Simmons, who was national committeeman from North Carolina, advised Bailey that he thought the movement to nominate Smith had stalled,[16] while Bailey, viewing the host of favorite-son candidates, speculated that Smith might not obtain the required two-thirds majority.[17] Smith never came close to losing the nomination after McAdoo's retirement, for no one else commanded equal national reknown, newspaper backing, organizational advantages, or financial support. Nevertheless, Simmons and many other Democrats deposed that prohibition and Catholic issues aroused hostility from so many influential groups that Smith should not be considered available. "I know my own motives and know that they are good and arise solely out of my interest in the maintenance of Democratic supremacy," Simmons confided, for "Democratic voters . . . are, I am convinced, unalterably and determinedly against Smith to such a degree as to divide our Party seriously in the State, if we should do so unwise a thing as to nominate him."[18] Undoubtedly correct in forecasting party division and sincere in striving to maintain Democratic control in North Carolina, Simmons' ultimate refusal to support his party's nominee would not only widen ensuing party splits but also destroy his personal control of the state organization.

From his original position in opposition, Bailey gradually warmed to the "Happy Warrior," but still asserted determination to avoid participation in the intraparty conflict. "I am devoting myself absolutely to the practice of the Law," he declared. "I do not wish anything to interfere with it. I had a long period of politics, enjoyed it

15. Bailey to Santford Martin, November 29, 1927, *Bailey Papers.*
16. Furnifold M. Simmons to Bailey, January 15, 1928, *Bailey Papers.*
17. Bailey to Furnifold M. Simmons, January 21, 1928, *Bailey Papers.*
18. Furnifold M. Simmons to Bailey, February 9, 1928, *Bailey Papers.* For a detailed analysis of Simmons' motives see Richard L. Watson, Jr., "A Political Leader Bolts—F. M. Simmons in the Presidential Election of 1928," *North Carolina Historical Review*, XXXVII (October, 1960), 516–543.

fully; have no regrets about it; am glad that I was in politics and rather glad that I am not now in office."[19] Like similar resolutions, this one dissolved with prospect of a good fight. Bailey clearly could not resist taking a stand on any controversial issue, particularly if it involved a major principle to which he gave allegiance. Nothing apparently gave him greater joy than to advocate an unpopular cause. In early April, Raleigh political circles reverberated with reports that Bailey would join the Smith forces. Although he possessed considerable political influence, his support brought heartiest welcome from Smith campaigners because he was a prominent Baptist layman and former editor of the *Biblical Recorder*.[20]

Bailey published an open letter on April 7 entitled *Why the Democrats Should Nominate Governor Smith for President*, which reviewed Smith's remarkable career and discussed major objections to his candidacy. "The nomination and election of Governor Smith to the Presidency," Bailey asserted, "would be an historical and most timely and salutary triumph of tolerance. The spirit of intolerance, which accounts for some of the opposition to him, is an inducement to me to be for him." He simply dismissed possibility of repeal of the Eighteenth Amendment, since Smith had promised that as president he would maintain and enforce the laws. "As matters stand," he pointed out, "insincerity and inefficiency are doing more to defeat the purposes of the 18th Amendment than could possibly be done by any other means." He candidly observed that for a time he had not favored Smith's candidacy, but that examination of Smith's life and career, meditation upon the questions involved, and consideration of the desperate need to rescue the country from Republicans prompted him to disregard minor differences. He warned that Democrats "may differ prior to the nomination, but in our differences it behooves us to utter no word calculated to make it difficult to present a united front in the approaching election."[21]

He immediately moved to establish himself as a leader of the campaign and to develop a statewide organization. Scheduled to speak on Smith's behalf late in April at Greensboro, he advised C. L. Shuping, his 1924 campaign manager, to form the nucleus of a

19. Bailey to Furnifold M. Simmons, January 21, 1928, *Bailey Papers*.
20. Asheville *Citizen*, April 7, 1928, p. 1.
21. Josiah W. Bailey, *Why the Democrats Should Nominate Gov. Smith for President* (Raleigh, 1928), *Bailey Papers*.

statewide organization by inviting key county leaders to confer at that time.[22] By mid-May he advised Judge Joseph M. Proskauer that "the friends of Governor Smith have formed a more definite organization and the work is going on in practically every precinct in the State."[23] Along with Bailey's achievements, however, came political blunders from others. Smith received enthusiastic indorsement in April at a political rally in Raleigh, but, according to Bailey, Representative John Kerr "made the fool statement that 90 percent of the people opposing Governor Smith were opposing him on religious grounds, but only two percent of them had the moral courage or intellectual honesty to admit it."[24] Despite its probable truth, this statement aroused previously lethargic voters to express their displeasure.

Intense personal rivalries and factional divisions within the Democratic party in North Carolina further complicated the political situation. Superficial appearances created the impression that the political machine opposed Smith, while actually the majority of party leaders supported him. This impression resulted from Simmons' vocal and irreconcilable stand against Smith, but the Senator no longer possessed great power over party apparatus despite his nominal leadership. Underneath the Smith contest, a struggle for Simmons' position as national committeeman had developed. Governor Angus W. McLean apparently wanted that post for himself, for Bailey observed that "McLean is not at present active against Governor Smith and would probably acquiesce in the Smith movement, if thereby he could be assured of becoming national committeeman."[25] More dangerous to Simmons was the challenge from leaders of Smith's campaign, who saw in Simmons' refusal to compromise with Smith's candidacy an opportunity to discredit the Senator.

Avoiding any action or statement attacking Simmons, Bailey assured him that advocacy of Smith's nomination did not mean that he opposed Simmons' re-election as national committeeman.[26] Suspicion that Smith leaders intended to destroy him induced Simmons in May to campaign actively for a delegation to the Democratic National Convention that would back Cordell Hull of Tennessee.[27] Bailey ac-

22. Bailey to C. L. Shuping, April 20, 1928, *Bailey Papers*.
23. Bailey to Joseph M. Proskauer, May 14, 1928, *Bailey Papers*.
24. Bailey to John J. Irving, June 7, 1928, *Bailey Papers*.
25. Bailey to Joseph M. Proskauer, May 14, 1928, *Bailey Papers*.
26. Bailey to Furnifold M. Simmons, April 28, 1928, *Bailey Papers*.
27. Watson, "A Political Leader Bolts," p. 519.

knowledged that Smith campaigners had blundered badly, for "when it appeared that the Smith forces would control the State Convention, certain Smith leaders announced that they were going to beat Senator Simmons for his place as National Committeeman and were going to put an end to his machine." He firmly believed that until challenged, Simmons had decided to oppose Smith only from the sidelines. Driven into a political corner, Simmons countered by enlisting such "moral forces" as the Anti-Saloon League, numerous Protestant ministers, and women's groups to capture precinct meetings and finally the state convention.[28]

With active backing from Simmons and Josephus Daniels, Cordell Hull's candidacy advanced rapidly. In initial manuevering, however, Smith forces emerged triumphant. In mid-May Hull backers demanded an informal preferential primary, but the Democratic Executive Committee refused the petition by a vote of 79 to 30.[29] Usually the seat of Simmons' power, the Executive Committee had definitely escaped his control. Simmons adamantly warned on May 23 that Smith's nomination "would mean the ruin of the Democratic Party in my State, the disruption of the Democratic Party in many states in the South. It would create a condition of chaos in the Democratic Party throughout the country from which we would not recover in 25 years."[30] Bailey averred privately that Simmons' course had itself damaged Democratic unity, but "I am inclined to forgive much on the ground that the Senator is an old man and I have made up my mind not to speak harshly of him. No one could ever have convinced me that he would have behaved as he has. Probably we are at the end of a political era in this State and in the history of the Democratic Party in our country and the present confusion is incident to that end."[31]

The struggle for North Carolina's delegation raged between precinct meetings of May 26 and district and state conventions of June 12. Bailey's friends encouraged him to stand for delegate-at-large at the state convention, but he argued that he could better serve by remaining aloof from personal contests. He pledged active support to William B. Jones, a former rival in Wake County politics, for delegate from his own district. His alliance with an old political foe

28. Bailey to John J. Irving, May 22, 1928, *Bailey Papers.*
29. *Ibid.*; Bailey to Lawrence Wakefield, May 18, 1928, *Bailey Papers.*
30. *Congressional Record*, 70th Cong., 1st Sess., pp. 9544 ff.
31. Bailey to Charles A. Webb, May 29, 1928, *Bailey Papers.*

greatly surprised friends,[32] but indicated his determination to bring about Smith's nomination and to strengthen his own political position by conciliating former opponents. Convinced that Simmons' days were numbered, Bailey cautiously avoided either overt criticism of the Senator or identification as an unwelcome aspirant for his office.[33] His refusal to attend the Houston convention sprang from realization that the delegates would confront the question of re-electing Simmons as national committeeman. "I would not like to vote against Senator Simmons in his old age for National Committeeman. I think such action would be interpreted as vindictive on my part," he confided, but "on the other hand, I would not like to be put in the position of having to vote for him."[34]

Delegates to the state convention at Raleigh assembled on the morning of June 12 in district conventions to elect national delegates. The Hull forces won a clear-cut victory, securing three-fourths of the delegates. In the afternoon the state convention elected four delegates-at-large and determined whether to indorse or to instruct for one candidate. Bailey, as chairman of the Steering Committee and floor manager for Smith, moved adeptly into the heated atmosphere of the convention where some seven thousand people had assembled. Fighting an uphill battle against the Hull faction, he saw the futility of securing a few extra votes for Smith at the expense of disrupting the party and losing the November election. The bitter campaign had revealed such deep-seated prejudices against Smith among so many elements that Bailey now sought to discourage further intraparty strife.[35]

Heading the delegates-at-large were Simmons and Daniels for Hull and former Governor Cameron Morrison for Smith. The Hull slate won by a vote of 1,073 to 880 for Smith. Bailey considered this a substantial victory for Smith, since Simmons and Daniels made personal fights, while Smith had only once visited the state. Smith leaders wanted proportionate representation on the basis of the voting, which would have instructed the delegates to cast 10 votes for Smith and 14 for Hull. The Hull faction opposed proportionate representation and demanded application of the unit rule to the entire

32. Santford Martin to Bailey, May 9, 1928, *Bailey Papers.*
33. Bailey to John J. Irving, May 24, 1928, *Bailey Papers.*
34. Bailey to C. L. Shuping, May 18, 1928, *Bailey Papers.*
35. Bailey to John E. Bellamy, June 15, 1928; Bailey to O. Max Gardner, June 15, 1928, *Bailey Papers.*

delegation. The size of the Smith vote, however, apparently convinced Hull managers that demanding unit rule might backfire. Daniels and Homer Lyon, floor manager for Hull, immediately proposed to Bailey not to proceed further if he would agree to a resolution merely indorsing Hull. Bailey refused and eventually won compromise terms of "no endorsement of Hull, no instructions, no unit rule, and a free delegation."[36]

He probably salvaged as much as possible for Smith in the state convention. He took pride in the compromise despite criticism that he should have pressed for proportionate representation. Pro-Smith speeches made by O. Max Gardner, Clyde Hoey, and Cameron Morrison as well as the size of Smith's vote and the failure to indorse or instruct for Hull greatly encouraged Bailey. He feared the potential Republican threat in the November election, however, for he believed that Simmons' course and utterances had put North Carolina in the doubtful column. "The character of the campaign against Smith by Mr. Simmons," he asserted, "has wrought irreparable harm to Smith as nominee of the party."[37]

Bailey's political fortunes received a substantial boost from his leadership at the state convention. Both Hull and Smith forces offered the position of elector-at-large for eastern North Carolina, but he protested that he had held that honor in 1908. The breach between Bailey and former Governor Cameron Morrison, created by Bailey's criticism in 1923, was repaired when, according to Bailey, "Morrison came up to me in public in the dining room of the Sir Walter [Hotel] Tuesday night and made his apologies."[38] Several days later Bailey wrote Morrison that "I prized your friendship and missed it. I have no doubt that I have said things that offended you and that I should not have said, and I very much regret them and am glad to say so."[39] He also observed that Simmons had been unable to command "even one man of sufficient political experience to act as floor manager and he had to depend upon his lifelong enemy, Josephus Daniels, for leadership on the floor."[40] Aligned against Simmons' slate for Hull had been not only the political organization of O. Max Gardner, the

36. Bailey to George Gordon Battle, June 16, 1928; Bailey to George R. Van Namee, June 13, 1928, *Bailey Papers*.
37. Bailey to John E. Bellamy, June 15, 1928, *Bailey Papers*.
38. Bailey to C. L. Shuping, June 14, 1928, *Bailey Papers*.
39. Bailey to Cameron Morrison, June 15, 1928, *Bailey Papers*.
40. Bailey to George R. Van Namee, June 13, 1928, *Bailey Papers*.

Democratic candidate for Governor, but also the "Old Guard" leaders like Morrison who usually formed the core of Simmons' strength. The "Simmons Machine is sunk, and without trace," gloated Bailey.[41]

The Democratic National Convention assembled in Houston two weeks later, but in the meantime Bailey grew increasingly nervous about the effect which Smith's "wet" views might have. "I have about made up my mind." he confided, "that unless Governor Smith gives positive and indubitable assurance that he will stand by the Eighteenth Amendment, make no recommendation for its alteration, we might as well make up our minds to let the electoral vote of this State go by, and concentrate our efforts on the election of State and local tickets."[42] Despite personal qualms, he quietly assured others that "there is not going to be any trouble on the subject of Prohibition this year. The National Platform is going to be just as strong as you could wish it, no matter who is nominated."[43] Believing that Smith would be nominated on the second ballot, he encouraged Smith supporters among the North Carolina delegation to persuade their colleagues to accept the inevitable and to make a fine showing for Smith on that final ballot.[44]

Following the Republican convention, which nominated Herbert Hoover for president, Bailey presented his views to national Democratic leaders on what the forthcoming Democratic platform should espouse. His efforts had a curious vagueness and superficiality testifying either to inadequate understanding of the nation's needs or to the veteran politician's reluctance to commit himself or his party. While he stressed the value of sound and timely ideas, those rare commodities did not grace his suggestions. Republican failure to relieve agricultural distress should be publicized, but Democrats should not indorse the McNary-Haugen Bill, which President Coolidge had vetoed despite advocacy by nearly all farm organizations. Democrats should not denounce protective tariffs, but should demand protection in the national interest rather than in the interest of special groups. The League of Nations issue should be avoided, but Republican incompetence in the Disarmament Conference should be exploited

---

41. Bailey to C. L. Shuping, June 14, 1928, *Bailey Papers.*
42. Bailey to O. Max Gardner, June 19, 1928, *Bailey Papers.*
43. Bailey to Santford Martin, June 19, 1928, *Bailey Papers.*
44. Bailey to John H. Small, June 20, 1928, *Bailey Papers.*

by pointing to the decline in United States naval strength relative to other great powers. Democrats could not criticize prosperity, but they should show where prosperity had been inequitably distributed. The Eighteenth Amendment should not be criticized, but Democrats should denounce Republican administration of the Volstead Act. Rights of states to regulate and administer their own affairs should be plainly enunciated, but assurance should be given that the federal government would prevent one state's policies from interfering with the policies of other states. In short, the Democratic platform "should be fresh in spirit, in terms and in form," he advised![45]

Senator Simmons apparently hoped to secure enough southern delegates to block Smith's nomination under the two-thirds rule, but his efforts proved fruitless. Smith received over one hundred votes more than he needed on the first roll call at Houston. In the South the only irreconcilables were North Carolina, South Carolina, Georgia, Florida, Alabama, and Texas.[46] Although the party's nominee was a wet, Catholic, urban New Yorker, southern delegates took some comfort in the nomination of Senator Joseph T. Robinson of Arkansas for vice-president and from the platform promise of "an honest effort" to enforce the Eighteenth Amendment. Southern misgivings increased when at convention's end, Smith telegrammed intention to modify the Volstead Act.[47] The Democratic platform differed but little from the Republican and conformed surprisingly to Bailey's uninspired suggestions. It criticized Republican failure to promote farm prosperity and promised unspecified agricultural relief. It did not mention the League of Nations, but did approve tariff protection. The only major difference was Democratic approval of an anti-injunction act, collective bargaining, and public control of hydroelectric power.

With Smith's nomination secured without recurrence of the dissension that had plagued the last Democratic National Convention, Bailey felt a deep sense of relief tempered only by uneasiness concerning Smith's approach to prohibition. His course was now quite clear. He would promote the candidacy of a man whom he sincerely believed would serve the country wisely as president, while simultaneously defending the principle of religious liberty. Many anti-Smith politicians now found themselves in an awkward position, but Bailey

45. Bailey to George Gordon Battle, June 18, 1928, *Bailey Papers*.
46. Watson, "A Political Leader Bolts," pp. 521–524.
47. Peel, *The 1928 Campaign*, pp. 34–35.

advised friends that "I am not inclined to say or do anything to make it difficult for Senator Simmons or any of his followers to fall in line. The time has come now to study the matters that make for peace and unity and victory."[48] Since bonds of party loyalty were strong, Democrats in North Carolina might have subordinated their differences to meet determined Republican efforts to capture the state. If so, the opportunity fell victim to mistakes on the national level which reinforced divisions.

The Democratic National Committee rubber-stamped Smith's choice for chairman, John J. Raskob—a Catholic, a militant opponent of prohibition, and a Republican industrialist. Smith apparently hoped that Raskob's appointment would attract business support, but it further alienated southern anti-Smith politicians and dismayed professionals who wished to subordinate Catholic and prohibition issues. Bailey immediately warned Smith's close associates that continued emphasis upon prohibition repeal would endanger North Carolina's electoral vote. He explained that while the state apparently had a Democratic majority of 100,000 votes on the basis of the 1920 and 1924 elections, the normal majority was about 60,000. In previous campaigns Republicans had little money and weak organization, enabling Democrats to win by larger majorities than usual. At present, Republicans had strong organizations, abundant financial assistance, and encouragement from influential Democrats and religious organizations. "On the face of it," he warned, "a change of 50,000 votes from one ticket to the other will mean Democratic defeat—but a change of less than that would do the work."[49]

The already difficult situation quickly worsened when Raskob reportedly declared that he had accepted the chairmanship to help relieve the country of "the damnable affliction of prohibition."[50] The Raskob statement antagonized Bailey, causing him to waver momentarily in support of Smith. "I predicated my support to Governor Smith on the assumption that the Eighteenth Amendment is not involved," he temporized, "and that Governor Smith would take the oath of office to enforce that amendment and carry out every oath."[51] Other southern Democrats reacted similarly. Josephus Daniels wrote

48. Bailey to D. W. Morton, July 2, 1928, *Bailey Papers.*
49. Bailey to Joseph M. Proskauer, July 12, 1928, *Bailey Papers.*
50. Watson, "A Political Leader Bolts," pp. 526.
51. Bailey to Josephus Daniels, July 20, 1928, *Bailey Papers.*

that he was "walking through deep waters" and quoted sympathetically from a letter he had received from Senator Carter Glass of Virginia: "Can you wonder that I am heartsick and could fervently wish that I were free from the moral constraints of party regularity?"[52] Raskob's statement was more than Simmons could stomach, for he resigned from the Democratic National Committee on July 25, 1928.[53] Dismayed by the reaction, Bailey asserted that if Smith would stand for constructive measures enforcing the Eighteenth Amendment, then North Carolina could still be held in line. "I think Senator Simmons should be left entirely alone," he noted. "Let him work out his own salvation. It may be that he will come around with a fair statement later on, but at present I do not think he is disposed to do anything."[54]

Simmons' fears that a "wet," urban, Catholic northerner would change the traditional character of the Democratic party gradually crystallized. He announced on August 20 that he would support the state Democratic ticket, but would not vote for either presidential candidate. Repudiating Smith, Simmons explained that not he but Smith bolted the Democratic party by altering platform and issues.[55] His stand distressed North Carolina Democrats and prompted some to consider asking Simmons to resign from the Senate, but Bailey's moderate view prevailed. "My judgment is," he counseled, "that we should ignore the Senator's attitude for the present. The more we stir this matter up the worse it will be for us. I think what we ought to do is to make a positive campaign for our cause disregarding all incidental matters."[56] At the Democratic State Executive Committee meeting on August 24, Cameron Morrison succeeded Simmons as national committeeman with the statement that "there is more to the Democratic party in North Carolina than prohibition and Senator Simmons, God bless him."[57]

Smith's acceptance speech on August 22 calmed fears of many southern leaders that he would advocate repeal of the Eighteenth Amendment. Smith pledged strict enforcement of prohibition laws and respect for the Constitution, but added that "I personally believe

52. Josephus Daniels to Bailey, July 21, 1928, *Bailey Papers*.
53. Raleigh *News and Observer*, July 26, 1928, p. 1.
54. Bailey to John H. Small, July 24, 1928, *Bailey Papers*.
55. Watson, "A Political Leader Bolts," pp. 527–528; New York *Times*, August 21, 1928, p. 1.
56. Bailey to C. O. McMichael, August 23, 1928, *Bailey Papers*.
57. Raleigh *News and Observer*, August 25, 1928, p. 1.

in an amendment to the eighteenth amendment which would give each state itself, only after a referendum vote of the people, the right, wholly within its borders, to import, manufacture or cause to be manufactured, and sell alcoholic beverages, the sale to be made only by the state itself and not for consumption in any public place."[58] Bailey responded with heartfelt relief, if not exultation, for he declared that "no man can estimate the force of such a speech of acceptance as Governor Smith made. He rang the bell and blew the bugle."[59] Bailey immediately began an arduous speaking campaign that stressed Smith's excellent record and defended him on issues of prohibition and Catholicism. Anticipating a long and bitter campaign, he noted that "probably the best thing that could happen to me would be something that would take me entirely out of politics. The thing takes not only my time, but is sapping my energies. However, my heart is in this campaign, and I am in for a fight to the hilt." He could resist neither the challenge of an uphill battle nor the excitement of a political campaign. "It is just as if I had been on a big drunk," the former Anti-Saloon League leader confessed, "and I must say that when I am going good I feel just about as good as if I had a pint of good old apple brandy in my system."[60]

The Democratic Executive Committee scheduled Bailey to speak almost every day, and sometimes twice a day, during the next two months. In mid-October he claimed 3,600 miles of travel throughout North Carolina in his speaking campaign.[61] He also wrote three pamphlets for distribution: *The Popularity of Governor Alfred E. Smith*, *Governor Smith and National Prohibition*, and *On Religious Liberty*. Reviewing Smith's public record in the first pamphlet, he certified that "it is remarkable that no one suggests a criticism of his private life and no one raises question of his honesty and fidelity as a public servant." He praised Smith not only for taking his work seriously, but also for advancing the cause of the humbler classes. "The wealthy know that he is honest, just and efficient"; he asserted, "the poor know that in him they have one who came up from the ranks, sympathizes with their cause, and knows how to serve their interests."[62]

58. Democratic National Committee, *Democratic National Convention, Official Report of the Proceedings, 1928* (Indianapolis, 1928), p. 277.
59. Bailey to I. M. Meekins, August 27, 1928, *Bailey Papers*.
60. *Ibid.*
61. Bailey to Herbert Lehman, October 17, 1928, *Bailey Papers*.
62. Josiah W. Bailey, *The Popularity of Governor Alfred E. Smith* (Raleigh, 1928), *Bailey Papers*.

Bailey demonstrated that Smith had been greatly misunderstood on the "Liquor Problem." He pointed out that questioning the soundness of the Volstead Act did not mean opposition to prohibition or to the Eighteenth Amendment. Woodrow Wilson had so disapproved the Volstead Act that he vetoed it as one of the last acts of his administration. Bailey argued that failure to enforce efficiently the amendment affected American reverence for the Constitution itself. He indorsed Smith's desire to give each state greater discretion in handling the enforcement problem, for "the principle of local self-government is the essential principle of Democracy." He testified that enforcement of prohibition during the eight years of Republican administration had been largely ineffectual, and asked candidly, "Do you think a thousand years of the present Republican policy would bring us any nearer to a solution?"[63]

His most acclaimed campaign contribution came from his unqualified defense of religious liberty. He presented an impassioned plea for devotion to the historic principles of the United States. The nation "had added to the three great liberties of the English-speaking peoples—The Right of Personal Liberty, The Right of Personal Security, and The Right of Personal Property—a fourth, Soul Liberty—that is, the freedom to worship God according to the dictates of one's conscience, untrammeled by any force whatsoever, political or otherwise." Even the best intentions and the highest motives could not justify suppression of liberty of opinion and of soul. Reviewing Article VI of the Constitution, he applauded the wisdom of the Founding Fathers in eliminating the religious test as a qualification for public office and in separating Church from State. "I cannot believe," he concluded, "that in my Party or my State it is possible that this great principle will at this late day be violated or called in question. . . . I can but believe that those who are proposing that it shall be violated have for some strange reason lost all sense of its place in American history and its value in American life, religious as well as political."[64]

While Bailey and other "regular Democrats," notably O. Max Gardner, Cameron Morrison, Josephus Daniels, Clyde R. Hoey, and Angus W. McLean, struggled to clarify issues and to arouse support for Smith, Democratic opposition to Smith grew increasingly power-

63. Josiah W. Bailey, *Governor Smith and National Prohibition* (Raleigh, 1928), *Bailey Papers.*
64. Josiah W. Bailey, *On Religious Liberty* (Raleigh, 1928), *Bailey Papers.*

ful and intemperate.[65] Regulars urged Smith to visit North Carolina in hope that a personal appearance would still the wildest rumors. On October 11 Smith made a brief stop at Raleigh, where he extemporaneously addressed a crowd estimated at 100,000 and then visited several other cities. Little went according to schedule on Smith's tour. Indicative of the candidate's own reaction was his later omission in his autobiography of his experiences in North Carolina. Widely divergent opinions were given on the value of Smith's personal tour, but his appearance and manner probably reinforced already existing sentiment for or against his candidacy.[66]

Addressing a meeting at New Bern, Simmons assailed Smith's relations with the corrupt Tammany Hall, denounced the subordination of Jeffersonian principles represented by the Raskob appointment, stressed the danger of urban-immigrant control of the Democratic party, and attacked Smith's intention to destroy the Eighteenth Amendment.[67] A powerful indictment of Smith's candidacy, Simmons' speech was widely circulated. His second major campaign address, however, fell far short of the mark. On October 25 he attempted to climax the campaign at Raleigh in a statewide radio address, but his three-hour-long and largely extemporaneous speech limped from one impassioned outburst to the next. Reviewing his long years of service and assailing Smith's record and principles, Simmons defied regular Democrats to read him out of the party by announcing that he would seek re-election to the Senate in 1930. "In God's name," he beseeched, "do not place upon the untarnished brow of the Democratic Party the brand of Liquor, Alienism, and Plutocracy."[68]

The passions that divided the Democratic party intensified in the closing days of the campaign. The bitterly personal intraparty squabble directed whispering campaigns against both Smith and Simmons. Cameron Morrison's statements of August 24 and October 31 indi-

65. Charlotte Observer, July 19, 1928; Raleigh News and Observer, September 7, 1928; Watson, "A Political Leader Bolts," pp. 528–529; S. C. Deskins, "The Presidential Election of 1928 in North Carolina" (unpublished doctoral dissertation, University of North Carolina, 1944), pp. 52–64.

66. Raleigh News and Observer, October 12, 1928, p. 1. See Alfred E. Smith, Up to Now (New York, 1929).

67. Raleigh News and Observer, October 13, 1928, p. 1.

68. Watson, "A Political Leader Bolts," pp. 534–535; Elmer L. Puryear, Democratic Party Dissension in North Carolina, 1928–1936 (Chapel Hill, 1962), pp. 3–20.

cated the changing attitudes toward Simmons. Morrison had originally declared temperately that "there is more to the Democratic
party in North Carolina than prohibition and Senator Simmons, God
Bless him." Later he won enthusiastic applause with the statement
that he hoped he "might live to beat Simmons as a candidate to
succeed himself" as an apology "to the people of the State for once
helping elect him."[69] Bailey's speeches remained remarkably free
from direct attacks on Simmons, although he quietly cultivated discontent among local party leaders against the bolter. By November,
Bailey had spoken in most principal cities and towns and in each case
had spent considerable time conferring with local leaders, who urged
him to run either for senator in 1930 or for governor in 1932.
Following the election, he boasted, "I am incomparably stronger in
the West now than I ever was."[70]

With Democrats fighting each other more actively than they
fought the Republicans, the election outcome should not have surprised anyone in North Carolina. Hoover received a majority of
62,969 votes over Smith out of a total vote of 635,150. North
Carolina voted Republican for the first time since 1872. Although the
Democratic slate of state officers won easy election, Republicans
seized forty-seven seats in the General Assembly and elected United
States congressmen in two districts.[71] Senator Simmons and the anti-
Smith Democrats had won a pyrrhic victory. The Democratic party
in North Carolina had split asunder in the raging passions and personalities of the campaign. Leaders faced problems of regrouping
their forces and re-establishing Democratic dominance. Was Senator
Simmons, "the bolter," to be allowed to continue his leadership or
should "regular Democrats" purge the party of fair-weather patrons?
Few Democratic politicians, however, emerged from the campaign
battles stronger then they had entered. The front page cartoon by
Berryman in the Washington *Star* symbolized the situation; it pic-
tured Josephus Daniels standing amid the wreckage of the "Solid
South" and proclaiming "We Need No New Leadership!"[72]

69. Raleigh *News and Observer*, August 25, 1928, p. 1. Charlotte *Observer*,
November 1, 1928, p. 1.
70. Bailey to Jesse H. Davis, November 7, 1928, *Bailey Papers*.
71. Edgar E. Robinson, *The Presidential Vote, 1896–1932* (Stanford,
1934), pp. 280–287.
72. See Washington *Star*, November 13, 1928, p. 1.

CHAPTER FOUR

SENATORIAL CANDIDATE

"If I should decide to run for the Senate should I announce within sixty days, or should I defer the announcement . . . ? Do you think all the forces opposed to Senator Simmons would concentrate upon my candidacy? How do you think I would run in an open field in your section?"[1] Political leaders throughout North Carolina received this inquiry from Bailey following the Republican triumph in November, 1928. While Bailey sought to rally forces of opposition to Simmons, the Senator himself began the difficult task of restoring his image as a loyal Democrat and his influence in party counsels by declaring magnanimously that he would consider "bygones as bygones" and allow "the dead past to bury its dead."[2] Bailey and others resolved, however, that Simmons' breach should neither be forgotten nor unpunished. Bailey's determination stemmed from many factors, but least important was vindictiveness. He could understand Simmons' original opposition to Smith, for he had felt similar qualms. He could excuse silent non-support from Simmons, who for twenty years had not actively participated in campaigns. Bailey could not forgive Simmons' encouragement of Democrats to split the ticket by voting for the Republican Hoover. This violated unwritten rules of politics in North Carolina. "His conduct in bolting the Convention, to which he was a delegate, is thoroughly dishonorable," Bailey explained, "and his attack upon the entire Democratic ticket (this is what his conduct amounted to) is indefensibly disloyal."[3]

Aware that Hoover intended to consolidate Republican gains in the South, Bailey suggested that "loyal Democrats" must redeem the disaffected by a policy of reconciliation, provide women voters and young Democrats a "true conception of the mission of the Democratic party in the South," lessen influence of Republican mill foremen over

1. Bailey to Jesse H. Davis, November 7, 1928, *Bailey Papers*.
2. Raleigh *News and Observer*, November 8, 1928, and December 4, 1928.
3. Bailey to Cameron Morrison, November 12, 1928, *Bailey Papers*.

workers, support a corrupt practices act to halt extensive use of money in elections, and require enrolment of voters by party affiliation to prevent Republicans from voting in Democratic primaries. To prevent Simmons from reuniting Democrats under his personal leadership, it would be necessary to insure that two of the three members of the state Board of Elections were "loyal Democrats," since the remaining Republican member would vote with Simmons; to support "loyal Democrats" for county chairmen, since they named county election officials; to canvass the General Assembly for sufficient votes to reform election and primary laws; to prepare to collect proxies quickly, since the Democratic State Executive Committee might convene at any time; and to chill hopes of all potential anti-Simmons candidates except one, since Simmons would be renominated if he faced a divided opposition.[4]

With questions of party control and leadership fresh in the minds of Democrats, Charles L. Shuping, campaign manager for Bailey in 1924, advised that "I have been planning for sometime to force concentration upon you. This can be done—but this is another matter about which there should be no delay. We should not be too sensitive about advancing plans."[5] Bailey agreed, but cautioned prudence, for "I realize that I am in pretty good position now. All the candidates for Governor would like to see me out of that race."[6] Bailey had excellent political prospects, but the situation throughout 1929 remained too fluid for concerted action. The political scene was bereft of the excitement engendered by the 1928 campaign, and the passions and bitterness of that contest faded for many Democrats. Bailey grew less confident of his chances of defeating Simmons. His inquiries indicated that both former Governor Angus McLean and Chief Justice Walter Stacey of the North Carolina Supreme Court would campaign for Simmons' office.[7] Bailey had to choose between the governorship, for which his support might be so strong that he would have no primary opposition, and a senatorship, for which he might face both Simmons and a host of other candidates. Safeguarding both prospects, Bailey

---

4. Bailey to R. A. Doughton, November 17, 1928, *Bailey Papers.*
5. C. L. Shuping to Bailey, November 20, 1928, *Bailey Papers.*
6. Bailey to C. L. Shuping, November 23, 1928, *Bailey Papers.*
7. See, for example, A. C. Jones to Bailey, December 5, 1928; R. A. Collier to Bailey, November 23, 1928; Bailey to Gallatin Roberts, January 30, 1929; Bailey to C. L. Shuping, January 30, 1929; Bailey to Gallatin Roberts, March 15, 1929; Robert R. Reynolds to Bailey, March 6, 1929, *Bailey Papers.*

devised a deceptively simple, if dangerous, maneuver. To supporters for governor, he expressed willingness to run, but emphasized the necessity of finding a suitable candidate to oppose Simmons. To supporters encouraging him against Simmons, he responded that he would run only if the party united on him, but that he did not want to lose his chance for governor. Bailey effectively prevented premature alignment of party leaders behind candidates for either position, or against him since no one knew his plans. This strategy made a virtue of necessity for it masked Bailey's own indecision.

Insisting that opposition to Simmons should be a party matter, Bailey constantly affirmed willingness to support whomever the party might choose. He warned that the opposition should organize rapidly and carefully, for Simmons would not be easily disentrenched in 1930. An editorial from the Greensboro *Daily News* aptly observed that "if Senator Simmons was 55 instead of 75 he would be slaughtered. That assumes that the displeasure at his course is of unquestioned volume. . . . The difficulty of displacing an elderly man, in North Carolina at least, has been one of the phenomena of latter years."[8] Anxious about organizational needs, Bailey authorized Shuping to poll leaders in all counties on the following questions:

(1) Would you support a candidate other than Senator Simmons for the Democratic nomination for the Senate succeeding Senator Simmons?

(2) Do you think a contest in the Democratic Party next year for the nomination for Senator desirable?

(3) In addition to the statement of your position, will you indicate your opinion as to the state of sentiment in the Party in your county?

(4) If you are opposed to Senator Simmons, whom do you prefer to run against him?[9]

Shuping immediately prepared a "Confidential" questionnaire addressed to "loyal Democrats who are interested as such in a real triumph for the party in 1930." The questionnaire was not intended to poll all Democrats in North Carolina on Simmons' renomination, but to consolidate opposition to Simmons and to stimulate interest in Bailey. Few Democrats would be unaware that Shuping had managed

8. Greensboro *Daily News*, July 15, 1929, p. 4.
9. Bailey to C. L. Shuping, July 16, 1929, *Bailey Papers*.

Bailey's campaign in 1924. Shuping later announced that of six hundred Democratic leaders answering the questionnaire only sixty-seven supported Simmons.[10]

Early in September, 1929, Bailey told friends that he would probably campaign for the Senate, but he feared that a 1917 pledge of continuing support and allegiance to Simmons might embarrass him and opposition forces. "I have been very much troubled," he disclosed, "by the fact that Senator Simmons has a very emphatic pledge from me to support him as long as he lives and a personal pledge not to run against him. I have no copy of the letter I wrote him. But I remember I made it very powerful and absolute and authorized him to make any use of it he might see fit."[11] Bailey emphasized that the pledge assumed that Simmons himself would remain loyal to the party; that it had been withdrawn in November, 1928, but not acknowledged by Simmons; and that he felt absolved from obligations, since Simmons had aligned with Republicans. For a year Bailey had optimistically planned and maneuvered to strengthen his position, but the pledge now seemed an insurmountable obstacle. While he considered himself released by Simmons' conduct, he realized that some people would not agree. "I do not care to pursue a course," he explained, "that would bring into discussion my honor."[12]

With Bailey apparently begging off, the contest with Simmons was put squarely before Judges Walter P. Stacy and W. J. Brogden, the only other prospects seriously considered by opposition leaders. Late in November, Bailey conferred at length with Stacy and Brogden, offering support to each, but neither would run without further assurances of winning. Bothersome to Bailey and, perhaps, also to Stacy and Brogden was the attitude of former Governor McLean, who had indicated interest in Simmons' office, but who had not joined opposition forces. "To tell you the truth," Bailey acknowledged, "the attitude of Governor McLean is embarrassing the unity movement in the opposition to Senator Simmons, and there are many who think that he is playing the game to reelect Simmons with a view to succeeding the Senator whenever the Senator may die."[13] Bailey feared that McLean

10. Greensboro *Daily News*, December 22, 1929, p. 1.
11. Bailey to W. B. Jones, September 13, 1929, *Bailey Papers*.
12. Bailey to C. L. Shuping, November 8, 1929, *Bailey Papers*.
13. Bailey to Robert R. Reynolds, November 29, 1929, *Bailey Papers*.

would wait until the opposition united behind one candidate and then enter the race to split the opposition and bring about victory for Simmons. In mid-December, however, McLean announced that he would not run under any circumstances as long as Simmons remained in the field. Stacy and Brogden continued to hesitate, undoubtedly because they already held high state offices and would have less to gain and more to lose than would Bailey. Bailey now declared that "I have dismissed from my mind the matter of my letter to Senator Simmons on the ground that I wrote it to a Democrat, and assuming that he would be faithful to the Party, and my view of the matter is that he forfeited all rights whenever he gave aid and comfort to the Republicans."[14]

Bailey's correspondence during the winter of 1929 made little mention of the stock market's collapse. Declines in stock prices did not affect Bailey, whose savings were largely in real estate. In early 1928 his financial statement listed total assets of $250,500, of which $200,000 represented one-half interest in the Bland Hotel of Raleigh, $20,000 represented approximately 250 acres of farm land and several city lots and houses, and most of the remainder constituted insurance policies. His stock holdings amounted to about $3,400, of which the majority was invested in local enterprises and fishing club interests.[15] Bailey could not be unaware that steady market decline testified to an end to booming prosperity, and provided means to attack successfully the Republicans, President Hoover, and those Democrats who had aided Hoover in 1928. Perhaps this realization prompted Bailey's re-evaluation of his political prospects in early December.

On Christmas Eve, 1929, Bailey recorded that all possibilities had been eliminated except for himself and Judge Brogden. He conferred for two hours with Brogden, Shuping, and Judge Heriot Clarkson on December 30, after which Brogden declared that for financial reasons he could not enter the race. Announcing his own candidacy for the Democratic party's nomination for United States senator, Bailey put the issue of party loyalty squarely before the voters. Without mentioning Simmons, Bailey asserted that "one who makes common

14. Bailey to A. F. Sams, December 3, 1929, *Bailey Papers*.
15. Bailey to E. B. Crow, Commercial National Bank, Raleigh, N.C., February 10, 1928, *Bailey Papers*.

cause with others in the interest of his own will ought to stand with them in the common decision. He cannot demand that they stand with him unless he means to stand with them."[16]

A week later Simmons formally announced candidacy, but declared that senatorial duties in addition to inadequate funds and physical stamina prevented him from conducting a personal campaign. He would run on his record of thirty years service and would depend upon friends and supporters.[17] He did not realize either the strength and organization of forces aligned against him or the weaknesses and confusion existing among groups to which he looked for support. He was accustomed to absentee campaigns, conducted by able political lieutenants, such as Bailey and A. D. Watts. By 1930, the latter was dead and the former his opponent, while Simmons' recent recruits did not have adequate campaign experience or political contacts. Simmons had always depended upon the unanimity of party apparatus and leadership behind his candidacy, but that had dissipated in the 1928 campaign. He could expect anti-Smith Democrats who had welcomed his leadership in 1928 to vindicate his judgment in 1930, but this again assumed that they could be effectively organized and that passions aroused two years before in a national battle could be revived for a state contest.

Bailey confidently believed himself master of the situation because he knew Simmons' methods and history. He asserted that Simmons had never been as strong a fighter as reputed, while the so-called Simmons machine was only mythical.[18] Recognition of his own strength and of Simmons' weaknesses shaped Bailey's personal conduct in the campaign. Although noted for his ability to express forcefully his views, Bailey submitted to the wise counsel of Shuping and others by remaining silent. This policy subordinated Bailey's own aggressive personality to the major issue of party loyalty and compelled Simmons' forces to initiate other issues that might bring the battle to Bailey. By mid-February, he rejoiced that the "policy of silence on my part is a source of great confusion to the other side.

16. Josiah W. Bailey, "Announcement of Candidacy," January 2, 1930, *Bailey Papers*; New York *Times*, January 3, 1930, p. 48.

17. Raleigh *News and Observer*, January 12, 1930, p. 1; New York *Times*, January 12, 1930, sec. 1, p. 26. For an illuminating account focusing on Simmons, see Richard L. Watson, Jr., "A Southern Democratic Primary: Simmons vs. Bailey in 1930," *North Carolina Historical Review*, XLI (Winter, 1965), 21–46.

18. Bailey to Gerald W. Johnson, January 16, 1930, *Bailey Papers*.

. . . They cannot get around a campaign projected on these lines."[19] Whether credit should be given to Bailey's silence or to the ineffectiveness of Simmons' supporters, the first two months seemed unnaturally peaceful.

Both sides concentrated on building campaign organizations. Simmons' forces had the difficult task of co-ordinating that loose alliance of "moral forces," which had held the balance of power in 1928, while the Bailey camp could build on already existing party apparatus. The advantage rested with Bailey from the beginning, since even in 1928 "regular" Democrats far outnumbered "bolters." Simmons' absenteeism deprived his organization of advice and direction needed to prevent untimely actions and internal dissension, but Bailey maintained strict vigilance over organizational efforts and statements. He utilized each day to extend privately the number and zeal of wellwishers and workers visiting him. "I have had some eight or nine hundred visitors from outside this county," he commented early in March, "and I can faithfully say that from early morning until the close of business for the day my office has been crowded with enthusiastic supporters from practically every county in the State. . . . We spend the days talking with friends and the nights answering letters."[20]

The contest grew increasingly bitter. The first overt sign appeared at the Jackson Day Dinner sponsored by Young Democrats in mid-March. The Young Democrats, founded in 1928 with a pro-Smith bias, invited the candidates to speak, but only Bailey personally accepted. Simmons sent a brief message in care of Congressman Homer L. Lyon of Whiteville, whose attempt to read Simmons' remarks met repeated jeering. Bailey's speech brought repeated ovations.[21] The significance of this occurrence could not be ignored by leaders of Simmons' campaign, for younger voters had arisen with little or no memory of Simmons' leadership in winning North Carolina from Republicans between 1898 and 1900. Simmons, seventy-six years old in 1930, appealed to many as an elder statesman, but to many others he seemed a relic of the ancient past with small conception of problems confronting a newer generation.

19. Bailey to Cameron Morrison, February 10, 1930, *Bailey Papers.*
20. Bailey to John H. Small, March 3, 1930, *Bailey Papers;* interview with C. L. Shuping, Greensboro, N.C., February 3, 1961.
21. Raleigh *News and Observer,* June 16, 1930, p. 1.

With Bailey silent and Simmons absent, the campaign revolved around charges and countercharges which eventually reached most North Carolinians through scores of pamphlets and broadsides. The records of both candidates received intense scrutiny leading inevitably to distortions. Neither side could claim lack of guilt, but Bailey's record was most vulnerable. Bailey forces stressed party loyalty, but their only instance of disloyalty from Simmons was his 1928 bolt of the Democratic national ticket. Modifying this issue to its corollary of party regularity, the Simmons backers cited statements of independence made by Bailey between 1895 and 1908 as editor of the *Biblical Recorder*. Bailey's ambivalent attitudes toward the Democratic party weakened his image of party regularity, but twenty-to-thirty-year-old statements did little to obscure Simmons' own break.

The most reasoned and powerful of comparisons for Simmons and against Bailey was the speech given by Charles A. Hines, state manager for Simmons. Hines's remarks—later published in a pamphlet entitled *Let Us Reason Together: Shall We Stone the Prophet?*—developed almost every charge against Bailey, but narrowly avoided the emotional extremes later attained by Simmons' followers. Hines charged that Bailey's record testified only to the consistency of his inconsistency:

> He has been on both sides of nearly all public questions; he has held office under a Republican administration, the worst this state ever had, and has served under a Democratic administration; he has called himself at one time an Independent and at another a Democrat; he has praised independence in politics of Bryan and Cleveland and denounced it in Simmons; he has been praised by a negro newspaper for voting for the notorious Jim Young to fill the place of a white Democrat, and has himself tardily joined forces with those who freed the state from negro rule; he has abused and criticised many leading Democrats of the state, yet calls himself a loyal party man; he has written editorials designed to cause Democrats to vote for McKinley rather than Bryan, yet says he himself has always voted the Democratic ticket. . . . We are further assured that he has always been a strong prohibitionist, yet when the good people of this state found that the neighborhood went beyond county lines

and demanded state prohibition, Mr. Bailey was wondering if local option was not the better way.[22]

Hines reaffirmed the threat of domination of the Democratic party by the corrupt Tammany organization, insinuating that Raskob and liquor interests financed Bailey's campaign. Here were the major issues of the campaign against Bailey: his early political irregularity, his lukewarm support of white supremacy, his reluctance to advocate state and national prohibition, and his alleged alignment with Raskob and Tammany. To out-of-state observers, North Carolinians appeared to be fighting the anti-Smith battle over again.[23]

Charges against Bailey's early political irregularity had some foundation, but statements taken out of context and brought forward in time by thirty years misled. Opponents made much of such statements as: "I am an Independent and Always Have Been" in reply to charges that he was a Republican in 1898; "Every Man Owes It to His Country to Vote as His Conscience bids Him" in 1900; "The slogan: 'My Party Right or Wrong,' Plays Right Into the hands of the Man Who Wants it Wrong" in 1904; "I am Independent in That I would Not Vote for Immoral Men or Measures if All the Democratic Parties in the World Should Support Them" in 1908.[24] Bailey made these statements and many more indicating an independent viewpoint, when as editor of a denominational newspaper he sought neutrality in partisan party politics, while bringing the full force of righteous concern to bear on political issues. Nevertheless, he admitted privately that "it was not my original purpose to edit the Biblical Recorder. . . . I was utterly unprepared for it, and I had everything to learn. . . . The miracle of my life is that I began editing . . . before I was 20 years of age and got away with the task as well as I did."[25]

Charges that Bailey had not given full support to the white supremacy campaign and that by implication he had favored Republican and Negro control constituted a serious threat, for it evoked emotional prejudices of almost legendary character. Typical of the attacks was a

---

22. Charles A. Hines, *Let Us Reason Together: Shall We Stone the Prophet?* (n.p., n.d.), *Bailey Papers.*
23. See, for example, Chicago *Tribune*, May 31–June 1, 1930.
24. William R. Dalton, *The Deadly Parallel* (n.p., May, 1930), *Bailey Papers.*
25. Bailey to R. D. Douglas, April 16, 1930, *Bailey Papers.*

broadside entitled *Bailey Stands by the Party, But Not the Democratic Party*, which featured a statement attributed to former Governor Aycock: "Lawlessness walked the State like a pestilence. Death stalked abroad at noonday. Sleep lay down armed—the sound of the pistol was more frequent than the sound of the mocking-bird. The screams of women fleeing from brutes closed the gates to our hearts with a shock."[26] The broadside imputed that Bailey had sneered at white supremacy, eulogized Governor Russell and the Republican party, opposed segregated facilities for whites and Negroes, and served on the State Board of Agriculture with the Negro Jim Young. Almost equally damning for Bailey was an anonymous circular entitled *Tammany and North Carolina Negroes Would Defeat Simmons*, which quoted extensively from an editorial written by Louis E. Anderson, the Negro editor of the *Carolina Times* of Durham. Anderson wrote that Simmons "will hold the Negroes up before the people of the State and [say] that he alone can save the State from the calamity of Negro domination," but that Bailey "is a different man, coming from a much younger and more intelligent school, [who] will not resort to such tactics to sway the people of the State. He is too much of a gentleman and represents a broader and more liberal-minded element."[27]

In rebuttal Bailey pointed out that the Democratic party under Simmons' leadership had printed and distributed seventy-five thousand copies of Bailey's white supremacy speech at Thomasville in July, 1898. He had upheld the constitutional amendment disfranchising the Negro, but after its adoption he had hoped "to have the negro question eliminated from politics in order that we might discuss other matters and bring about peace. . . . I did not oppose separate cars for white and colored races, but expressed regret that the negro question had come up again." He had served with the Negro Jim Young on the State Board of Agriculture in 1897, but had resigned in 1898 to support white supremacy, after which the new white supremacy legislature re-elected him in 1899 to board membership. Observing that the Democratic party had sent him out to sponsor its causes in every election since 1908, Bailey asked, "Is it possible that the Democracy of this State will now permit the advocates of Senator Simmons to

26. T. J. Ray, *Bailey Stands by the Party, But Not the Democratic Party,* *Bailey Papers.* Also see Raleigh *News and Observer,* May 2, 1930.
27. *Tammany and North Carolina Negroes Would Defeat Simmons* (1930), *Bailey Papers.*

besmirch my political record and destroy my political character after the Party has used me so long?"[28]

Bailey's attitude toward Negroes in 1900 had been advanced for the time. He had willingly supported disfranchisement to restore the state to Democratic and white leadership, but had never approved the demagoguery of politcans who used Negroes to obscure need for reforms. In 1930 he realized, of course, the political dynamite embodied in the Negro issue and allowed his supporters to use it when necessary, but he would have preferred that the issue never be raised at all. Bailey's attitude toward the Negro was decidedly paternalistic. He commented late in 1930, "I do not think the negro race would care to govern in the South, nor do I think that any of their friends would care to have them govern. All of us rejoice in their progress, and we have great attachment to them as individuals."[29] This attitude was illustrated in Bailey's attachment to his chauffeur, Joseph Washington Holloway, who traveled with Bailey throughout the campaign and, according to Bailey, "found the greatest joy in my success, and, when I won, his friends congratulated him as heartily as my friends congratulated me. . . . There is something more here than the political relation, and something much deeper than the relation of master and servant. There is not a chance that our chauffeur or our nurse will ever suffer as long as I have means."[30]

Accusations that Bailey had not been and was not in full accord with either state prohibition or national prohibition were accurate, but lacked effectiveness because of Bailey's well-publicized leadership in temperance campaigns as executive chairman of the North Carolina Anti-Saloon League between 1903 and 1907. He had always contended that local option would best control liquor traffic, but in 1930 declared himself "for the Volstead Act and any other act that may strengthen it. I am for the Amendment to the Constitution and do not for a moment entertain any thought that it will ever be repealed. . . . I may add that I practice what I preach, and am a total abstainer."[31] Perhaps the kindest observation would be that Bailey overgilded the lily in the heat of the campaign, for he disliked the Volstead Act,

28. Bailey to F. S. Worthy, April 23, 1930, *Bailey Papers.*
29. Bailey to George H. Bruce, November 25, 1930, *Bailey Papers.*
30. *Ibid.*; Bailey's "Last Will and Testament" dated July, 1929, reads in Item V: "I give to Joe Holloway, for life, my house and lot on East Davie Street, in the City of Raleigh," *Bailey Papers.*
31. Bailey to Walter Yokely, April 14, 1930, *Bailey Papers.*

disapproved the Eighteenth Amendment on principle, and pursued a personal policy of temperance rather than abstinence. He expressed his views on prohibition most clearly in private correspondence after the primary, when he pointed out that "the matter has taken a political turn that tends to prevent fair consideration of the ways and means of alleviating the evil." Bailey committed himself publicly to stand upon the Democratic platform and its prohibition pledge, while privately he admitted hoping "to bring about more moderate views on either side, all with the view to diminishing this great evil in the most effectual way possible."[32]

The corollary of the attempt to place Bailey in the antiprohibition camp was the charge that Raskob, Smith, and by implication the Catholic Church financed Bailey's campaign. At first the charge was made only obliquely, as in Charles Hines's question, "Now that Mr. Bailey is a candidate for office in a year in which it is a matter of record that Raskob's money will be used either for or against him, if there is a chance of electing a 'wet' or defeating a 'dry,' do we hear Bailey saying that he is for or against the Raskob program? No, this is a 'quiet campaign' "[33] More to the point was an eight-page pamphlet authored by John D. Langston asserting that "the Fight on Simmons Is a Liquor Fight."[34] The most exaggerated piece of propaganda portrayed the *Al Smith–Raskob–Bailey: Idea of Happiness* as "standing at a bar with one foot on the brass rail," while children wept for their degenerate fathers.[35] Apparently no direct connection existed between Bailey and Raskob's money, but Bailey did receive contributions from out-of-state business friends and their friends. For example, a letter from Herbert W. Jackson, president of the Virginia Trust Company of Richmond, enclosed "a New York check for $425.00 which Mr. John M. Miller and I have gathered up from a few of our friends here . . . all of whom know about you though most of them do not know you personally."[36] Evidence of this nature leaves some doubt as to Bailey's accuracy in stating after the primary that "I know of my own knowledge that no money came into this State for my campaign from outside. There was no connection between Mr.

32. Bailey to Gerald W. Johnson, June 23, 1930, *Bailey Papers*.
33. Hines, *Let Us Reason Together*.
34. John D. Langston, *The Issue Clearly Defined: The Fight on Simmons Is A Liquor Fight* (n.p., 1930), *Bailey Papers*.
35. *Al Smith—Raskob—Bailey: Idea of Happiness* (n.p., n.d.), *Bailey Papers*.
36. Herbert W. Jackson to Bailey, March 28, 1930, *Bailey Papers*.

Raskob and me and no funds came from him."[37] While Bailey probably did not suffer as greatly from lack of funds as did Simmons, Bailey noted just before the primary that he had "no money for workers and heelers, notwithstanding all the insinuations about Raskob and that sort of thing."[38] Bailey found references to Catholic support highly amusing, for rumors had spread that he was on the Vatican payroll with a salary of ten thousand dollars a month.[39]

Simmons' supporters also attempted to discredit Bailey with farmers and laborers. They accused him of advocating higher taxes for farmers in 1919, when he stated that "if you want some revenue right badly, assess the lands of North Carolina, thirty-three million acres of them, at their market value, as is your constitutional duty and you will get some revenue—all you need."[40] The statement had been lifted out of context, for Bailey had argued against a state income tax proposal on grounds that the federal government already collected enormous income taxes. He had insisted that North Carolina could raise its revenue by the simple and fair expedient of equalizing tax valuations between one county and another, since hogs were taxed at sixty cents in one county and three dollars in another. Bailey pointed out that when the legislature met in August, 1920, he had been employed without compensation by the Farmers' Union to resist passage of the so-called Revaluation Act, which would have transferred tax burdens from railroads and other corporations to farms and small homes.[41] Efforts to discredit Bailey with farmers fell flat in view of his repeated statements urging reduction of taxes on real estate between 1920 and 1930.

The attempt to place Bailey in an antilabor position had even less success, although Bailey felt less sympathy for laborers than for farmers. The Simmons forces widely distributed a broadside entitled: *The Labor Vote Be Hanged*, which first appeared in the Charlotte *Observer* as a letter signed by O. W. Dickens, Salisbury, North Carolina. Apparently from a Bailey supporter, the letter declared that with assistance from "the powerful forces of Northern Democracy," including Smith, Raskob, Du Pont, and Roosevelt, Bailey could win

37. Bailey to Livingston Johnson, August 14, 1930, *Bailey Papers.*
38. Bailey to John E. White, May 27, 1930, *Bailey Papers.*
39. Bailey to George Gordon Battle, June 25, 1930, *Bailey Papers.*
40. *Bailey Advocated Higher Taxes for Farmer* (n.p., 1930), *Bailey Papers.*
41. *Bailey's Great Record As a Democrat and As an Opponent of Taxation of Farms and Small Homes* (n.p., 1930), *Bailey Papers.*

without Daniels, McLean, and Gardner of North Carolina. "Further-more," Dickens stated, "let the labor vote and the common factory hands in the furniture shops and mills and tobacco plants be hanged. We can put Bailey in without them."[42] An intensive search of tele-phone directories and city and county records failed to disclose a resident of Salisbury named O. W. Dickens. The Bailey leaders responded with a four-page pamphlet exposing *An Attempted Fraud and Fake Intended to Deceive the Labor Vote of North Carolina,* which Simmons forces found highly embarrassing.[43]

Bitterly fought on many issues, the campaign centered upon the single issue of party loyalty. Each side might debate which candidate had the best record or had served in greatest measure, but Bailey's managers constantly stressed that under Simmons' leadership the state had given the Republican Hoover its electoral vote. Hoover bore responsibility for what was derisively called "Hoover Prosper-ity"—the business depression which had shut down or placed on part-time virtually all of the 633 textile mills and 100 furniture factories in North Carolina.[44] When the Negro issue broke into the campaign, Bailey partisans countered that Simmons had been respon-sible for Hoover, whose wife had insulted Southerners by receiving at a White House tea the wife of the Negro congressman from Illinois, Oscar De Priest.[45] Each side charged the other with conducting "whispering" campaigns to discredit its candidate. Simmons later claimed that his defeat had been accomplished in part by rumors that he had become senile and incapable of performing senatorial duties.[46] Bailey was charged with political and personal indiscretions which reflected upon his character and thoroughly enraged him. Bailey repeatedly confronted Shuping with lengthy statements denouncing his opponents' allegations, but each time Shuping persuaded him not to inject himself personally into the campaign.[47]

Shuping and his lieutenants, under Bailey's guidance, created a tight-knit campaign organization reaching into almost every precinct

42. O. W. Dickens, *The Labor Vote Be Hanged* (n.p., 1930), *Bailey Papers.*

43. *An Attempted Fraud and Fake Intended to Deceive the Labor Vote of North Carolina* (Raleigh, 1930), *Bailey Papers.*

44. *Why Defeat Simmons? The Answer to a Question Propounded by Mr. Ed. M. Land* (Raleigh, 1930), *Bailey Papers;* New York *Times,* June 1, 1930.

45. J. W. Bunn, *Simmons Raises Negro Racket* (Raleigh, 1930), *Bailey Papers.*

46. Rippy, *F. M. Simmons,* pp. 68–69.

47. Interview with C. L. Shuping, Greensboro, N.C., February 3, 1961.

and exploiting almost every source of discontent. He employed seven campaign workers with salaries of fifty dollars a week to co-ordinate activities of local organizations, supply printed materials and funds to bolster local efforts, and watch developments in the Simmons camp.[48] Bailey's organization had the added advantage of controlling election machinery. So serious was this that Simmons' campaign manager requested the state Board of Elections to appoint to county boards one Democrat to represent Simmons and one to represent Bailey in certifying the votes. Judge Crawford Biggs, chairman of the state board, rejected the request on grounds that in case of division the Republican member required by law would cast the deciding vote.[49] Bailey wrote gleefully to Biggs that his answer "not only successfully defends the course of the Board, but, without appearing to do so, shows up the conspiracy of the other side. My judgment is they made fools of themselves and there will be a tremendous reaction against them."[50] The conspiracy implied that the Republican member would vote with the Simmons member to reward the Senator for his 1928 assistance to the Republican party. The request may not have brought tremendous reaction, but it vividly signaled that the machine which had buttressed Simmons' power over many years had now passed to new hands.

The Negro issue reappeared in the last week of the campaign when the Wake County manager for Simmons, Bart M. Gatling, charged that Bailey forces registered over four hundred Negroes in Raleigh as Democrats in order to defeat Simmons. Bailey's managers countercharged that Negroes had been registered by the Simmons faction in an effort to raise the race issue against Bailey. They produced testimony from one Negro that he had registered as a Democrat in order to vote for Simmons "in gratitude for the senator's help in electing Hoover, who 'has given the black man more political and social recognition than any other President.' "[51] Bailey himself urged his supporters "not only in Raleigh, but elsewhere, to prevent Republicans both white and colored from taking any part in the Democratic primary."[52] His statement was obviously designed to confuse the issue thoroughly.

Two days before the primary, both Simmons and Bailey appealed

48. Puryear, *Democratic Party Dissension*, p. 31.
49. Raleigh *News and Observer*, March 30, 1930, p. 1.
50. Bailey to J. C. Biggs, March 31, 1930, *Bailey Papers*.
51. Chicago *Tribune*, May 31–June 1, 1930.
52. Raleigh *News and Observer*, May 30, 1930, p. 1.

personally to the voters. Simmons issued a statement calling attention to his thirty-year record of service to party, state, and nation, while Bailey declared in a speech at Raleigh that the Democratic party could not be preserved by advising young Democrats to vote for Hoover.[53] Both candidates testified, thereby, that the real issue of the campaign was Simmons' break with the national ticket in 1928. Bailey's speech was his first direct appeal for votes, but not, as many observers have indicated, his only personal appearance during the campaign. As early as mid-March he noted: "I am already filling up the last weeks of the campaign with commencement appointments. I shall do very extensive travelling after I have obtained a little rest."[54] On May 27, 1930, he recorded: "I have just returned from a trip, having made about 28 speeches and travelled some six or seven thousand miles in the State."[55] These commencement addresses put Bailey before thousands of North Carolinians in a "non-political" capacity, while presenting opportunities to meet and encourage campaign workers and well-wishers.

As the primary approached Bailey projected a public image of confidence, but privately felt many doubts. All reports indicated that he would win by a large majority, but growing personal attacks and constant demands for money led him to question the outcome. "Come what may, I shall not be disturbed," Bailey confided to his old friend John E. White, for "I set out to do my duty as I saw it by the Democratic Party, and I have no regrets."[56] Bailey had no regrets. On June 7, 1930, the people of North Carolina gave Bailey a plurality of about seventy thousand votes over Simmons. He carried eighty-four of the hundred counties and eight of the ten congressional districts.[57] For Simmons, of course, defeat provided a bitter and heartbreaking climax to thirty years of service in the United States Senate and forty years of leadership in the Democratic party of North Carolina.

Simmons found great difficulty in believing that North Carolinians would have renounced his leadership except under great and, perhaps, subversive coercion from his enemies. His colleague, Senator Lee S. Overman, reported to Bailey on June 13, 1930, that "Senator

53. *Ibid.*, June 6, 1930, p. 1.
54. Bailey to Clyde Hoey, March 14, 1930, *Bailey Papers*.
55. Bailey to John E. White, May 27, 1930, *Bailey Papers*.
56. *Ibid.*
57. Raleigh *News and Observer*, June 15, 1930, p. 1.

Simmons is telling everyone, indiscriminately Republicans and Democrats alike, in explaining his defeat that he had the election won up to Friday, but your agents went over the state and spent about a quarter of a million dollars in securing an organization which caused his defeat."[58] Senator J. Thomas Heflin of Alabama, who had also bolted in 1928, took to the Senate floor on June 12 to praise Simmons and to explain the defeat in stronger language: "The Tammany tactics were employed, and the Raskob agents were there. They whispered it around that Senator Simmons was very feeble and would not live out his present term. That was the dirty and slimy work of Raskob agents."[59] Bailey took no notice of Heflin's accusations and adopted a cordial and magnamimous attitude toward his fallen leader Simmons. "There was, to be sure," he observed, "no motive of punishing Senator Simmons. . . . But there was a motive of setting the Party right—of getting it back to its base—and that motive was in the breasts of thousands."[60] In reply to the committee headed by Senator Nye which investigated fraud charges against Bailey, he asserted that the accusation had absolutely no foundation in fact, and the committee itself eventually found no evidence to support the charges.[61]

Bailey's victory in the Democratic primary virtually assured his election as senator in November, but the Republican party by no means conceded the November election. The Republicans had in George M. Pritchard, the winner of the Republican senatorial primary, an able and experienced candidate, who had served several terms in the House of Representatives. Republicans undoubtedly hoped that the sharply defined factionalism among Democrats would carry over into the November election. Bailey exerted himself throughout the summer and fall, however, to bring about reunification and victory. Typical of Bailey's approach was his address at Carthage on September 15, in which he emphasized that Democrats "may divide in our primary on candidates, but we unite on our principles in the election."[62] He scored the Republican party for accepting credit for prosperity in 1928, while denying responsibility for depression in 1930. He insisted that Republican policies and

58. Senator Lee S. Overman to Bailey, June 13, 1930, *Bailey Papers*.
59. *Ibid.*
60. Bailey to Joseph M. Proskauer, June 20, 1930, *Bailey Papers*.
61. New York *Times*, October 14, 1930, 52:2.
62. Josiah W. Bailey, "An Address to the Voters of North Carolina," Carthage, N.C., September 15, 1930, *Bailey Papers*.

programs had contributed to, if not caused, the depressed condition of agriculture and industry.

Bailey charged that the Coolidge-Hoover administrations had neglected the farmers and had broken all promises to assist agriculture. Republicans had destroyed the farmers' world market by tariff measures, and then protested that farmers had overproduced. Republicans had idled the government's huge power and nitrate plant at Muscle Shoals, while exacting duties on nitrates for fertilizers imported from Chile. Republicans had done nothing to relieve tobacco farmers from heavy taxes levied during the World War, but had reduced similar taxes in the North. The Farm Relief Board under Republican administration had led farmers to plant wheat and cotton upon promises of fair prices, but had withdrawn assurances after the planting. The farmer had not been the beneficiary of Republican farm relief, but its victim. Republican policies had been equally injurious to industry, for the Coolidge-Hoover administrations had encouraged flagrant abuses of the monetary system. The great speculative orgy had concentrated all free money in Wall Street, thereby draining the banks of cash, depriving farmers and merchants of credit, and paralyzing industry for want of funds or credit. The Federal Reserve System created by Woodrow Wilson and a Democratic Congress might have prevented this monopolization of money and credit, but that institution had suffered from mismanagement and misuse under Republican leadership. Depending upon predatory interests for financial support, the Republican party could never serve the people.[63]

On Election Day, November 4, 1930, the weather was the worst in many years, with a blizzard in western North Carolina and with windstorms and rain in the east. Notwithstanding severe conditions, the Democratic party in North Carolina turned out in full strength to give Bailey a 113,073 vote plurality over his opponent Pritchard. Bailey's total vote of 323,620 was the largest majority ever given a North Carolina senatorial candidate until that time.[64] With this victory, Bailey at the age of fifty-six years attained his first and only elective office. Only the passage of years would disclose what he would make of this opportunity and how well he would serve the people of North Carolina. He intended to follow his own common sense, rather than the popular clamor, in searching for and adopting

63. *Ibid.*
64. Raleigh *News and Observer*, November 14, 1930, p. 1.

governmental policies. "I shall go to the Senate with no view to cultivating popularity," he vowed, for "I have never seen the man who could divine what is popular." Prophetic of his senatorial career was his remark that "I have gone uphill and up-stream these thirty years. I shall continue in the same direction."[65]

65. Bailey to Gerald W. Johnson, June 23, 1930, *Bailey Papers*.

CHAPTER FIVE

FRESHMAN SENATOR

FOR THE first time in almost three decades North Carolina would be represented by two fledgling senators, Bailey and Cameron Morrison, the latter having been appointed to fill the unexpired term of Lee S. Overman.[1] Both had long been stalwart defenders of the Democratic party, but while Morrison had served as governor between 1921 and 1925, Bailey had never before held high elective office. An article in the *Nation*, evaluating and comparing North Carolina's new senators, painted Morrison as a colorful champion of the people's cause and Bailey as a diligent scholar, whose "devotion to abstract principles of right and wrong, and specifically to righteousness in civil and political affairs, borders on fanaticism." Describing Bailey as a Baptist lawyer who rarely smiled and who might be taken for an ascetic, the article maintained, "His lean, angular face and cold, piercing eyes suggest Cassius, who thought too much. He is a brilliant but painstaking student whose mind quickly cuts through to the heart of a thing, with a logic that is irrefutable, and a command of language probably unequalled by any other living North Carolinian." After briefly reviewing their respective records, the article concluded that Morrison and Bailey "will be found casting their ballots more frequently with the liberal (not radical) than the conservative blocs."[2] Bailey's political career as a spirited crusader for worthy, but temporarily unpopular, causes had given him a reputation in some quarters as a liberal reformer and in others as a dangerous radical. Bailey himself was devoted to ideals of individualism, hard work, self-help, sound money, a balanced budget, strong local government, and administrative

1. Cameron Morrison, governor of North Carolina between 1921 and 1925 and Democratic national committeeman between 1928 and 1932, was appointed in 1930 by Governor O. Max Gardner to fill the unexpired term of the late Senator Lee S. Overman, who had served in the United States Senate since 1903.
2. Weimar Jones, "North Carolina's New Senators," *Nation* (January 7, 1931), pp. 11–12.

efficiency. He opposed revolutionary change, but perception of the exigencies of public welfare somewhat tempered his conservative attitude. The new senator could be expected to pursue a course in which his desire to meet pressing national needs would often conflict with his preference for trusted individualistic traditions.

Senator-elect Bailey had not yet recognized the seriousness of the nation's economic collapse. Convinced of the basic soundness of the economy, he asserted confidently on December 20, 1930, that the business tide had turned for the better.[3] He equated the depression chiefly with unemployment which had stemmed from "the breakdown of our foreign commerce" and a "blundering national policy." A secondary cause was excess production: "If I am right about this, so long as we are capable of producing more than we can consume, some sort of new order is predicated, and this order ought not to take the direction of socialism or communism." Reaffirming "the American principle of individual initiative and competition," Bailey stressed that curtailing working hours and reducing agricultural and industrial output would impair the American standard of wages and living. The economic task facing the nation was to maintain this standard, while stimulating employment through increased international commerce. Tariff problems seemed basic to foreign trade difficulties, for "the characteristic of the age is retaliatory tariffs. . . . Back of it all lies the fact that our continent is now pretty well occupied, and, if we have an outlet for our commerce, it must be foreign . . . and our problem is how to compete with the workers of other nations."[4] He apparently never considered that maldistribution of wealth might be a major flaw in the domestic economy or that its consequence might be loss of consumer purchasing power.

To meet the depression in North Carolina, Bailey proposed retrenchment. He advised reduction of taxation and expenditures. As for relief measures, he contended, "Let us place the responsibility where it rests. The disposition to look to the State for relief ought to be candidly met so far as the State may meet it; but the people ought also to know that the county commissioners and city authorities have a greater opportunity here than the legislature."[5] Frugality and thrift were in Bailey's mind the only foundation for recovery. He seemed

3. Raleigh *News and Observer*, December 21, 1930, p. 1.
4. Bailey to Santford Martin, January 9, 1931, *Bailey Papers*.
5. Bailey to O. Max Gardner, January 3, 1931, *Bailey Papers*.

unaware that as unemployment rose and as banks failed, even the thriftiest might find their savings dwindling. Nor did he yet perceive that as depression intensified and as relief burdens grew heavier, treasuries of local governments would be depleted. Along with unemployment, overproduction, and breakdown of foreign trade, Bailey thought that excessive expenditure was no small reason for depression, for "we have been spending money like wild men in a governmental way and individually."[6] These views, of course, remarkably resembled those expressed by Herbert Hoover and industrial leaders.

The depression grew grimmer through the winter of 1930–31. Hoover's management-labor pact to maintain employment collapsed as industry curtailed production and increased layoffs. Unemployment rose from 4,340,000 in 1930 to 8,020,000 persons in 1931, affecting almost 16 per cent of the civilian labor force. Bank failures increased from 1,352 in 1930 to 2,294 in 1931, wiping out several million savings accounts.[7] Yet Bailey noted in February, 1931, that "the danger is in such a situation that ill-informed and inconsiderate men will get into the leadership and bring to pass measures that will not only not accomplish the purpose desired, but will actually do lasting injury to all of us."[8] Several months later Clarence Poe, editor of the *Progressive Farmer* and a close personal friend, informed Bailey that sagging agricultural prices stimulated growing restiveness among North Carolina farmers. Poe also reminded Bailey that both the Declaration of Independence and the Constitution had been expressions of radical movements.[9] Bailey largely agreed with Poe's interpretation, but he also recognized that both documents had been "founded upon human experience and produced by men who had a due appreciation of the past." The true liberal sought the welfare and progress of mankind with a just, but not an absolute regard for history. As for growing popular restiveness, he reaffirmed, "What I most fear is that demagogues will mislead our people, and next to that I fear that men will espouse causes without having sufficiently tested them."[10]

As the bitter summer of 1931 passed with increased popular

6. Bailey to Clarence Poe, February 17, 1931, *Bailey Papers*.
7. U.S. Bureau of the Census, *Historical Statistics of the United States, Colonial Times to 1957* (Washington, 1960), pp. 73, 116, 636, 724.
8. Bailey to A. D. McLean, February 6, 1931, *Bailey Papers*.
9. Clarence Poe to Bailey, May 8, 1931, *Bailey Papers*.
10. Bailey to Clarence Poe, May 12, 1931, *Bailey Papers*.

clamor for governmental action, Senator-elect Bailey considered the role of the Democratic party in the approaching Seventy-second Congress. He suggested that although the Hawley-Smoot Tariff might be attacked, the protective policy should be continued since the United States could little afford to open its gates to nations closing theirs. He proposed a reconstructed Federal Farm Board with greater funds and power to provide financing, marketing, and voluntary crop control. Regulation of public service corporations could be demanded, but the Democratic party should support policies encouraging individual initiative. The Federal Reserve System should be liberalized to require less security of member banks and to increase funds available for credit. The voluntary principle ought vigorously to be upheld and the dole strongly opposed in matters of unemployment relief. The federal budget should be balanced by exhausting the powers of the income tax, rather than by creating a sales tax. A moderate devaluation of the dollar might be considered to relieve the debtor class, but disturbance of the gold standard would be dangerous. The United States should follow a foreign policy based upon avoidance of entangling alliances, approval of the World Court under the Root formula, and insistence upon payment of international debts. Since the Democrats were badly divided on prohibition, the final statement of position should be left until the national convention, and even then a battle must be avoided between "wets" and "drys."[11]

The Seventy-second Congress convened on December 7, 1931, with a Democratic House of Representatives and a Republican Senate. The Senate had 48 Republicans, 47 Democrats, and 1 Farmer-Laborite. So narrow was the margin that Hoover advised Senator James Watson, the Republican majority leader, to let the Democrats "organize the Senate and thereby convert their sabotage into responsibility." Hoover believed that he could deal more effectively with Democratic leaders "if they held full responsibility in both houses, than with an opposition in the Senate conspiring in the cloakrooms to use every proposal of mine for demagoguery."[12] His impressions of cloakroom conspiracies were not unfounded. Democrats, looking to the 1932 election, accused Hoover of sole responsibility for the depression. The only important legislation approved in the first month

11. Bailey to Joseph T. Robinson, November 4, 1931, *Bailey Papers*.
12. Herbert Hoover, *The Memoirs of Herbert Hoover* (New York, 1952), III, 101.

was a resolution to establish the one-year moratorium, declared by
Hoover in June, 1931, on the payment of debt installments owed the
United States by foreign governments. The House passed the resolution of December 18, after first including a specific provision placing
the Congress on record against outright cancellation of foreign obligations. The Senate voted 69 to 12, with Bailey's support, in favor of
both the resolution and the non-cancellation provision on December
22, just before adjourning for the Christmas holidays.[13]

Bailey remained silent during the first month of the congressional
session, but he felt considerable pressure from constituents both for
economy in government and for increased governmental expenditures.
He had slowly equated the daily financial statistics in the New York
Times with the human reality. Room 145 in the Senate Office Building overflowed with constituents seeking Bailey's advice, looking for
jobs, and demanding relief for distressed businesses and farms.[14] On
January 4, 1932, President Hoover urged prompt action by the
reassembled Congress on the non-partisan recovery program set forth
in December. Congress speedily approved without record votes the
Federal Land Bank and Reconstruction Finance Corporation Bills.
Called upon later to explain support for Hoover's program, Bailey
declared that both measures were Democratic in origin. In regard to
the bill doubling the capital of Federal Land Banks and extending
credit facilities, he averred, "The Federal Land Bank System is a
product of the Democratic Party and I consider that in increasing its
efficiency we are simply following the lead of Woodrow Wilson."
The Reconstruction Finance Corporation Bill, he contended, was "not
one of Mr. Hoover's bills, having been first suggested by Mr. McA-
doo [D., Calif.], and put forward as a non-partisan measure, necessitated by the emergency in which we found ourselves." He acknowledged, however, that Senate Democrats might have taken issue with
many provisions of the bill had time permitted.[15]

Bailey blamed Hoover for deliberately waiting from March to
December to call Congress into session. Faced with grave national

13. *Congressional Record*, 72nd Cong., 1st Sess., p. 1126.
14. Interview with Thad S. Page, Alexandria, Va., November 21, 1961;
Bailey to Tyre Taylor, December 28, 1931, *Bailey Papers*.
15. Bailey to C. O. McMichael, March 4, 1932, *Bailey Papers*; See, however,
Gerald D. Nash, "Herbert Hoover and the Origins of the Reconstruction
Finance Corporation," *Mississippi Valley Historical Review*, XLVI (December,
1959), 455–468.

emergency, he pointed out that Democrats might have been charged with obstructive tactics had they chosen to prepare a substitute to the Reconstruction Finance Corporation Bill. Since the chief object of the bill was "to arrest the downward progress and to allay the hysteria and demoralization, to stop the failing of the banks," he felt impelled to vote for the bill despite reservations.[16] He questioned whether people would return their money to banks under any circumstances, since confidence had been greatly shaken. Noting the businessman who exchanged paper currency for gold and placed the gold in a safety deposit box, Bailey observed that this man was only "one of thousands . . . proceeding by way of wrecking this Country, but these men will not return their money to circulation in response to any Act of Congress. Frightened and ignorant people are very dangerous and are not amenable to considerations of reason."[17]

The Senate fought its first major political battle in February over the La Follette–Costigan Relief Bill, authorizing a modest grant of $375,000,000 to states for direct aid to individuals. The bill was defeated 48 to 35, with 27 Republicans and 21 Democrats voting against it. Support came chiefly from the minority bloc of progressive western Republicans and from dissident liberal Democrats impatient with Hoover's doctrine of local responsibility for relief. Opposing the bill, Bailey announced that "the money would have gone to New York, Boston, Chicago, Detroit, Cleveland, and other great cities."[18] He also contended that responsibility for relief rested primarily upon individuals, municipalities, and states, and only at last resort upon the federal government. In view of his repeated demands for a balanced budget and for economy in government, his vote against direct relief probably stemmed more from these considerations than from fear that funds would be distributed unfairly. In early March he did concede that "undoubtedly this Congress will find it necessary to take action with a view to relieving the debtor class, not by way of moratorium but by way of correcting the appreciation of the gold dollar." According to his figures, the gold dollar was worth $1.65 in terms of farm products as compared with the year 1926, and $1.51 in terms of 784 other commodities. "It is morally wrong," he averred, "to require

16. Bailey to C. O. McMichael, March 4, 1932, *Bailey Papers.*
17. Bailey to E. S. Parker, Jr., January 25, 1932, *Bailey Papers.*
18. *Congressional Record*, 72nd Cong., 1st Sess., p. 4052; Bailey to C. O. McMichael, March 4, 1932, *Bailey Papers.*

debtors to pay their debts on this basis, and to undertake to do so is to provide moral grounds for repudiation." Believing that no man deserved an unearned increment on money, he saw relief for the growing debtor class in currency devaluation that would restore commodity prices to former values.[19]

Bailey strongly advocated currency control in his first general speech in the Senate on April 15, 1932. Obtaining the floor late in the afternoon, he analyzed the effects of a resolution introduced by Senator McKellar, which provided for a 10 per cent reduction in governmental expenses. Retrenchment in public expenditures and economy in government, although needed, might worsen already existing confusion and might magnify the disaster of the depression by adding to the seven to ten million persons already unemployed. Yet if retrenchment and economy were not pursued, at least a billion dollars of new taxes would be imposed upon the American people. The nation could not bear this tax increase, since the existence of unemployed workers over some twelve months had exhausted relief funds provided by individuals, communities, and states. "So far from the lapse of time diminishing that great army of helplessness, of fear, and of unrest," he acknowledged, "there is every evidence that that great army in the United States is increasing."[20]

These facts had not become apparent to him at once, he confessed, but "if these are the realities of the situation—and they are—there is a responsibility here, and we must meet it." He favored cutting administrative expenses, but not public works appropriations. He proposed a program of public construction to employ a million men during the next ten months. Funds could be provided by a bond issue due in the future and amortized annually. Public works could provide only temporary employment, however, for Bailey now realized that appreciation of the gold dollar had unstabilized America's financial structure. The United States Congress had never had many powers, but "there is one power which it will not exercise, and that is an absolutely fixed, expressed, clear, and unequivocal power . . . to regulate the value of money." Reminding his colleagues that a man paid in 1932 almost

19. Bailey to Brevard Nixon, March 16, 1932, *Bailey Papers*. See also Bailey to Clarence Poe, February 24, 1932; Bailey to J. Allen Taylor, June 20, 1932, *Bailey Papers*.

20. *Congressional Record*, 72nd Cong., 1st Sess., pp. 8312–8314.

$1.60 in return for each dollar borrowed in 1926, Bailey recommended deliberate devaluation. "We will not get out of this situation, we will not solve our appropriation question, we will not raise our taxes, we will die in a blind alley," he concluded, "unless the Congress of the United States excercises that power, and excercises it, in the name of God, without delay."[21]

The McKellar resolution providing for 10 per cent reduction of funds for the Treasury and Post Office departments came to a vote on April 18. Bailey voted for the reduction, which the Senate approved 37 to 31 after exempting appropriations for public buildings. In a press conference immediately afterward, Bailey reaffirmed his commitment to a policy of governmental economy and scorned efforts of certain administrative leaders and federal employees to prevent the reduction. He testified that he had received hundreds of letters and telegrams from North Carolinians threatened from Washington with loss of appropriations for various public projects. "There is a battle on in this country between the bureaucrats at Washington and the representatives of the people in Congress," he declared. His "propensity for battle" prompted him to exclaim pugnaciously: "I know of only one way to respond to a threat, and this is defiance. I shall go straight forward for economy, regardless of this stimulated propaganda proceeding out of the bureaus at Washington for the purpose of frightening our people, and thereby bringing pressure on me."[22]

The Revenue Bill of 1932 rapidly became the most controversial business before Congress. With governmental expenditures exceeding income for the first time in a decade, the tax bill had been designed to produce $1,118,000,000 in revenue, but was practically rewritten on the House floor. The Senate Committee on Finance began consideration on April 1, but became involved in battles over inclusion of import taxes on oil, coal, lumber, and copper. By a close committee vote, the import taxes were written into the bill reported to the Senate on May 9. In the subsequent division Bailey voted against import taxes on oil and coal, but supported taxes on lumber and copper. He also opposed an amendment offered by Senator Hull to prohibit increases of the protective tariff for two years. The Hull amendment was defeated 42 to 35, with all Republicans against and

21. *Ibid.*
22. Raleigh *News and Observer*, April 19, 1932, p. 6.

all but two Democrats for. The two Democrats straying from the fold were Edwin Broussard of Louisiana and Bailey.[23]

President Hoover appeared at the Capitol in person on May 31 to urge a balanced budget and to warn of the danger in further delaying the revenue bill. He charged that "if tax and economy legislation . . . had been promptly enacted there would have been less degeneration and stagnation in the country." He now favored "an extension for a limited period of the many special excise taxes to a more general manufacturers' excise tax" and would support Congress if it should be adopted.[24] He referred to an amendment offered by Senator David I. Walsh of Massachusetts, imposing a general manufacturers' excise or sales tax of 1¾ per cent of the sale price of every article by the manufacturers instead of special excise taxes already in effect. The Senate Finance Committee, meeting immediately after Hoover's address, reported Walsh's substitute unfavorably. When the substitute came to a vote, Bailey explained that hitherto he had voted consistently with the committee under the impulse of duty, but that the special excise taxes were "vexatious, obnoxious, injurious, and ineffectual." Approving the substitute, he held that the manufacturers' excise tax would reach out lightly, and although it would touch millions of people, "they would rejoice in their opportunity to make a contribution to the welfare of our country in a time like this."[25] The Senate rejected the substitute and passed the revenue bill.

Bailey's votes brought criticism from North Carolina's newspapers. The Raleigh *News and Observer* found his votes for import taxes on lumber and copper and his vote against the Hull amendment both surprising and disappointing. Josephus Daniels, the editor, asserted that when Bailey campaigned for the Senate, he "vigorously denounced the Hawley-Smoot tariff act and severely criticised Mr. Hoover for signing it. Now he has cast three votes against the letter and spirit of his own utterances."[26] Bailey did not consider his votes incompatible either with his former statements or with Democratic policy. The Democratic party stood for a protective tariff, competitive in character, which could maintain the American standard of living

23. *Congressional Record*, 72nd Cong., 1st Sess., pp. 10782, 10799, 10908, 10945, 11127.
24. William S. Myers (ed.), *The State Papers and Other Public Writings of Herbert Hoover* (New York, 1934), II, 197–203.
25. *Congressional Record*, 72nd Cong., 1st Sess., pp. 11662–11663.
26. Raleigh *News and Observer*, May 31, 1932, p. 4.

and level of wages. His vote against the Hull amendment had not been prompted by desire to raise tariff walls, but by cautious determination to protect the right of the United States to adjust its protection policy in relation to other nations' policies. The lumber industry in North Carolina, he divulged, had suffered from imports from Canada and Russia. The Katanga mines, which employed African labor at ten cents a day, shipped and sold copper to the United States for three cents per pound below cost of production in America. These facts justified his vote to impose an import tax. No one had wished to vote for special taxes, but the issue had been whether to balance the federal budget.[27]

Three months before the Democratic National Convention, Bailey drew closer to the Roosevelt organization. Considering organization for the Roosevelt campaign in North Carolina, he did not favor appointment of a manager at present, but suggested to Roosevelt and James A. Farley that Charles L. Shuping could informally look after Roosevelt's interests.[28] Following Alfred E. Smith's fighting Jefferson Day speech, Farley asked Bailey to report the reaction in Washington. Bailey promptly responded that Smith had "struck Governor Roosevelt a very hard blow, not so much by what he said as by the manifestation of his determination to beat him at any cost." Reports circulated that the New York delegation would not support Roosevelt under any circumstances and that Smith held fully two hundred votes.[29] By late April the Roosevelt bandwagon bogged down as Smith won the Massachusetts primary by a three-to-one vote over Roosevelt. Several days later Roosevelt carried a majority of Pennsylvania's delegates, but Smith again showed surprising strength. John N. Garner captured the California primary early in May, with Roosevelt a poor second and Smith a strong third. Although set back by these developments, the New York Governor would have nearly a majority of delegates at the national convention. The problem of

27. *Ibid.*, June 3, 1932, p. 4; Bailey to J. W. Davis, August 2, 1932, *Bailey Papers.*

28. Bailey to Franklin D. Roosevelt, April 12, 1932, *Bailey Papers.* Since mid-November 1931, Bailey had conducted a heavy correspondence with Roosevelt.

29. Bailey to James A. Farley, April 25, 1932, *Bailey Papers.* In his Jefferson Day Speech, Smith declared: "I will take off my coat and fight to the end against any candidate who persists in demagogic appeals to the masses of the working people of this country to destroy themselves by setting class against class and rich against poor!" New York *Times*, April 14, 1932, p. 1.

lining up two-thirds of the delegates became more pressing. Fred J. Paxon, a close friend of Bailey and Roosevelt, approached Bailey with a suggestion that the two-thirds rule be abrogated. Bailey replied that he opposed this rule, but thought it unwise to seek a change in the midst of the nominating race. Such a venture would provoke resentment and retaliation at a time when their chief goal should be to unite the party.[30]

The political situation in North Carolina was delicate for Bailey. His senior colleague, Cameron Morrison, was engaged in a bitter primary battle. Morrison's opponents were Frank D. Grist, Thomas C. Bowie, and Robert R. Reynolds. Grist was a strong supporter of Furnifold M. Simmons, but Bowie and Reynolds had supported Bailey in his 1930 campaign against Simmons. Bailey felt considerable pressure from Morrison to support him, but determined to remain neutral. "I am for him," he commented, "but I shall not go to the extent of doing anything that would give the other candidates just ground for criticism."[31] The fact that Reynolds campaigned on a "wet" platform in a state in which prohibition remained an emotional issue further complicated the senatorial race. The implications for the national scene were manifold in Bailey's view and moved him to assert, "We are trying to proceed by way of unity and harmony with the view to carrying North Carolina Democratic in the election. The fact that the State is dry and our Country is wet tends to make this somewhat difficult and would really put the State in jeopardy, if we should have a bad fight in the convention like we did in 1928." Nevertheless, he repeatedly assured Farley and Roosevelt that sentiment in North Carolina favored Roosevelt and that the delegation would support him. Bailey also conferred with McAdoo of California and Garner of Texas at their request, frankly advising them to make no moves in North Carolina.[32]

In late June the Winston-Salem *Journal* reported that "if North Carolina has any Democratic 'bosses' now they are O. Max Gardner and Josiah William Bailey. . . . For the present, it is apparent that Governor Gardner has the edge on Senator Bailey."[33] While the term "bosses" conjured up stronger images than perhaps existed in reality,

30. Bailey to Fred J. Paxon, May 13, 1932, *Bailey Papers.*
31. Bailey to J. S. Manning, March 21, 1932, *Bailey Papers.*
32. Bailey to Fred J. Paxon, May 13, 1932, *Bailey Papers.*
33. Winston-Salem *Journal*, June 29, 1932, p. 4.

Gardner and Bailey did effectively control the state organization of the Democratic party through their numerous friends and appointees. This alliance was extremely cordial. Gardner usually deferred to Bailey's strong wishes, while Bailey showed little disposition to compete with Gardner in manipulation of party politics. In the state primary contests of 1932 Gardner successfully concentrated his forces behind the candidacy of J. C. B. Ehringhaus for governor, while Bailey lent silent support. Neither Bailey nor Gardner gave the full support of their organizations to Senator Morrison, apparently because neither considered it necessary. Morrison himself was superbly confident, but in the first primary on June 4 he received fewer votes than Reynolds. Awakened from complacency, the Gardner-Bailey forces rallied behind Morrison in the second primary, but the trend to Reynolds had become irresistible. Reynolds, who in Bailey's words was "wringing wet," had caught the imagination of the distressed by promises to vote for payment of the soldiers' bonus, by attacks upon the wealthy, and by promises to redistribute wealth.[34] Reynolds' victory did not upset the balance of political power in North Carolina, but it would be necessary, particularly for Bailey, to find means of accomodating Reynolds on patronage matters.

Leaving for the Democratic National Convention in Chicago on June 21, Bailey jumped into the preconvention scramble for delegates. Roosevelt had almost a majority of the delegates pledged or instructed for him but still fell some two hundred votes short of the required two-thirds. James A. Farley sent out a questionnaire from the Roosevelt headquarters in the Congress Hotel requesting information on delegation committee assignments and voting preferences. Bailey promptly responded for the North Carolina delegation that C. L. Shuping had been assigned to the Committee on Permanent Organization, A. D. McLean to Rules and Order of Business, Josephus Daniels to Credentials, and Bailey himself to the Resolutions and Platform Committee. He estimated that Senator Thomas J. Walsh of Montana would receive twenty votes for permanent chairman, while only six votes would go to Jouett Shouse. He judged that a motion to adopt the majority rule in selection of candidates would receive only four and one-half votes, while twenty-one and one-half would be cast for retention of the two-thirds rule. In a postscript he scrawled this

---

34. Bailey to Gerald W. Johnson, July 6, 1932, *Bailey Papers.*

message for Farley: "If anything beats Roosevelt it will be this immature movement to change the rule."[35]

The fight against the two-thirds rule created a major crisis on June 24 when Senator Huey P. Long rose at the first meeting of Roosevelt forces with a resolution to abolish the rule. Roosevelt's supporters immediately split, with such liberals on this point as Josephus Daniels of North Carolina, John Rankin of Mississippi, and Burton Wheeler of Montana in favor, and with conservatives such as Bailey, Pat Harrison of Mississippi, and William B. Bankhead of Alabama in opposition.[36] As dissension weakened the Roosevelt movement, Bailey worked to hold the delegates together. Edward J. Flynn, one of Roosevelt's most trusted advisers, later recalled that "the day after our intention became known Senator Josiah W. Bailey of North Carolina stormed into our headquarters, thoroughly enraged at what we had started. He told us that we would not only lose the votes of North Carolina, but that we would alienate every other Southern state if we persisted in raising the question of two-thirds rule. Farley and I took a lesson in national politics then and there."[37] Bailey wired Roosevelt a strongly worded telegram in which he warned, "I regret necessity of saying that the fight on two-thirds rule affects your supporters' sense of your character and threatens to demoralize your friends here and to defeat you if nominated."[38] Several hours later, Roosevelt issued a statement from Albany disclaiming any intention to change the rule.[39] Bailey subsequently commented that North Carolina had turned the tide of battle, but noted that the fight had started again when the Committee on Rules submitted a resolution to abrogate the two-thirds rule on the sixth ballot. "When this happened," he recorded, "I went to bat and talked directly with Governor Roosevelt. He stood with us and we forced the Committee on Rules to rescind its action."[40]

35. Mimeographed questionnaire from Farley filled out by Bailey, June 1932, *Bailey Papers*.
36. Arthur M. Schlesinger, Jr., *The Crisis of the Old Order* (Boston, 1957), p. 299; Frank Freidel, *Franklin D. Roosevelt: The Triumph* (Boston, 1956), p. 299.
37. Edward J. Flynn, *You're the Boss* (New York, 1947), p. 90.
38. Bailey to Franklin D. Roosevelt, June 27, 1932, telegram, *Bailey Papers*.
39. Flynn, *You're the Boss*, p. 90.
40. Bailey to Robert Lathan, July 6, 1933, in personal collection of Thad S. Page, Alexandria, Va.

With the two-thirds rule context retired for the 1932 convention, the delegates turned to nominating and electing their candidates for president and vice president. On Thursday, June 30, 1932, Roosevelt's name was placed in nomination, along with the names of Alfred E. Smith, John N. Garner, and several "favorite sons." Three ballots and forty-eight hours later the so-called "Stop Roosevelt" coalition collapsed, although the Smith forces remained irreconcilable. Shortly before the fourth ballot, Garner released his large bloc of Texas and California delegates to Roosevelt, whose total vote climbed to 945 out of 1,148. Roosevelt decisively secured the Democratic nomination for president, while Garner became the unanimous choice of the convention for vice president. Breaking a long-standing tradition, Roosevelt immediately wired the convention that he would fly to Chicago to accept the nomination in person. He declared in his acceptance speech that "our Republican leaders tell us economic laws—sacred, inviolable, unchangeable—cause panics which no one could prevent. But while they prate of economic laws, men and women are starving. We must lay hold of the fact that economic laws are not made by nature. They are made by human beings." He further affirmed the Democratic party's role as "the bearer of liberalism and of progress and at the same time of safety to our institutions," promised retrenchment and economy in the federal government, gave assurances that the new administration would "assume bold leadership in distress relief," and pledged himself and the party "to a new deal for the American people."[41]

The nomination settled and the campaign underway, Bailey returned to North Carolina after adjournment of Congress on July 16. He had fought unstintingly for Roosevelt, but disapproved both the tone and the timing of the acceptance speech. Writing to Farley in mid-August, he suggested that Roosevelt had erred in addressing the convention and implied that the speech itself had not been well-considered. He particularly disliked the statement that economic laws were man-made, for "while there is dispute on this subject, the accepted doctrine for 150 years is that fundamental economic laws are natural laws, having the same source as physical laws. . . . I realize, of course, that the more modern view is that there are no

41. Samuel I. Rosenman (ed.), *The Public Papers and Addresses of Franklin D. Roosevelt* (New York, 1938), I, 647–659.

stable and reliable laws of economics, but I do not subscribe to this view."[42] Disappointed, if not disillusioned, with Roosevelt, Bailey nevertheless campaigned throughout North Carolina for the entire Democratic ticket. He repeatedly charged that neither Hoover nor the Congress had done anything to relieve the economic depression and called for general tax reduction, a reasonable devaluation of the gold dollar, a balanced budget, and "a new deal for the country—a new deck and a new dealer."[43] Four weeks later Roosevelt, the original new dealer, carried forty-two states with 472 electoral votes, while Hoover won only six states with a total of 59 votes.

Democrats in the lame-duck Congress made no pretense of cooperation with President Hoover and engaged in lengthy discussions concerning their course following transferal of power in March, 1933. At a closed conference of Democratic senators shortly after the convening of the second session of the Seventy-second Congress on December 5, Senator Huey Long delivered a furious tirade demanding immediate steps to decentralize wealth and to initiate his "Share-Our-Wealth" program. Columnist Drew Pearson, in describing the conference, noted that the "dapper, fastidious, conservative" Bailey showed increasing impatience with Long's harangue and icily interrupted, "If I correctly interpret the Senator's proposition, I am against it." Long, after eyeing Bailey briefly, drawled, "Maybe so, but the people of North Carolina are not."[44]

42. Bailey to James A. Farley, August 13, 1932, *Bailey Papers.*
43. Raleigh *News and Observer*, October 12, 1932, p. 2.
44. *Ibid.*, December 15, 1932, p. 9.

CHAPTER SIX

THE NEW DEAL EMERGES

"MANY CONCESSIONS will be made to popular demands. The strong men in financial circles have made so many blunders and done so many things that cannot be defended, it is likely that the socialistic and populistic ideas will prevail much more fully than is good for us," predicted Bailey on the eve of Franklin D. Roosevelt's inauguration.[1] By March 4, 1933, the American economy approached complete paralysis as unemployment reached new heights, trade and industry verged on full stops, and bank closings touched the financial nerve center of New York City. In this atmosphere of calamity and challenge, the expectant eyes of a distressed nation turned to Roosevelt. Affirming that "the only thing we have to fear is fear itself—nameless unreasoning, unjustified terror which paralyzes needed efforts to convert retreat into advance," Roosevelt pledged vigorous and immediate action. He confidently expected speedy approval by Congress of recovery legislation, but warned that should Congress fail he would ask for "broad Executive power to wage a war against the emergency, as great as the power that would be given to me if we were in fact invaded by a foreign foe."[2]

Between March 9 and May 12, the Congress approved six measures: (1) the Emergency Banking Bill, providing for reopening closed banks and giving the government power to control currency movements, (2) the Beer-Wine Revenue Bill, legalizing sale of low-alcoholic-content beverages, (3) the Economy Bill, cutting government spending, (4) the Reforestation Unemployment Bill, establishing the Civilian Conservation Corps, (5) the Federal Emergency Relief Bill, appropriating $500,000,000 for direct-relief grants, and

1. Bailey to James Hinton Pou, February 28, 1933, *Bailey Papers*.
2. Roosevelt, *Public Papers and Addresses*, II, 11–15. For an interesting examination of the use of the imagery of war to justify New Deal actions, see William E. Leuchtenburg, "The New Deal and the Analogue of War," in John Braeman *et al.* (eds.), *Change and Continuity in Twentieth-Century America* (New York, 1966), pp. 81–143.

(6) the Agricultural Adjustment Bill, providing for farm relief and including the Thomas Amendment conferring powers of monetary expansion on the President. Bailey supported only the first, third, and fourth, but he especially applauded the President's apparent determination to reduce regular governmental expenditures as a means of balancing the federal budget. Speaking for the Economy Bill, he declared that "excessive debt and excessive taxes—Federal, State, and local—were the underlying causes of the depression and . . . are no less the principal obstacles to overcoming it." Although many of his colleagues spoke lightly about budget balancing, Bailey believed this the most serious proposition before the country, since unbalanced budgets demanded increased taxation and resulted in business uncertainty and unstable commodity prices.[3]

Of the three opposition votes, only two brought criticism, for Bailey's dissent on the Beer-Wine Revenue Bill corresponded to general sentiment in North Carolina. Critics severely rapped Bailey's rejection of the Federal Emergency Relief Bill, pointing to his supposed disinterest in the unemployed. Bailey explained that the bill discriminated against North Carolina, which could not afford to put up two dollars for every one dollar of federal matching funds. He contended that North Carolina would therefore pay taxes benefiting richer states, while receiving little in return. Critics remained dissatisfied, however, for they anticipated immediate relief efforts rather than eventual tax increases or disproportionate distribution. Bailey thought Roosevelt inconsistent in establishing two budgets, one reducing regular expenditures and the other increasing emergency spending. Nor did the President's facile explanation that the emergency was temporary ease Bailey's concern over rising deficits.[4]

Nothing in Bailey's early failures to support New Deal legislation created greater disapproval in agrarian North Carolina than his opposition to the Agricultural Adjustment Act. He agonized over his proper course, for he approved the greater portion of the bill, particularly the Cotton Option Plan to lift cotton prices and dispose of surpluses and the agricultural credit provision to relieve farm-mortgage burdens. Comparing the complex array of provisions to a sandwich with attractive top and bottom layers, he found the middle portion quite indigestible. "The processing tax and the price-fixing

3. *Congressional Record*, 73rd Cong., 1st Sess., pp. 278–280.
4. *Ibid.*, p. 536. See also Bailey Press Release, May 7, 1933, *Bailey Papers*.

theory," he charged, "are the most veritable concoction of legislative confusion and ineffectiveness . . . the most far-fetched and far-reaching vagaries that ever gave promise of passage by the Congress."[5] Bailey opposed at least five features of the bill: (1) tariff rates on certain articles higher than those of the Smoot-Hawley tariff, committing the nation irrevocably to the protective tariff, (2) sales taxes on necessities such as cotton goods, flour, and hog products, (3) processing taxes levied by the secretary of agriculture and appropriated for crop reduction with no recognition of the tax source, (4) the secretary of agriculture's power to fix prices of farm products and to penalize anyone paying less, and (5) the so-called Thomas Amendment, which provided three different methods of inflating the currency.[6]

Bailey concluded that the bill would pass, but believed that the common judgment of the Senate opposed it: "I have never since I have been here heard a bill advocated on this floor with less enthusiasm and denounced in the cloakrooms with more ardor than this has been."[7] He recounted that at one point Senator William E. Borah interrupted floor debate on the price-fixing amendment in order to bring up the question of the recognition of Russia, but a colleague walking into the cloakroom remarked that "the question now was whether Russia would recognize us." Another remarked that "we were no longer expected to have the courage of our convictions, but only to have the courage of President Roosevelt's convictions."[8] To his own constituents Bailey declared that "I am not here, as I understand it, to take legislation blindfolded from any source. . . . But if it shall appear at length that the President has avoided the features of the Bill that I could not support . . . I hope my critics will take note of the fact."[9] Bailey's critics did not take note. The Agricultural Adjustment Bill underwent extensive revision in conference where the President had the price-fixing amendment stricken. Later, Roosevelt

5. *Congressional Record*, 73rd Cong., 1st Sess., pp. 1866–1877. See also Bailey to Josephus Daniels, May 5, 1933, *Josephus Daniels Papers*, Library of Congress, Washington, D.C.
6. Raleigh *News and Observer*, May 7, 1933, p. 1. See also Bailey to Eric W. Rogers, May 12, 1933; Bailey to N. L. Duncan, May 5, 1933, *Bailey Papers*.
7. *Congressional Record*, 73rd Cong., 1st Sess., pp. 1866–1877.
8. Bailey to Tom P. Jimison, May 10, 1933, *Bailey Papers*.
9. Raleigh *News and Observer*, May 7, 1933, p. 1. See also Bailey to Josephus Daniels, May 5, 1933, *Daniels Papers*.

gave public assurances that he would not impose the higher tariffs, that he would postpone the processing taxes for 1933, and that he would not invoke authority to issue printing-press money.[10]

In the third month of the special session, the pressure of legislative duties lightened when Bailey and other southern senators held the floor for several days to reply to an impolitic speech made by Secretary of Labor Frances Perkins. A professional social worker from New York and the first woman Cabinet member, Secretary Perkins irritated southerners with an address to the girls' work section of the Welfare Council of New York. "When you realize the whole South of this country is an untapped market for shoes," she stated, "you realize we haven't yet reached the end of the social benefits and the social good that may come from further development of the mass production system . . . a social revolution will take place if you put shoes on the people of the South." Rising to defend the South, Bailey good-naturedly ridiculed Secretary Perkins by observing that even mules in the South wore shoes. He brought out the Census Bureau's report to show that shoe sales in the South compared favorably with northern sales, if one considered the climate. In reciting a history of the South since the Civil War, he specified that for sixty years the North had taxed the South to pay for that war.[11] The incident had many humorous elements, but Perkins' lack of political discretion impressed Bailey, who commented four years later: "It is a great pity to think that anybody could be so highly educated as she is and yet be so ignorant."[12]

Congress enacted some fifteen major laws, many without record votes, before adjournment in mid-June. Among these were the Securities Act, requiring full financial disclosure of issues in new securities; the Home Owners' Loan Act, providing for refinancing of home mortgages; the Glass-Steagall Banking Act, separating investment banking from deposit banking; the Emergency Railroad Transportation Act, establishing a federal co-ordinator; and the Farm Credit Act, reorganizing agricultural credit activities. Although these laws passed by voice vote, Bailey's letters indicate that he supported all.[13]

10. Bailey Press Release, May 12, 1933, *Bailey Papers*; Bailey to Josephus Daniels, May 17, 1933, *Daniels Papers*.
11. *Congressional Record*, 73rd Cong., 1st Sess., p. 4157.
12. Bailey to J. S. Manning, January 29, 1937, *Bailey Papers*.
13. See, for example, Bailey to Louis Graves, May 23, 1933, *Bailey Papers*. *Congressional Record*, 73rd Cong., 1st Sess., p. 5599.

The Tennessee Valley Authority Act, providing for development and operation of federal properties in the Tennessee Valley, passed the Senate on May 3. If present, Bailey would probably have voted for the bill, since he had previously expressed approval.[14] Early in June the Senate indorsed a joint resolution abrogating the gold clause in public and private contracts. Bailey strongly supported the resolution as a necessary step toward devaluating the currency and placing the nation on a competitive trade basis. He also approved the National Industrial Recovery Act, which provided codes of "fair competiton" for industry under federal supervision and for a three billion dollar public works program.[15] Neither the public record nor Bailey's correspondence indicated the reasons for his support of the NIRA beyond its program to aid business recovery. On the basis of his position on other New Deal measures, he should have opposed the codes of "fair competition" as price-fixing devices and the public works program as evidence of deficit spending.

Reviewing the accomplishments of Congress in responding to Roosevelt's leadership, Bailey observed that "all of the money that has been asked for has been granted. All of [the] constructive measures which have been recommended have been enacted, and all the power that has been called for has been given."[16] Bailey himself had supported many New Deal programs, but his critics naturally remember only his key opposition votes. This oversight stemmed partially from the temper of the times, which prompted Josephus Daniels to advise: "All these measures Mr. Roosevelt is stressing in the extremity are experiments. Most of them will be temporary, but, my dear friend, with the conditions as terrible as they are . . . I think we ought to take every chance, and Democrats ought to vote together."[17] Bailey's two major opposition votes involved the popular farm relief and unemployment relief bills and were conspicuous when few other Democrats voted "Nay." Resigned to criticism, he fully expected the passing of time to vindicate his position. Speaking only as a conservative could in a period of rapid change, he remarked that "after some

14. Bailey may not have been enthusiastic in support of TVA, but he paid close attention to a joint resolution of the General Assembly of North Carolina urging development of the project. Bailey to P. V. Parks, January 22, 1936, *Bailey Papers.*
    15. *Congressional Record,* 73rd Cong., 1st Sess., pp. 4929, 5424.
    16. *Ibid.,* pp. 5599–5603.
    17. Josephus Daniels to Bailey, May 10, 1933, *Bailey Papers.*

forty years of it [criticism], I do not see much difference between going up stream and down. In fact, it is a little pleasanter going up stream, if, for no other reason, you do not have to move so fast."[18]

Bailey disapproved the continuing transferal of power from Congress to the President. In his analysis, the powers of Congress, already greatly limited by the Constitution, had been surrendered one by one to the Executive. Authority to regulate the value of money had been given up with the Thomas Amendment to the AAA. Direct congressional control of appropriations had been lost by permitting the President to make such allocations from lump sums as his discretion allowed. Power to regulate commerce between the states slipped further under Executive direction with passage of the Railroad Coordination Act. The Constitution reserved control of local matters for the states, but Congress had given the federal government power to regulate all industries, businesses, and farming operations through the NIRA and AAA. If this trend should continue in the name of emergency, it would lead to "the subversion of the Government and the abandonment of the representative trust imposed in the Members of Congress."[19]

Besides his strictly legislative duties, Bailey confronted an endless stream of visitors and delegations seeking government jobs, asking special favors, and offering suggestions for projects in North Carolina. He regretted time taken from study of proposed legislation. "I do not object to a man who comes with some business and presents it and gets out," he asserted, "but these boys who chew the rag and kill time are as pestiferous as the lice and locusts of Egypt."[20] He particularly disliked job-hunters who appeared with the information that they could do "most anything." Bailey wanted a straightforward answer and would go to great efforts to satisfy a deserving person. After hearing this evasive answer several times, however, he would usually glare across his desk and ask bluntly if the applicant could "play the fiddle." This retort usually created a bitter enemy, but typified Bailey's impatience with patronage. He intrusted most patronage requests to his administrative assistants, Thad S. Page and, in 1936, A. Hand James, with the comment that "he hadn't been elected to the

18. Bailey to R. L. Gray, May 10, 1933, *Bailey Papers*.
19. Bailey to H. S. Williams, May 19, 1933, *Bailey Papers*.
20. Bailey to Thad S. Page, December 29, 1941, in personal collection of Thad S. Page, Alexandria, Va.

Senate to be an employment agency."[21] Nevertheless, Bailey's office processed tens of thousands of requests from North Carolinians between 1933 and 1946. In October, 1933, he asserted that "of course there are thousands of our people who are being disappointed in their desire to get upon the public payroll. . . . [B]ut I am doing the best I can to get good men and first class Democrats placed. I counted up recently and we have gotten 142 appointments at Washington since March 4th."[22]

On official patronage matters, Bailey consistently consulted with other members of Congress from North Carolina. He worked particularly well with Representatives Robert L. Doughton and Lindsay Warren, but could not satisfy everyone. Congressman Frank Hancock from the Fifth District frequently charged that the Works Progress Administration in North Carolina constituted a "one man setup" operating for Bailey's "political welfare." Bailey did have some influence, of course, in the appointment of George W. Coan, Jr., as state administrator of WPA, but he had no intention of building a political machine of officeholders. He held the policy that recommendations from congressmen on behalf of appointees in their own districts should have consideration superior to that of senators and publicly advised all persons seeking jobs under WPA to communicate with their congressmen rather than with him. "When our government goes into the business of distributing money for work or for relief," he insisted, "the partisan view must be dismissed."[23]

In matters of patronage falling exclusively within the prerogatives of North Carolina's senators, Bailey experienced difficulty at first in co-operating with Robert R. Reynolds. Lack of unity between Bailey and Reynolds on recommendations contributed in June of 1933 to the loss for North Carolinians of the positions of commissioners and assistant commissioners of internal revenue. Realizing that their public quarreling over patronage not only hurt North Carolina but also weakened their political power, Bailey and Reynolds worked out a compromise. Bailey appointed the collector of internal revenue, the

21. Interviews with James Hinton Pou Bailey, Raleigh, N.C., November 2, 1961, A. Hand James, Raleigh, N. C., November 1, 1961, and Thad S. Page, Alexandria, Va., November 21, 1961.
22. Bailey to Josephus Daniels, October 25, 1933, *Daniels Papers*.
23. Raleigh *News and Observer*, June 23, 1935, p. 1; Bailey to Lindsay Warren, August 26, 1933, and Bailey to Lindsay Warren, August 19, 1935, *Bailey Papers*.

United States marshal for eastern North Carolina, and the United States district attorneys for eastern and middle North Carolina, while Reynolds named the collector of customs, the district attorney for western North Carolina, and the marshals for western and middle North Carolina. Staying on good terms with the governors of North Carolina, Bailey worked with them throughout his senatorial career to develop the inland waterways system, seaports on the eastern coast, and the Great Smoky Mountains National Park. When receiving delegations, however, he often appeared less than tactful. On one occasion he greeted the governor and several members of the General Assembly with the question: "Well, what kind of raid on the United States Treasury are you planning today?"[24]

Economic activity revived under the impact of cheap government credit and the contagion of confidence generated by Roosevelt between March and July. North Carolinians especially welcomed the rise in farm prices, for production of cotton and tobacco had risen above the 1932 level. Concerning the World Monetary and Economic Conference in London, Bailey noted: "The President . . . fears, as I think, that the stabilization of currencies at this time might bring on a reaction and might arrest the advance of prices on farm commodities."[25] His analysis proved accurate when Roosevelt disrupted the London conference by refusing to consider re-establishment of an international gold standard and by announcing for a policy of national expediency. Although the Roosevelt administration had engaged in passive dollar devaluation, this proved inadequate when in midsummer the slight economic boom collapsed and farm prices fell abruptly. Roosevelt embarked on a positive program of devaluation in order to raise prices. Bailey indicated the urgent need for such devaluation on October 24: "To fail to raise the prices of agricultural commodities while the crops are coming in will be fatal. . . . Instant action is required."[26] An executive order on the following day authorized purchase of domestically mined gold. Since the world market remained below the domestic price, the United States soon began to buy foreign gold on the London market. As a result of these currency manipula-

24. Interviews with A. Hand James, Raleigh, N.C., November 1, 1961, and Thad S. Page, Alexandria, Va., November 21, 1961.
25. Greensboro *Daily News*, June 23, 1933, p. 1.
26. Raleigh *News and Observer*, October 25, 1933, p. 2. Also see Bailey to Josephus Daniels, September 5, 1933, *Daniels Papers*.

tions, the dollar was devalued to 59.06 cents by January 31, 1934.[27]

Late in November, Bailey observed that reduction in dollar values had been reflected in increased prices of cotton and tobacco abroad, but that reduction had not been effective at home. "North Carolina is profitting by the operation as no other State is," he asserted, "and the disparity between prices paid by North Carolina farmers and prices received by them is being corrected."[28] He feared, however, that when depreciation became effective in the United States, the effect of correcting disparity would be lost. Such operations appeared so salutary that the voting public would demand further inflationary measures. Nevertheless, he could not resist arguments for dollar devaluation that might provide justice between debtor and creditor. He instructed farmers how to benefit from the new monetary policy. He explained that the present advantage for cotton and tobacco producers was temporary, since both Great Britain and Japan were buying heavily to accumulate stockpiles. He also thought that the dollar would be stabilized at a less advantageous point in relation to foreign currency values by the next harvest. For these reasons farmers should use their unexpectedly good returns to pay off debts and taxes. He further suggested that all farm mortgage indebtedness be refinanced through federal land banks and that farmers negotiate with creditors to obtain cash discounts.[29]

Bailey's thoughts turned increasingly to the task of completing the nation's economic recovery. "Altogether our country is having a bad setback," he noted in late November. "It looks like Congress is going to meet under very trying conditions. Business index is now only four points above January 1933. This means we have lost a great deal that we thought we had gained." He hoped for substantial stimulation of commerce and industry within the next five months, provided the AAA and the NIRA proved successful. The new year would bring better cotton prices if acreage could be reduced to thirty million acres and stabilized. The National Recovery Administration had made some headway, but "enthusiasm for it is dying out and I have reason to believe that the Government is not going to put it forward as hard

27. Broadus Mitchell, *Depression Decade* (New York, 1947), p. 152.
28. Bailey to W. T. Shore, November 28, 1933, *Bailey Papers.*
29. Laurinburg *Exchange*, December 7, 1933, p. 4. Also see Raleigh *News and Observer*, December 22, 1933, p. 2.

and fast as it once appeared." The President would soon need to stabilize the dollar, for fear had spread throughout the country of inflation like that of revolutionary France or of postwar Germany. Roosevelt would stop short of danger, Bailey reaffirmed, for he "is rather bold and venturesome, but nobody would say he is a wild man or a fool."[30]

Congress proved in 1934 almost as compliant to Roosevelt's recommendations as during the Hundred Days. On deficit spending and inflation it often seemed more radical than the President, but as the economy slowly revived in midyear, the spirit of co-operation faded with the sense of emergency. Bailey began the session as a strong advocate of the President's proposal for stabilizing the dollar. At Majority Leader Joseph T. Robinson's request, he presented Roosevelt's monetary policy to the Senate.[31] He recalled shortly thereafter that the situation had given him opportunity to defend Roosevelt, since "I took the view that the legislation was constructive and moderate and that it was aimed in the direction of the President's pledge and the Democratic platform."[32] The Gold Reserve Act passed the Senate on January 27, 1934, under strong administration pressure, by a vote of 66 to 23, with Senator Glass the only Democrat to join the twenty-two Republicans opposing the measure.[33]

Recovery legislation, particularly amending and correcting laws passed in the hectic 1933 session, took up much of the congressional session. Bailey was recorded or announced in favor of the Vinson Naval Parity Act, approving navy buildup to the treaty limits of 1922 and 1930; the Emergency Air Mail Act, empowering the postmaster general to conduct the air mail service directly; the Philippine Independence Act, providing for inauguration of a new Philippine government and for independence in ten years; the Securities Exchange Act, to establish a commission to regulate securities; the Trade Agreements Act, authorizing the President to negotiate trade agreements with foreign governments without the advice and consent of the Senate; the Silver Purchase Act, authorizing the President to nationalize silver; the Electric Rate Investigation Resolution, ordering the Federal Power Commission to report on rates charged by private and

30. Bailey to Josephus Daniels, November 28, 1933, *Daniels Papers*.
31. *Congressional Record*, 73rd Cong., 2nd Sess., pp. 1387–1391. Also see Bailey to James A. Farley, July 19, 1934, *Bailey Papers*.
32. Bailey to Josephus Daniels, February 6, 1934, *Daniels Papers*.
33. *Congressional Record*, 73rd Cong., 2nd Sess., p. 1489.

municipal corporations; the Municipal and Corporate Bankruptcy Acts, relaxing bankruptcy proceedings and giving federal aid; and the National Housing Act, establishing the Federal Housing Administration and providing for home financing and mortgage insurance. He also voted for the Revenue Act of 1934, which, among other things, partially shifted the tax burden from small-income taxpayers in the "earned income" class to those whose incomes came primarily from "unearned sources," but he balked at voting for the amendment providing for the making of individual tax returns.[34]

Agriculture remained the area of greatest legislative effort. Bailey approved the Crop Loan Act, directing the Farm Credit Administration to make loans in 1934 for crop production and harvesting; the Grazing Act, providing for federal regulation of grazing on the public domain; the Frazier-Lemke Farm Bankruptcy Act, extending the time farmers might remain in possession of their indebted farms and facilitating agreements between farmers and creditors; and the Jones-Costigan Sugar Act, which amended the AAA by placing sugar beets and sugar cane among the basic farm commodities and authorized quotas for sugar imports. Impatient with the avalanche of "pork-barrel" amendments, he ultimately refused to sanction the Jones-Connally Farm Relief Bill. As the farm relief bill passed the House it applied only to beef and dairy cattle, but the Senate included peanuts, rye, barley, flax, and grain sorghum, with Bailey giving strong support to peanuts. He reached an impasse, however, when Senator La Follette of Wisconsin secured an amendment adding $150,000,000 for dairy cattle to the $200,000,000 already provided. Bailey not only voted against the La Follette amendment, but also the Jones-Connally Farm Relief Bill itself, which nevertheless passed by a two-vote margin.[35]

Bailey's opposition to the Bankhead Cotton Control Act rested on fundamental disagreement with the nature of the bill, which placed production of cotton on a compulsory rather than a voluntary basis. He vehemently denounced the bill for proposing to take from the people inalienable rights, asserting that the country faced a crucial decision on whether "it is going to be a free republic or it is going to be a regimented socialistic communism, and if this legislation goes through the latter will be indicated." So forceful were his remarks

34. *Ibid.*, pp. 3813, 4506, 5164, 6574, 7746, 8714, 10395, 11060, 12013.
35. *Ibid.*, pp. 4151, 6937, 12381.

that the bill's managers could not prevent a rash of last-minute amendments. Bailey himself secured adoption of five amendments, of which one provided that no farmer be required to reduce his acreage below six acres, and another changed the base period for the reduction from five to ten years. The Cotton Control Bill passed the Senate, but the conference committee eliminated Bailey's emasculating amendments. Reiterating his attack, Bailey declared for the record: "I want the statement to go forth to the people of North Carolina that the President of the United States has sent no message to the Congress concerning this bill. . . . And further, the Secretary of Agriculture . . . has said that he prefers the voluntary principle of crop control . . . and . . . that he looks with suspicion upon propositions to regiment agriculture in America."[36]

He also opposed additional appropriations for the Civil Works Administration and ratification of the St. Lawrence Seaway Treaty. On the CWA Bailey objected to further increases in public debt, but his stand against the treaty was more complex. First, he doubted the wisdom of spending large sums of money to open the Great Lakes to ocean-bound shipping since the United States had ceased to be a grain-exporting country. Second, he believed the plan to develop cheap power and low freight rates in the thousand-mile area between Chicago and New York lacked equity, when the federal government would do nothing to provide similar benefits for North Carolina, which had long sought a seaport that could deliver the state from the domination of the railroads. As Bailey put it: "I do not see how the Administration can afford 180 million dollars for a Seaway and at the same time refuse us the one million dollars we need." Although reluctant to bargain about such matters, he planned to recommend to the President construction of a port terminal at Morehead City.[37]

Newspapers in North Carolina harshly criticized Bailey's negative votes, but often condemned him just as heartily for siding with Roosevelt. In one outstanding case, Congress passed the Independent Offices Appropriation Bill, which restored cuts made in veterans' pensions and federal employees' salaries by the Economy Act of 1933. Roosevelt immediately vetoed the bill for violating his administration's policies of economy, but Congress took advantage of Roose-

36. *Ibid.*, pp. 5420, 6618.
37. Bailey to Josephus Daniels, February 12, 1934, *Daniels Papers.*

velt's absence while vacationing in Florida by overriding the veto. Closing debate for the administration, Bailey admonished: "With my latest breath I should like to bear witness to this, that the American people do not have a chance to get out of the depression until their Government balances its Budget." Nevertheless, the Senate lined up 63 to 27 against sustaining the veto. On a purely party basis the vote showed thirty-three Republicans, twenty-nine Democrats, and the one Farmer-Laborite for overriding the veto. The twenty-seven senators supporting the President were all Democrats, but of the thirty-two members facing re-election in 1934 only six sustained the veto.[38]

Bailey had been identified by mid-1934 as an outstanding member of the conservative wing of the Democratic party. The Washington *Post*, running front-page interviews with Democratic senators critical of New Deal policies, placed Bailey number four on its list, preceded only by Senators Glass and Byrd of Virginia and Tydings of Maryland. While the ordering of anti-New Deal Democrats was exaggerated in Bailey's case, he did find most congenial the views of conservative Democrats. A warm personal camaraderie developed between Bailey and Walter F. George of Georgia, Harry F. Byrd of Virginia, Peter G. Gerry of Rhode Island, and Millard E. Tydings of Maryland. Continuing dialogue and agreement among the five senators resulted in remarkable similarity in their approaches to most issues. Bailey left word with his secretaries that he could always be paired when absent from a roll call the same way that George or Byrd voted. The five senators suspected Roosevelt's political motivations and his experimental approach to national problems. Correspondence between them almost always demonstrated outspoken and sometimes intemperate criticism of Roosevelt and his policies.

Bailey's image was further tarnished when on June 11, he unexpectedly became the chief inquisitor of Rexford G. Tugwell, Roosevelt's nominee for under secretary of agriculture. Attending the Senate Agricultural Committee at the request of its chairman, Ellison D. Smith, Bailey subjected Tugwell to a two-hour interrogation of a speech made to the American Economic Association in 1931 in which Tugwell had favorably described the Russian policy of economic planning. Tugwell contended that Bailey did "not make any distinc-

38. *Congressional Record*, 73rd Cong., 2nd Sess., pp. 5601–5605. Also see Raleigh *News and Observer*, March 29, 1934, p. 1.

tion between a scientist describing something and a politician advocating something."[39] Bailey later declared to the Senate:

> Now, put him in that office yonder; exalt him after he has made this speech and declaration, and you notify the farmers of America that at least there is one man in the American government in high position who repudiates private ownership; who . . . [says] first that the government shall control the land of the farmer, and second that the government shall decide which farmers are efficient and which are inefficient; and third, that the inefficient farmer shall not be permitted to farm.[40]

Why Bailey accepted Smith's invitation to present the case against Tugwell was never fully explained, but Smith's motives became quite obvious later. He succeeded in pressing Roosevelt to nominate for United States Marshal for South Carolina one of his henchmen whose reputation was marred by homicide. Making the trade with Smith, Roosevelt later remarked to Tugwell: "You will never know any more about it, I hope, but today I traded you for a couple of murderers!"[41]

The Tugwell episode brought editorial censure from Bailey's hometown newspaper and caused speculation on future political opposition. The *News and Observer* editorialized: "The truth about the Tugwell incident seems to be that Senator Bailey was asked to make the fight. But his critics say that he would not have been asked had he not been regarded as a foe of Roosevelt policies and that the invitation was not one which required an acceptance."[42] Considerable demand was heard for a Democratic candidate to contest Bailey on a platform of 100 per cent support of Roosevelt. Most conjectures about a potential rival centered on Representative Lindsay C. Warren, but nothing in fact came of this. Bailey insisted that his investigation of Tugwell had been magnified out of proportion and claimed complete support of Roosevelt's recovery program. Taking a leaf from Roosevelt's regular and emergency budgets, Bailey distinguished between miscellaneous legislation, which he had opposed, and recovery legislation which he had supported. By such differentiation, Bailey defended both his vote against the St. Lawrence Seaway Treaty, a legacy of the

39. New York *Times*, June 12, 1934, p. 1.
40. *Congressional Record*, 73rd Cong., 2nd Sess., pp. 11439–11442.
41. Rexford G. Tugwell, "The Compromising Roosevelt," *Western Political Quarterly*, VI (June, 1935), 339.
42. Raleigh *News and Observer*, June 16, 1934, p. 5.

Hoover administration, and his opposition to the Bankhead Cotton Control Bill, which Roosevelt had neither proposed nor encouraged.[43]

In mid-1934 Bailey confidently looked for a conservative legislative trend, since the nation had recovered from the depths of the depression. He thought that Roosevelt would now welcome opportunities to withdraw radical emergency measures and to return to a more customary course. He no longer expressed fears of impending alteration of the federal government toward socialism, but noted prophetically:

> There are a good many young lawyers in the various Departments who have no attachment to American institutions. If they could have their way, they would throw the country into communism, each one hoping to play the part of Stalin. I think they are all in for a spanking in due season and that in a few years from now, each one will swear he never had such thought as he had today.[44]

Bailey correctly saw the superficiality of much of the New Deal's progress and held that eventual retraction of government cushions would bring a harrowing period of readjustment. New Deal policies reflected unwillingness to suffer the people to experience the natural readjustment process, paying the price of survival as they went. He questioned whether the hardship of transition could be either softened or finally averted, but suspected that a decided relapse would bring such panic and hysteria that democracy itself might fall victim. Observing that Hoover had tried some measures and that Roosevelt sought every measure of artificial stimulation, he concluded that "assuming that either of them has understood that in the final analysis we will have to go down to the bottom and take our losses, it must also be said of them that each of them feared violent revolution and each sought to avoid it by compromise with fate."[45]

Bailey published a lengthy analysis of Roosevelt's recovery program in July, 1934, in which he reviewed the orderly and conservative character of the administration's attack upon the forces of depression. For the first time in the Republic's history all its power and

43. Bailey to J. A. Parham, June 19, 1934, in Raleigh *News and Observer*, June 20, 1934, p. 1; also Bailey to James A. Farley, July 19, 1934, *Bailey Papers*.
44. Bailey to Fred Starek, April 9, 1934, *Bailey Papers*.
45. Bailey to H. S. Williams, May 19, 1934, *Bailey Papers*.

resources had been mobilized under a single leadership against an economic disaster. "Risk is involved," he avowed, "grave risk, but who will say that it was not necessary to the preservation of the people and their Republic? And who will say that at the present hour it is not justified by its consequences?" Yet the nation could no longer depend on emergency measures. It must rely instead on restoration of business as the means to permanent recovery. Banking, business, and industry should assume responsibility for establishing normal conditions, for if the federal government exhausted its resources in a solitary effort to relieve prolonged emergency conditions, a serious movement to nationalize and socialize all business might follow. Revival of business and private initiative would end the emergency and allow government to resume its normal functions of order and justice. The United States would profit by its experience with the depression, for "we will return to reliance upon private enterprise and individual initiative, but not to greed, not to unconscionable profits, not to speculation, not to evil practices, not to oppression. This, as I understand, is the essence of the New Deal." Far from abandoning the historic character of American institutions and traditions, Roosevelt had in Bailey's opinion sought to preserve it.[46]

He thought that Roosevelt desired to turn to the right, but that he dreaded the hour when artificial expenditures must cease. Noting that Roosevelt would face re-election in 1936, Bailey suspected that the President anticipated sufficient narrowing of the gulf between current and desirable conditions by 1936 to make possible a graceful transition from the artificial to the substantial. The American people would not yet tolerate a return to normality, but in two years would they be more inclined to abandon governmental spending programs? Would not unnatural emphasis on money spending necessarily compel a ruinous policy of inflation? Within the next six months, Bailey asserted, the President must decide whether to balance the budget, as he had promised, by July 1, 1936. Although many people expected the President to turn to the left, he noted, "I do not see how he can get the consent of his mind to run into destructive inflation."[47]

Bailey gave his personal loyalty to Roosevelt and hoped for conservative leadership from the President, but many so-called conservatives organized opposition to the New Deal in the summer of 1934.

46. Raleigh *News and Observer*, July 8, 1934, p. 3.
47. Bailey to Harry F. Byrd, October 5, 1934, *Bailey Papers.*

Most vocal of the reactionary organizations was the American Liberty League, chartered in August, 1934, under the leadership of such Democratic politicians as Al Smith and John W. Davis, and of such industrialists as Sewell L. Avery and the Du Ponts. The league chiefly sought the downfall of Roosevelt and the New Deal, but it also formally dedicated itself to teach about the rights of property and persons, the duty of an administration to encourage private enterprise, and the responsibility of government to protect ownership and use of property.[48] Shortly after its formation, Roosevelt declared unequivocally: "I am not for a return to that definition of liberty under which for many years a free people were being gradually regimented into the service of the privileged few."[49] Nevertheless, during his first two years as President, Roosevelt pursued a course generally consistent with conservatism and in public speeches favored nearly all goals which conservatives such as Bailey desired, although Roosevelt's love for experimentation in government and his opportunism often vied with stated concepts.[50]

Dire predictions from former politicians and industrial magnates about regimentation of society failed to move the people, when they had suffered so long from governmental inaction and irresponsible business practices. As the congressional elections of 1934 approached, voices of dissent from standpat conservatives swelled. Nonetheless, many conservative party loyalists held the line for Roosevelt. Bailey, opening the Democratic campaign in North Carolina, declared that for the first time in America's history a political party which had been in power for two years did not need to defend itself to the people. "If conditions in the State or the country as a whole are better today," he maintained, "it is because of the Democratic Party. We chose Roosevelt our President and gave him the power to give a New Deal."[51] In the general election on November 4, 1934, the people of the United States showed themselves overwhelmingly in agreement with Bailey's analysis as they boosted Democratic strength in the House from 313 to 322 and from 59 to 69 in the Senate.

48. Frederick Rudolph, "The American Liberty League, 1934–1940," *American Historical Review*, LVI (October, 1950), 19–33.
49. Roosevelt, *Public Papers and Addresses*, III, 413–422.
50. James M. Burns, *Roosevelt: The Lion and the Fox* (New York, 1956), pp. 234–241. Burns presents a thoughtful analysis of Roosevelt as a conservative.
51. Raleigh *News and Observer*, October 18, 1934, p. 12.

CHAPTER SEVEN

RELUCTANT NEW DEALER

"THE PRESIDENT is going to be the great stabilizing force between the extremists and the reactionaries during the coming session of Congress," suggested Bailey on January 1, 1935.[1] The State of the Union clearly confirmed Bailey's view. Roosevelt reaffirmed his intention to channel the American people's desire for change through tested liberal traditions. Stressing the need for social justice, he sought a general security program of unemployment and old-age insurance, conservation of natural resources, and public works and work relief projects. He proposed consolidation of federal regulatory administration over all forms of transportation, renewal and clarification of purposes of the National Industrial Recovery Act, restoration of sound conditions in public utilities through abolition of unethical practices of holding companies, tapering off of federal emergency credit activities, and improvement in taxation forms and methods. "We can, if we will," Roosevelt concluded, "make 1935 a genuine period of good feeling, sustained by a sense of purposeful progress."[2]

Congress proved completely unresponsive to the President's lighter touch. Roosevelt suffered his first defeat when the Senate fell short of the two-thirds majority required for United States adherence to the protocols of the World Court. Bailey not only favored membership on the World Court, but delivered the strongest speech of any administration supporter during the debate, winning Roosevelt's enthusiastic commendation. Replying directly to William E. Borah (R., Ida.), who led the opposition, Bailey repelled suggestions that membership would lead the country into war. "To reject the character of jurisdiction outlined here," he argued, "is to reject the principle of justice in international relations; and to reject the principles . . . is to reject the

1. Raleigh *News and Observer*, January 2, 1935, p. 2.
2. Roosevelt, *Public Papers and Addresses*, IV, 15–25.

principle of justice altogether, because justice is not a national affair."[3]

The only measure in Roosevelt's program approved between January and June was the $4,880,000,000 Public Works Relief Bill. Conservatives wished to reduce the appropriation so it would be impossible to substitute work relief for the dole. Liberals hoped to increase the bill's coverage and to give workers on relief projects the prevailing wage paid by private employers in the project area. Neither proposition was acceptable to Roosevelt, but the "prevailing wage" amendment presented the greatest threat. The amendment passed by a single-vote margin of 44 to 43.[4] By upholding the President, Bailey won considerable praise in North Carolina, where the Raleigh *News and Observer* noted that the positions of Bailey and Robert R. Reynolds, the junior senator, had reversed. Bailey's support of Roosevelt had been doubtful in 1934, while Reynolds seemed an administration stalwart. Reynolds had voted, however, against the President on both the World Court issue and the prevailing wage amendment. "Senator Reynolds," now admitted the *News and Observer*, "has always been considered somewhat of a political free lance, while Senator Bailey has supported President Roosevelt politically, although differing with him at times, both publicly and privately on economic questions." [5]

The Public Works Relief Bill eventually passed the Senate without the prevailing wage amendment, but not before conservatives from both parties attempted to reduce the initial appropriation. Bailey voted for an amendement offered by Harry F. Byrd to reduce work relief funds to one billion dollars, and when that failed, for an amendment proposed by Alva B. Adams to reduce funds to two billion dollars, which also failed.[6] Bailey supported the Public Works Relief Bill four days later, explaining somewhat illogically that his fear that North Carolina would be taxed for the relief of other states had prompted his budget-cutting efforts. The money would provide work for the unemployed where they were most numerous, which to Bailey meant "it will be spent in places like New York, Chicago and San

3. *Congressional Record*, 74th Cong., 1st Sess., pp. 794–799. For Bailey's radio appeal for the World Court, see New York *Times*, January 29, 1935, p. 2.
4. *Congressional Record*, 74th Cong., 1st Sess., p. 2395.
5. Raleigh *News and Observer*, February 24, 1935, p. 1.
6. *Congressional Record*, 74th Cong., 1st Sess., pp. 3966–3969.

Francisco, where the bulk of the relief money has been spent."[7] He seemed unaware that reduction would not correct disproportionate distribution, but only decrease relief funds for everyone—including North Carolinians.

While Roosevelt maintained his hands-off policy, Huey Long made slashing attacks upon administration leaders. He demanded senatorial investigation of Postmaster General James A. Farley on grounds that he personally profited from post-office construction contracts in New York.[8] Several days earlier Bailey had written Farley that if he ever needed a friend on Capitol Hill, Farley could count on him.[9] Bailey immediately prepared a detailed and scathing reply, but postponed his remarks when Long, after concluding a two-hour tirade against a motion to refer his resolution to committee, unexpectedly agreed to the motion. Bailey's willingness to tangle with the Louisiana Kingfish was notable, since few senators wished to face Long's demagogic tactics of ridicule and threat. Even the Senate, however, could not tolerate Long's outburst on March 5, when the Louisianan violently assaulted Roosevelt, Farley, Joseph T. Robinson, and NRA head Hugh Johnson. In the subsequent exchange between Long and Robinson, Bailey projected himself into the fray when Long pointed in Bailey's direction while asking a rhetorical question. Discussing destitution in the country, Long asked, "You will take my word for it, won't you?" This was too much for Bailey, who immediately stood and, as gasps echoed from the galleries, asserted quietly: "I am utterly unwilling to take your word for that or anything else!" The ensuing colloquy heard Long threaten to campaign in North Carolina against Bailey in 1936, and Bailey suggest that the Tarheel State would welcome Long's interference with tar and feathers.[10] Several months later, Bailey subjected Long to a dose of his own ridicule and sarcasm. Declaring that Long's autobiography, *Every Man a King*, was first of a trilogy, Bailey predicted that the second volume would be entitled "Every Man a Kingfish" and the third "Every Man a Sucker." He read aloud from the autobiography an apt description of Long in the Farley matter—a small dog that always barked noisily up a tree, but invariably emitted a false alarm.[11] Farley latter testified that "Bailey's frank and full exposition . . . was tremendously im-

7. Raleigh *News and Observer*, March 19, 1935, p. 12.
8. *Congressional Record*, 74th Cong., 1st Sess., p. 1782.
9. Bailey to James A. Farley, February 7, 1935, *Bailey Papers*.
10. *Congressional Record*, 74th Cong., 1st Sess., pp. 2933–2956.
11. *Ibid.*, pp. 7362–7374.

portant in influencing the Senate vote, and I have always been grateful to him on that account."[12]

Despite abusive sniping between Bailey and Long, they were personal friends. Long often called at night upon Bailey in his Mayflower Hotel apartment where they would banter about their exchanges over drinks. Bailey frequently invited Long on fishing trips out from Morehead City in the Gulf Stream. A standing joke in the Bailey family centered on a statement made by Long during one fishing expedition. Long, expounding his plans to become the dictator-president of the United States, was asked what his first move would be when he achieved his goal. He allegedly replied that the very first thing would be to have Senator Bailey shot. Bailey greatly enjoyed this comment, but confided privately that he thought Long had been perfectly serious. Nevertheless, both men enjoyed each other's company, and this strange relationship between arch-radical and convinced conservative continued until Long's assassination on September 8, 1935.[13]

Huey Long was not the only would-be messiah to feel the lash of Bailey's tongue during 1935. He delivered a withering attack in April upon Father Charles E. Coughlin, the Catholic radio priest of Detroit, declaring that "there is nothing more sinister in our life right now than that Coughlin . . . stirs the depths of hate throughout the land of liberty, matches class against class, foments the fires of revolution, to crucify the American people upon his damnable ambition." Although affirming respect for the ministry, whether Protestant or Catholic, he asserted that when a minister entered the political arena to stir up fountains of hate in a distressed land among a suffering people, someone must "snatch the halo from his brow and throw it into the nearest spittoon."[14] Bailey's attack held his colleagues and the galleries in rapt attention, but did not prevent Senator Matthew M. Neely of West Virginia from denouncing Bailey's irreverence and comparing Coughlin to Christ, an analogy which indicated the hold Coughlin had established upon the imaginations of many Americans.[15]

On May 1 Bailey informed Roosevelt that he had prepared suffi-

12. James A. Farley, *Behind the Ballots* (New York, 1938), pp. 247–248.
13. Interviews with James Hinton Pou Bailey, Raleigh, N.C., November 2, 1961, and Mrs. Josiah W. Bailey, Raleigh, N.C., February 7, 1962.
14. *Congressional Record*, 74th Cong., 1st Sess., p. 6379; New York *Times*, April 26, 1935, p. 3.
15. *Congressional Record*, 74th Cong., 1st Sess., p. 6773.

cient data to explode Long's "Share-Our-Wealth" program and awaited only a suitable opportunity to state the facts. He believed that such a statement would serve a good purpose, since Roosevelt's policies clearly provided a more extensive and more equitable distribution of annual income than would Long's. He also warned that Father Coughlin was no true friend of the President. "He professes to support you under the 'Roosevelt or Ruin' slogan, and at the same time and in the same speech, he gives out utterances calculated to destroy the National faith in yourself." As for himself, Bailey acknowledged that he differed with Roosevelt in one important respect: "I think all efforts should be bent towards recovery and only those reforms should be undertaken now which are indispensable to recovery." He particularly questioned the wisdom of extending federal power into local fields.[16]

Federal legislation against lynching had long been a major objective of the National Association for the Advancement of Colored People and in 1935 was sponsored by Robert M. Wagner (D., N.Y.) and Edward P. Costigan (D., Colo.). Roosevelt gave little support to the Anti-lynching Bill, but he had previously stated that lynchings were violations of ethics and of law which called "on the strong arm of Government for their immediate suppression."[17] Southern Democrats responded to a motion to consider the bill with the traditional filibuster. Bailey denounced the legislation as a force bill and used statistics prepared by Tuskegee Institute to show that lynchings in the United States had dropped since Reconstruction from two hundred to less than twelve a year. Giving the federal government power to fine people and to imprison police officers for not suppressing lynching altogether was unfair unless applied to all other crimes of passion.[18] The filibuster succeeded, but the subject of lynching continued to embarrass Bailey.

Shortly after Bailey asserted that North Carolina needed no federal incentive to prevent lynchings, one occurred in Franklin County on July 30. Walter White, secretary of the NAACP, promptly wired Bailey that "thoughtful Americans including many white citizens of

16. Bailey to Franklin D. Roosevelt, May 1, 1935, *The White House Papers*, The Franklin D. Roosevelt Library, Hyde Park, New York, hereafter cited as the *Roosevelt Papers*.

17. Roosevelt, *Public Papers and Addresses*, III, 12–13.

18. *Congressional Record*, 74th Cong., 1st Sess., pp. 6448–6457; Bailey to C. C. Spaulding, August 19, 1935, *Bailey Papers*.

North Carolina do not believe that lynching can be stopped except by Federal action. The eyes of the world will be upon you and your state to see if you spoke truthfully when you filibustered against the Costigan-Wagner bill."[19] Bailey spiritedly replied that federal action would not have stopped the lynching and expressed utter contempt for White's suggestion that he had spoken other than truthfully. Bailey displayed his emotional bias in his concluding remark to White: "You ought to go out and make an honest living instead of trying to attend to other people's business and taking up collections from people who are deluded by the folly which you put forward."[20] He deplored the lynching, but insisted that even if federal action might have prevented it, he preferred to respect the powers and the character of his state rather than to invoke the federal government's aid in preserving civilization in North Carolina.[21]

While Congress and President drifted without purpose or program, Senator Robert M. Wagner almost single-handedly evolved a national labor policy. In 1934 he had proposed a bill designed to strengthen the program of self-organization for labor initiated by Section 7a of the NIRA, but through Roosevelt's efforts the bill had been sidetracked. Reintroducing the bill as the National Labor Relations Bill in 1935, Wagner secured its adoption in mid-May by a vote of 63 to 12 after only perfunctory debate. Eight Republicans and four conservative Democrats—including Bailey, Byrd, Tydings, and Edward R. Burke of Nebraska—opposed the measure. Bailey thought the bill would intensify antagonism between capital and labor and might produce rather than prevent strikes.[22] The bill passed the Senate with relative ease, but met concerted resistance from southern Democrats in the House. Roosevelt did not become interested until the National Labor Relations Bill passed the Senate and applied pressure only after the Supreme Court invalidated the NIRA, including what legal support the act had given to unionization.[23]

The Supreme Court in May 1935 threatened the whole New Deal

19. Walter White, secretary of the NAACP, to Bailey, telegram, July 31, 1935, *Bailey Papers.*

20. Bailey to Walter White, August 15, 1935, *Bailey Papers.*

21. Bailey to C. C. Spaulding, August 19, 1935, *Bailey Papers.*

22. *Congressional Record*, 74th Cong., 1st Sess., p. 7681; Bailey to J. L. Horne, Jr., April 10, 1935, *Bailey Papers.*

23. For Roosevelt's attitude toward the Wagner Labor Relations bill, see: Burns, *Roosevelt: The Lion and the Fox*, pp. 218–220; Schlesinger, *The Coming of the New Deal*, pp. 400–406.

structure. The court held the Railroad Pensions Act, which provided for compulsory retirement of elderly railroad employees, to be contrary to the due process clause of the Constitution as well as an unwarranted extension of the commerce power. Three weeks later the court nullified the NIRA as an improper delegation of legislative power to the President, and as an unjustified attempt to extend the commerce clause to industry only indirectly touching interstate commerce. Roosevelt responded to the NIRA decision with a carefully reasoned dissent. His administration had made sincere efforts to help all groups, including business, labor, and agriculture, but these efforts had necessitated some compulsion through federal regulation. This control had been instituted under the general theory that the interstate commerce clause authorized it, because the many separate facets of economic and social activities affected the internal commerce of the entire United States. The commerce clause had literally been written in the horse-and-buggy age, while New Deal legislation had been framed in light of present-day civilization.[24] Opposition from the bench destroyed the indecision which had plagued Roosevelt's course. "I had hoped that circumstances would move him towards the Right," Bailey observed, "but the circumstances went the other way. His statement on the subject of the Supreme Court decisions arrayed the business element against him in an emphatic and almost unanimous way."[25] Bailey was essentially correct in his analysis, but business elements had for more than a year opposed the New Deal. The NIRA had been the government's chief vehicle for direct aid to business. Henceforth, business would benefit only indirectly from governmental action to help agriculture and labor. Circumstances had moved Roosevelt farther to the left.

Under impetus of Roosevelt's renewed leadership, Congress quickly enacted every major presidential recommendation. The National Labor Relations Bill was forced through the House before the end of June. The Social Security Bill, establishing comprehensive programs of old-age pensions, unemployment insurance, and public health services, passed with heavy majorities. Amendments to the AAA attempted to protect the Agricultural Adjustment Act from

---

24. Roosevelt, *Public Papers and Addresses*, IV, 200–202. For court decisions, see *Railroad Retirement Board* v. *Alton Railroad Company*, 295 U.S. 330; *United States* v. *A.L.A. Schecter Poultry Corporation*, 295 U.S. 495.
25. Bailey to James Hinton Pou, June 21, 1935, *Bailey Papers*.

judicial veto. The Banking Act of 1935 strengthened further the nation's banking structure. The Neutrality Act of 1935 passed with Roosevelt's approval and declared unlawful export of munitions and arms to belligerents. The Guffey-Snyder Bituminous Coal Act, creating a "little NRA" for the coal industry, had little opposition, despite fears that it would meet the NIRA's fate. The Public Utility Holding Company Act, providing for drastic control of holding companies and increasing powers of the Tennessee Valley Authority, was approved under intense administration pressure. A radically new tax policy became part of the Revenue Act of 1935 and instituted estate and gift taxes as well as a progressive corporation income tax. Roosevelt again succeeded in mustering sufficient votes in the Senate to prevent Congress from overriding his veto of the Veterans' Bonus Bill.[26]

Bailey did not actively support all the measures, but neither did he publicly oppose any except the Guffey Coal Bill. Influenced by the approaching election year, Bailey either approved the President's program or refrained from voting at all. "I think the better course," he confided, "is to keep one's thoughts to himself in such circumstances and to try to deal prudently with the situation as it develops."[27] Josephus Daniels more cogently summed up Bailey's course: "It seems to me as if he deliberately made up his mind to follow Glass and Byrd, doing just enough to keep in touch with the pie counter until the election in the fall of 1934. He then saw the trend of public opinion and rushed in to be the great champion and defender of the New Deal."[28] Expediency was not the sole motive behind Bailey's acquiescence. He still held high personal regard for Roosevelt and feared the consequences for the nation if the Roosevelt administration were not continued. "At worst it is much better than any Republican Administration would be. Things may not be going just to suit us, but we can all afford to be patient with the President while he struggles to do the best in a great emergency."[29]

When Congress adjourned, Bailey concentrated on his own 1936 campaign and prospects for Roosevelt and the Democratic party in

26. See E. Pendleton Herring, "First Session of the Seventy-Fourth Congress," *American Political Science Review*, XXIX (December, 1935), 985–1005.

27. Bailey to James Hinton Pou, June 21, 1935, *Bailey Papers*.

28. Josephus Daniels to Jonathan Daniels, September 10, 1935, *Daniels Papers*.

29. Bailey to Stacy Brewer, May 11, 1935, *Bailey Papers*.

the nation. Bailey's candidacy appeared in most satisfactory condition with strong support from western North Carolina and with major state leaders working actively for him. Rumors that Josephus Daniels, who was currently serving as ambassador to Mexico, might campaign against Bailey on a liberal platform somewhat clouded Bailey's political horizon.[30] However, Bailey maintained a friendly correspondence with Daniels on matters of political interest. In August he informed Daniels that his correspondence indicated increasing restlessness in North Carolina, but that farmers and workers solidly supported the President.[31] Relaying this information to Roosevelt, he cited an Asheville *Citizen-Times* poll indicating that Roosevelt would receive 68 per cent of the state's vote, as against 58 per cent in 1932. He thought that Senator Borah would run stronger than any other Republican candidate, but that North Carolina would give Roosevelt full support in 1936.[32] Roosevelt promptly replied that Bailey was "right about the prospective advancement and also that we should capitalize on it. As a matter of fact, the country is coming to realize this also and with the realization there will be less attention paid to the silly cries of destruction, radicalism, unconstitutionality, etc."[33]

Bailey usually returned to North Carolina to fish off the coast or to vacation in the mountains after Congress adjourned. Stopping at a small resort outside Franklin for a brief rest, he quickly tired of the unaccustomed inactivity and resolved to visit friends in town. Never having learned to drive, he called his chauffeur, Joe (Joseph Washington) Holloway, a Negro who served the Bailey family for forty years, but unexpectedly found Joe reluctant to make the trip. Growing impatient with excuses, he finally discovered that Negroes in the neighborhood had planned a testimonial dinner for Joe that night. Curiosity whetted, he accepted Joe's invitation to attend instead of visiting his own friends. At dinner Bailey learned that the Negroes greatly admired Joe's services in securing jobs for many of them on public works projects. Bailey realized at length that Joe had been his contact man for Negroes in western North Carolina, putting in a word for his friends and learning of job opportunities each morning as he drove the Senator to the Capitol. Afterward Bailey noticed that when-

30. Bailey to James Hinton Pou, June 21, 1935, *Bailey Papers.*
31. Bailey to Josephus Daniels, August 19, 1935, *Daniels Papers.*
32. Bailey to Marvin McIntyre, August 20, 1935, *Bailey Papers.*
33. Franklin D. Roosevelt to Bailey, August 29, 1935, *Roosevelt Papers.*

ever he spoke in a town, Joe would slip off to hold his own street corner audience. He believed that he received a large portion of the Negro vote in western North Carolina simply because Joe lobbied for him.[34]

Roosevelt used his annual message to the Congress on January 3, 1936, to kick off the presidential campaign. Following the World War, government had been dominated by financial and industrial groups, he asserted, but the New Deal had restored power to the people. Yet these same groups sought now to restore their selfish power by stealing the "livery of great national constitutional ideals to serve discredited special interests."[35] An unqualified success as a keynote speech for the 1936 political campaign, Roosevelt's address left much to be desired as a message on the state of the Union. Unlike previous messages, the President proposed no new policy, program, or legislation.

Congress did not long lack legislative objectives. On January 6, the Supreme Court knocked down the Agricultural Adjustment Act. Conversing with Roosevelt four days later, Bailey found him hopefully considering several alternative plans. The Supreme Court had found it necessary to define the powers of Congress, Bailey observed, but "I do not think they meant to tell us that the farmers could not be relieved . . . only to tell us that they could not be relieved in the way proposed."[36] The AAA had been a commodity price-raising program with agricultural conservation incidental to production control. The new Soil Conservation and Domestic Allotment Act dealt with the farm rather than the commodity and made nationwide soil conservation the indirect means of regulating production. The substitute agricultural plan quickly won Bailey's enthusiastic backing and passed the Senate in mid-February.[37] The Soil Conservation and Domestic Allotment Act at least partially filled the gap left by the invalidated AAA and became a permanent part of national agricultural policy.

The remainder of the languid and undistinguished session covered legislative measures relating only incidentally to the New Deal program. Under intense election-year pressure Congress repassed the controversial Veterans' Bonus Bill, alloting two billion dollars for

34. Interview with James Hinton Pou Bailey, Raleigh, N.C., November 2, 1961.
35. Roosevelt, *Public Papers and Addresses*, V, 8–18.
36. Bailey to J. L. Burgess, January 14, 1936, *Bailey Papers*
37. *Congressional Record*, 74th Cong., 2nd Sess., p. 2164.

immediate payment of adjusted-service compensation certificates not due until 1945. The Senate approved the bonus bill and later overrode Roosevelt's perfunctory veto. In each case Bailey reversed his previous position and yielded to veterans' demands. Political discretion dictated by the threat that Josephus Daniels might seek the Democratic senatorial nomination with veteran support motivated Bailey's sudden about-face.[38] He also supported the Walsh-Healy Government Contracts Act, establishing minimum wages and maximum hours and prohibiting child labor in industries working on government contracts; the Merchant Marine Act, preventing use of foreign labor to maintain low labor standards for seamen; the Strike-breaker Act, prohibiting interstate transportation of persons to interfere with labor stoppages; and the Commodity Exchange Act, authorizing governmental control over speculation, manipulation, and unreasonable price fluctuations. He followed administration leaders in supporting the First Deficiency Appropriation Act, necessitated by the obligations of the Veterans' Bonus Act and by contracts made under the invalidated AAA. He also deserted conservative colleagues by opposing amendments to strike provisions for rural rehabilitation and to return relief administration to the states.[39]

The Democratic senatorial primary in North Carolina troubled Bailey. Josephus Daniels continued to test the measure of popular support which his candidacy might elicit. On January 28, 1936, the editor of the Winston-Salem *Journal*, Santford Martin, informed Daniels that "I am among a great host of Democrats in North Carolina who hope you will come home soon and assume the leadership of the liberal forces. . . . With you as their candidate, the true Democrats of North Carolina would certainly march to victory in the June primary."[40] Daniels, remembering only opposition votes, privately stated in reference to Bailey that "it is a tragedy that so often in North Carolina, with a people who want equality and justice, we have been represented by men who 'gave the promises to the ear and broke it to the hope.' "[41] He asserted his feelings about Bailey even more bluntly in a handwritten note to his son on January 31. He approvingly noted that a *News and Observer* correspondent had suggested

38. Bailey to C. L. Shuping, February 10, 1936, *Bailey Papers*.
39. Bailey to J. M. Broughton, April 25, 1936, *Bailey Papers; Congressional Record*, 74th Cong., 2nd Sess., pp. 8293, 8400, 8517, 8519.
40. Santford Martin to Josephus Daniels, January 28, 1936, *Daniels Papers*.
41. Josephus Daniels to Larry I. Moore, January 28, 1936, *Daniels Papers*.

that North Carolinians visit former Senator Furnifold M. Simmons and cry out: "Senator, we are sorry." As for himself, Daniels concluded, "My conscience is clear for I voted for him. I am glad I am not responsible even by one vote for Bailey. I want to see him defeated so much that I can hardly stay here and let . . . [several indecipherable words follow]."[42]

Charles L. Shuping, the Democratic national committeeman for North Carolina, took Daniels' potential candidacy so seriously that he inquired of Bailey if he had not placed too much credence upon the friendly attitude of the White House. Bailey responded that Daniels had failed as an ambassador and now desperately sought a way out. His best solution would be to campaign as the President's friend and apostle of the New Deal, but he was not likely to receive encouragement from the President. Roosevelt would need North Carolina's support in the fall and would take no step endangering its electoral vote. "I do not believe that Mr. Daniels will run," Bailey concluded, "but this is based only on the information that he has not received sufficient encouragement. It may be that he will take a different view, and we should be prepared for an announcement from him at any time between now and the first of April."[43] By early April Daniels had decided against opposing Bailey, despite encouragement from many citizens who wished North Carolina to be "in the front ranks of the New Deal" and to see Daniels "hold up the banner of true liberalism and progress." After serious reflection he noted: "I have become convinced that I would not be justified in departing from the resolution not to run for office to which I have held since I became an editor. . . . I can better serve in the lines wherein I have sought to promote sound public policies for half a century."[44]

Bailey still had three contenders for the Democratic nomination for senator, but his chief opposition came from Richard T. Fountain. A former lieutenant governor of North Carolina, Fountain campaigned on a platform of total commitment to the New Deal and accused Bailey of obstructing Roosevelt's recovery program. The other two candidates were William H. Griffin, a minor government employee in Washington, D.C., who used a sound truck to denounce Bailey's

42. Josephus Daniels to Jonathan Daniels, January 28, 1936, photostat in *Bailey Papers*.
43. Bailey to C. L. Shuping, February 10, 1936; C. L. Shuping to Bailey, February 7, 1936, *Bailey Papers*.
44. Daniels to Edward M. Land, April 8, 1936, *Daniels Papers*.

voting record, and David Strain, a Durham real estate man, who conducted a comparatively quiet campaign. Replying to a friend who described the opposition as "presumptuous," Bailey asserted that "ballyhoo and back-slapping are very acceptable substitutes for capacity and intelligence," but did not menace his renomination.[45] He made no speeches and communicated only once with the voters to cite support of thirty-nine separate administrative measures between 1933 and 1936. He ignored completely his opposition, but encouraged friends and political appointees to carry the burden of organization. His personal secretary, Thad Page, jotted down a revealing list of Bailey's campaign maxims:

> Never argue with your audience—reason cannot take out of their minds what reason did not put there. Forty per cent vote against, therefore groundswells rise on organized prejudices. He who defends himself is lost! He who praises himself disgusts. The grapevine invites no replies. A good grapevine is better than a dozen newspapers. People love reform but hate reformers. The boy who stood on the burning deck was not elected. Resolve all doubts in inaction. The enemies in one campaign may be the friends in the next.[46]

Whatever the merits of Bailey's campaign philosophy, his strategy did no harm in North Carolina, where he received on June 6 a total of 247,365 votes as against 184,197 for Fountain, 26,171 for Griffin, and 13,281 for Strain.[47]

Bailey's first primary victory attested the strength of his and his friends' control of the party apparatus in North Carolina. Most influential was O. Max Gardner's political assistance. After serving as governor between 1929 and 1933, Gardner effected the election of J. C. B. Ehringhaus for governor in 1932 and in 1936 successfully pushed the candidacy of his brother-in-law Clyde R. Hoey. Gardner thus maintained his influence in Democratic party councils. Many North Carolinians, responding in part to Gardner's actual influence and in part to the myth nurtured by insurgent candidates, considered Gardner to have replaced Simmons as the political "boss" of the state

45. W. L. Poteat to Bailey, March 14, 1936; Bailey to W. L. Poteat, March 16, 1936, *Bailey Papers.*
46. "Campaign Maxims of Senator Josiah W. Bailey" (1936), in personal collection of Thad S. Page, Alexandria, Va.
47. Raleigh *News and Observer,* June 13, 1936, p. 1.

Democratic party. Whether under Simmons or Gardner, however, the course of North Carolina politics continued to depend upon a purely practical and shifting alliance of political leaders. The relationship between Bailey and Gardner reflected this mutual agreement and co-operation. Thus Bailey could write Gardner following the first primary, "I am very deeply grateful for your powerful and friendly interest in behalf of my renomination. I know what you did and I shall never forget it."[48] While Gardner could write to Bailey between the first and second gubernatorial primaries that "your friends up here will never forget your loyalty and leadership in this critical period. It is a source of great satisfaction to us all to know that you are in Raleigh and doing everything in your power for Clyde Hoey."[49] Following Hoey's victory in the second primary over the insurgent candidate Ralph McDonald, Gardner confided to Bailey:

> As you know, I did not deserve and certainly did not covet to be made the object of McDonald's main assault. It was his idea that he could make great progress with our people by taking certain facts and convict me as a creator of a machine. . . . I have never understood his strategy in leaving you out of the picture. . . . He knew that you were against him but he was afraid to publicly array you against him. I think he hoped to dull your blade by these tactics. If this was his idea, we know that he failed utterly.[50]

While Gardner's influence behind the scenes was undoubtedly greater than that of any other North Carolina politician during New Deal years, Bailey's position in the so-called Gardner machine was by no means subordinate. The continuity of his long Senate terms and the nature of his office as a pipeline to federal funds made Bailey a force to be reckoned with and appeased when necessary. Indicative were the efforts of Gardner and Hoey following the second primary of 1936 to persuade Bailey to accept Representative Lindsay Warren for the state Democratic party chairmanship. Despite repeated appeals and assurances of continuing loyalty from Gardner and Hoey, Bailey quietly, firmly, and successfully opposed naming Warren to the post. He apparently suspected that the politically ambitious War-

48. Bailey to O. Max Gardner, June 17, 1936, *Bailey Papers.*
49. O. Max Gardner to Bailey, July 1, 1936, *Bailey Papers.*
50. O. Max Gardner to Bailey, July 7, 1936, *Bailey Papers.*

ren might use that influential office to build potential support for a
senatorial bid against Bailey in 1942.[51] On the national level, Gardner's activities as a major corporation lawyer and lobbyist in Washington for North Carolina industrial interests were often noted. Gardner influenced Bailey, however, not by any political strings that he
manipulated but rather through the personal friendship, political
agreement, and mutual pro-business outlook shared by both men.

The New Deal suffered further reverses from three decisions by
the Supreme Court in May, 1936. The court invalidated 5 to 4 the
Guffey-Snyder Bituminous Coal Act, a decision which left conditions
in the coal industry chaotic and cast doubts on the constitutionality of
the National Labor Relations Act. In another 5 to 4 decision, the
Supreme Court held that the Municipal Bankruptcy Act was an
unconstitutional infringement by the federal government on the rights
of states to deal with their municipalities. A week later, when it
invalidated a New York State minimum wage law, the court held that
the states could not regulate the wages of labor. These decisions,
Roosevelt charged in a press conference on June 2, created a
" 'no-man's-land' where no Government—State or Federal—can function."[52]

The Republican party also attacked the New Deal at its national
convention in Cleveland, Ohio, on June 9. Denouncing regimentation
and socialism, the Republican platform solemnly warned: "America
is in peril. The welfare of American men and women and the future
of our youth are at stake. We dedicate ourselves to the preservation of
their political liberty, their individual opportunity and their character
as free citizens, which today for the first time are threatened by
government itself."[53] Although approving unemployment relief, collective bargaining, and social legislation, the convention assumed a
revivalistic stance, which in Herbert Hoover's words devoted the
Republican party to "a holy crusade for liberty which shall determine
the future and the perpetuity of a nation of free men."[54] As leader of

51. O. Max Gardner to Bailey, July 27, 1936; Bailey to Clyde R. Hoey, July
27, 1936; Clyde R. Hoey to Bailey, August 3, 1936; Bailey to Clyde R. Hoey,
August 6, 1936; Clyde R. Hoey to Bailey, August 7, 1936, *Bailey Papers*.

52. Roosevelt, *Public Papers and Addresses*, V, 191–192.

53. Eugene H. Roseboom, *A History of Presidential Elections* (New York,
1957), 447; Republican National Committee, *Text Book of the Republican
Party, 1936* (Chicago, 1936), chap. xi.

54. Herbert Hoover, *Addresses upon the American Road, 1933–1938* (New
York, 1938), pp. 173–183.

this "holy crusade," the convention chose Alfred M. Landon, the mildly progressive governor of Kansas, on the first ballot and largely without opposition. Franklin Knox, publisher of the Chicago *Daily News* and a former Theodore Roosevelt Progressive, won second place on the ticket.

The Democratic convention, meeting in Philadelphia, June 23–27, lacked the fervor that motivated Republicans. Satisfied with their record, Democrats renominated Roosevelt and Garner and pledged continuation of New Deal policy. The century-old two-thirds rule, which had threatened Roosevelt's nomination in 1932 and had given the solid South a determining voice, was abrogated. The platform, prepared by the White House, proudly pointed to the three-year recovery brought about by humanizing policies of the federal government and held as self-evident truth that "the test of a representative government is its ability to promote the safety and happiness of the people."[55] Bailey, who presided over many meetings of the platform committee, headed a subcommittee that made the two principal changes in the White House version. The first softened the plank dedicating the party to renewed efforts to stamp out monopolistic concentrations of economic power. The major change engineered by Bailey, however, struck out a sentence deploring creation of a "No Man's Land" by the Supreme Court decisions. Bailey contended that in America a no man's land necessarily existed—"that is the land of rights reserved to the people, the individual and inalienable rights reserved to the people in the Declaration of Independence."[56] Accepting renomination, Roosevelt charged that "the royalists of the economic order have conceded that political freedom was the business of the Government, but they have maintained that economic slavery was nobody's business." The Democratic party held that freedom was not a half-and-half affair. Citizens must be guaranteed equal opportunity in the market place as well as in the polling place. "Economic royalists" complained that the New Deal sought to overthrow American institutions, but in reality they feared destruction of their despotic power.[57]

While Landon and Knox stumped the country during the summer,

55. *Official Report of the Proceedings of the Democratic National Convention, June 23–27, 1936* (Philadelphia, 1936), pp. 192–198.
56. Bailey to Burton K. Wheeler, April 15, 1937, *Bailey Papers.* See also Raleigh *News and Observer*, June 27, 1936, p. 1.
57. Roosevelt, *Public Papers and Addresses*, V, 230–236.

Roosevelt deserted the political arena in late July for a two-week vacation cruise off the New England coast. He embarked on a "non-partisan" trip through nine states in late August to inspect personally the distressed conditions in drought areas of the Great Plains. Bailey enjoyed a brief political blackout between July and September and wrote glowing reports to friends of the abundance of dolphin, mackerel, and amberjack taken on fishing trips. In early September he canvassed the state for the Democratic party and appeared at Charlotte and Asheville with Roosevelt during the President's brief visit to North Carolina. Reviewing the *Literary Digest*'s polls showing a trend toward Landon, he noted that "as I read Mr. Landon, he is a far more dangerous man than many seem to think. He is ready to promise anything. He may talk for economy, but his program will call for an endless amount of money. . . . The man on the outside can always out bid the man on the inside."[58] Bailey not only spoke on Roosevelt's behalf throughout North Carolina and in several other states, but also debated the President's fiscal policy with Ogden L. Mills, former secretary of treasury under Herbert Hoover, before the Life Underwriters Association of New York City. Closing the campaign in North Carolina on November 2, Bailey defended Roosevelt against Landon's charge that the President was a would-be dictator, who sought to override the Supreme Court.[59]

When the votes were counted, Roosevelt had won every state but Maine and Vermont. In North Carolina the President polled 616,141 votes to Landon's 223,284. Bailey, who throughout the fall had never referred to his Republican opponent, Frank C. Patton, won 563,968 votes to Patton's 233,009, while the Democratic candidate for governor, Clyde R. Hoey, polled 542,139 votes as against 270,843 for his Republican rival, Gilliam Grissom.[60] Josephus Daniels, who watched the election closely, but who misapprehended the votes cast in North Carolina, commented on November 10 that he "of course expected Roosevelt would lead but did not suppose he would receive 133,000 more votes than Hoey, and 215,000 more than Bailey. The latter vote was a great vote of rebuke and protest and I hope that Senator will regard it as a mandate to go to Washington and back up the progres-

58. Bailey to Harry F. Byrd, September 28, 1936; Bailey to Harry B. Hawes, September 9, 1936, *Bailey Papers*.
59. Raleigh *News and Observer*, September 4–November 2, 1936.
60. *North Carolina Yearbook, 1937* (Raleigh, 1938), pp. 37–38.

sive program which must be carried out."[61] However, Bailey's 330,-959-vote majority over his Republican opponent was by far the greatest majority ever given a candidate for governor or senator in North Carolina. Nor did Bailey propose to abandon his conservative course. If anything, the election stiffened his resolve to lead conservative forces toward national victory in 1940.

Roosevelt's landslide victory impressed Bailey as a great manifestation of the people's power, but left him concerned that democracy would run riot. "The trouble about it all is," he declared, "when democracy gets free to do what it pleases, it usually does the wrong thing."[62] He surmised that Roosevelt would correctly interpret his vote as overwhelming justification of his course. Very probably Roosevelt would lead more emphatically than ever, but Bailey did not think this meant that would undertake extreme measures. Bailey rejoiced that conservative leadership might now pass from the Republicans, for "there are Democrats in the Senate—Glass, George, Adams, Burke, Moore, King, Gerry, perhaps Smith, and surely myself, and some others of whom I have hopes, who can put forward the conservative policies and create the background for the contest in 1940." Preparing to lead conservatives in the Senate, he mused, "if I could feel that I were going to have my way, I believe that I could create the proper issues and the proper background for a real victory in 1940."[63]

In any conservative coalition for the next presidential election business interests would need to play a skilful part. Conservatives had ruined their cause in 1936 by imprudently allying with the American Liberty League and thereby justifying Roosevelt's proclamation that he battled economic royalists. "Businessmen must learn to think politically," Bailey advised, "and where they have no one in their organizations who can think politically, they ought to get someone." The issue in 1940 would be between conservatism and radicalism, but he believed the conservatives would triumph. The world struggled with Ricardo's iron law of wages. Roosevelt had halted the law's operation by borrowing money and distributing wealth, but no man had ever arrested the law except temporarily. Adam Smith had been

61. Josephus Daniels to Jonathan Daniels, November 10, 1936, *Daniels Papers.*
62. Bailey to Earle Godbey, November 20, 1936, *Bailey Papers.*
63. Bailey to J. E. S. Thorpe, November 13, 1936, *Bailey Papers.*

content to let the law operate, as all people faced its consequences, while Karl Marx recognized the law but sought to adjust society by leveling all. Conservatives, Bailey hoped, would find middle ground between the extremes.[64]

On November 21 Bailey testified that his fundamental conception of government had not changed. He had read new articles on the Constitution and reread old ones, since he believed that constitutional questions would dominate the next several years. "I sometimes think we are to fight all over again all of the battles we fought in the original conventions," he asserted.[65] He would not tolerate any tampering with the Supreme Court, its membership or its jurisdiction, and doubted whether he could consent to constitutional amendments.[66] Roosevelt would have abundant opportunity to change the tenor of the Supreme Court's decisions, but should he fail by way of death on the bench, Bailey speculated that he would likely demand amendments to extend the police power of the federal government or to revise the membership of the court.[67]

64. *Ibid.* See also: Bailey to Joseph P. Tumulty, November 17, 1936; Bailey to John Nance Garner, December 10, 1936, *Bailey Papers.*
65. Bailey to William E. Borah, November 21, 1936, *Bailey Papers.*
66. Bailey to Walter F. George, November 19, 1936, *Bailey Papers.*
67. Bailey to J. E. S. Thorpe, November 13, 1936, *Bailey Papers.*

CHAPTER EIGHT

COURT CHAMPION

"In his famous Reflections on the Revolution in France," Bailey observed, Edmund Burke "remarked of certain leaders in that revolution that they took a constitution in hand as savages 'took a looking glass.' This is a precise description for our time. . . . [T]he same curiosity, the same wonder and the same failure to apprehend what it [the United States Constitution] means and what it is for."[1] Such was Bailey's immediate response to Roosevelt's demand for co-operation from Congress and the Supreme Court in realization of new legislation broadening and amplifying the New Deal. Addressing an overwhelmingly Democratic Congress on January 6, 1937, Roosevelt insisted that, while the Constitution did not need revision, the Supreme Court should take "an increasingly enlightened view with reference to it."[2] His demand for co-operation and his implied warning of constitutional revision foreshadowed the events of 1937. Bailey thoughtfully noted that Roosevelt had raised a great constitutional issue, but no one appeared shaken by the threat. The idea of "co-operation" between the Supreme Court and the Executive was utterly repugnant. The desired co-operation should properly come from Congress in framing legislation within its powers. The American people asked only that questions pending in the Supreme Court be free from political influence and that judges follow the ancient injunction to "do justice, love mercy and walk humbly before the Lord."[3]

Between January, 1935, and December, 1936, the Supreme Court had voided the Railroad Pensions Act, the Farm Mortgages Act, the National Industrial Recovery Act, the Agricultural Adjustment Act, the Bituminous Coal Act, and the Municipal Bankruptcy Act. Doubt had also been cast on the constitutionality of such federal statutes as the National Labor Relations Act and the Public Utility Holding

1. Bailey to Johnston Avery, January 7, 1937, *Bailey Papers*.
2. Roosevelt, *Public Papers and Addresses*, V, 639.
3. Bailey to George Sutherland, January 11, 1937, *Bailey Papers*.

Company Act.[4] In six of the cases the court had divided either 6 to 3 or 5 to 4 with conservative justices prevailing. "The reactionary members of the Court," contended Roosevelt, "had apparently determined to remain on the bench as long as life continued—for the sole purpose of blocking any program of reform."[5] Determining to reconstitute the recalcitrant court, Roosevelt proposed appointment of an additional judge for every federal judge over the age of seventy who refused to resign or retire. The proposal limited appointments for the entire federal bench to fifty and banned raising the membership of the Supreme Court above fifteen.[6] The Judiciary Reform Bill or "Court Packing" bill, as opponents dubbed the proposal, met congressional hostility from the outset. Roosevelt concealed his plans until just a few hours before formally presenting the bill, which caught many members of Congress unprepared. He also neglected to secure advance commitments from the agricultural and labor leaders most concerned with the conservative court's threat to liberal legislation. The most damaging aspect of the proposal, however, was its disingenuous and incorrent argument that overcrowded dockets and aged judges required judicial reorganization.[7]

Several weeks earlier Bailey had declared that "the modern attack upon the Supreme Court . . . is in no small measure an effort to strike down the judicial power of the Court and thereby to give to Congress unlimited power and therefore to take from the people their rights and from States their powers."[8] On February 8 he avowed opposition to any attempt whatever to enlarge the number of justices and asserted that the American people would perceive and resent any effort to subject the court to political influences.[9] Anti-court-plan Democrats gathered shortly afterward at a dinner given by Senator Millard E. Tydings of Maryland to organize themselves into a compact opposition machine. The steering committee consisted of Bailey, Harry F. Byrd (Va.), Edward R. Burke (Neb.), Walter F. George (Ga.), Bennett C. Clark (Mo.), Tom Connally (Tex.), Frederick Van Nuys (Ind.), David I. Walsh (Mass.), Peter G. Gerry (R.I.),

4. Robert H. Jackson, *The Struggle for Judicial Supremacy* (New York, 1941), p. 181.
5. Roosevelt, *Public Papers and Addresses*, VI, lxi-lxii.
6. *Ibid.*, pp. 51–66.
7. *Ibid.*; Joseph Alsop and Turner Catledge, *The 168 Days* (New York, 1938), p. 69.
8. Bailey to C. J. Agrafiotis, January 19, 1937, *Bailey Papers*.
9. Bailey to editor of the New York *Times*, February 8, 1937, *Bailey Papers*.

Burton K. Wheeler (Mont.), and Tydings. With Gerry acting as the organization's whip and Wheeler providing public leadership, the steering committee worked tirelessly and efficiently to secure commitments from their unannounced colleagues. Each day the committee culled attitudes of senators for possible changes and prepared lists showing the progress of the fight.[10]

Over a nationwide radio network on February 13 Bailey calmly and deliberately bared the subterfuges which Roosevelt had used to conceal his real purpose. The President had first argued that the Supreme Court had fallen behind in its work, but Roosevelt's own solicitor general had officially stated that "the work of the Court is current and cases are heard as soon after records have been printed as briefs can be prepared." Roosevelt had contended secondly that the court declined petitions in many cases, indicating thereby necessity for six additional justices, but again the solicitor general had testified that "a very large majority of the cases on the appellate docket do not possess sufficient merit to warrant consideration on the merits." The third point made by the President touched the subject of age and mental and physical capacity as related to the first two considerations, but ironically, "the ages of the Justices was [sic] cited as the reason for conditions that do not exist." There had been division in the Supreme Court, but no one attributed this division on either side to age or infirmity. Reviewing Roosevelt's statements concerning the Supreme Court, Bailey found that "we have no difficulty in perceiving the obvious fact our President seeks to reconstitute the Supreme Court of the United States in the clear intention of bringing about a new interpretation of the Constitution." The President's zeal had obviously carried him far beyond wisdom and right, for the remedy was infinitely worse than the difficulty to which it was addressed. Granting even that Roosevelt's motive was worthy and his objective desirable, his method was nevertheless indefensible. If President or Congress ought to have more power, and the people and states less, then a constitutional amendment should be submitted to the people. The court and the Constitution stand or fall together, Bailey warned, for "to weaken either is to weaken the foundations of our Republic; to destroy either is to destroy the Republic."[11]

10. Tom Connally, *My Name Is Tom Connally* (New York, 1954), p. 189.
11. Josiah W. Bailey, "The Supreme Court, the Constitution, and the People," *Vital Speeches of the Day*, III (March 1, 1937), 290–295.

Among many plaudits received for his initial speech, Bailey valued most that of Associate Justice George Sutherland, who wrote that he was "unable to refrain from breaking the silence which is supposed to enshroud the judiciary to tell you how deeply your words moved me. I am quite sincere in saying that in my judgment there never has been a better speech."[12] By late February, Bailey judged that anti-court-plan senators controlled the situation, for they had forty-two votes and expected others. They would be weaker on a compromise bill authorizing appointment of two additional justices, but at least thirty-five senators would oppose to the end any measures compromising the independence of the Judiciary. Meanwhile, the controversy served to educate the people in the value of the court and the Constitution. For the first time in years, he exclaimed in some amazement, the people read the speeches of senators, and radio networks begged for speaking engagements. He hopefully watched for signs that the President would either admit his error, or at least recognize the necessity of improving his unhappy position.[13]

Instead of abandoning his proposal, Roosevelt shifted his tactics by departing from his original devious approach in favor of a direct appeal to the country. He explained in a fireside chat on March 8 that he hoped "to bring to the decision of social and economic problems younger men who have had personal experience and contact with modern facts and circumstances under which average men have to live and work." He wished to prevent surrender of the country's constitutional destiny "to the personal judgment of a few men who, being fearful of the future, would deny us the necessary means of dealing with the present." Then, speaking confidentially and as a friend, Roosevelt reassured his followers, "You who know me can have no fear that I would tolerate the destruction by any branch of government or any part of our heritage of freedom."[14] After a full month of conducting his court proposal through administrative lieutenants, Roosevelt at last assumed leadership, but popular response to his appeals was not impressive.

From the outset the people indicated reluctance to abandon their traditional veneration of the Supreme Court, despite disapproval of

12. George Sutherland to Bailey, February 22, 1937, cited in Joel Francis Paschal, *Mr. Justice Sutherland* (Princeton, 1951), p. 201.
13. Bailey to George Sutherland, February 26, 1937, *Bailey Papers*.
14. Roosevelt, *Public Papers and Addresses*, XI, 113–133.

some of the court's decisions. Of the tens of thousands of letters received by Bailey, the vast majority censured the President's proposal, although many favored constitutional amendments permitting Congress to override Supreme Court decisions. Others, however, bitterly attacked Bailey's disloyalty to Roosevelt, while one influential North Carolinian demanded that he either "Represent or Resign."[15] Severe newspaper criticism by an old friend, W. O. Saunders, editor of the Elizabeth City *Independent*, prompted a personal reply from Bailey, which so impressed Saunders that he published the letter. To the charge that he looked not to pressing current needs but to the past in making his decisions, Bailey responded:

> History . . . teaches me that second thoughts are more to be trusted than first thoughts; that reason is better than impulse; that the long view is better than the view of apparent immediate self-interest; that the best friends of the people are not those who appeal either to their prejudices or emotions, nor who agree with them just to please, nor those who make the loudest professions of interest in them; that one who would serve them must study measures and seek the right; that men engaged in the tasks of life have but little time for study or meditation, and that if someone does not study for them they will learn only at the cost of bitter experience; and that one honest man who will tell them the truth is worth ten thousand who are content with them rather than take their criticisms or their curses. And history also tells me that in the long run only the men who are willing to pay this price receive the rewards of a grateful posterity, or the satisfaction of duty done.[16]

Subsequently, the letter, which Saunders entitled "The Hard Way," was reprinted in newspapers throughout North Carolina and the nation. Typical of the reaction was that of Newton D. Baker, secretary of war under Woodrow Wilson, who wrote that nothing recently had moved him as deeply. "As against the independent, thoughtful, and conscientious representative on the one side and the messenger boy on the other, no wise constituency will long hesitate," Baker

15. Josephus Daniels to Jonathan Daniels, March 13, 1937, day letter, *Daniels Papers*; Raleigh *News and Observer*, March 22, 1937, p. 4.
16. Bailey to W. O. Saunders, March 1, 1937, *Bailey Papers*; Raleigh *News and Observer*, March 22, 1937, p. 7.

affirmed, "and the messenger boy has the added infirmity that he may mistake a noisy minority opinion or a hastily formed judgment for a real expression of matured public will."[17] So great was demand for the letter that Bailey mimeographed and mailed upon request almost one million copies.[18]

If the administration's mistakes and the opposition's growing strength were not enough to defeat the court proposal, the issue of an anti-New Deal Judiciary was almost destroyed by the Supreme Court itself. On March 29 the court upheld the Railway Labor Act, the revised Frazier-Lemke Farm Mortgage Moratorium Act, and the Washington minimum wage law, which was similar to the New York minimum wage law invalidated by the court in 1936.[19] The last decision nonplused Roosevelt's liberal supporters who had to approve the court's interpretation while maintaining that legislative reform of the court was necessary since the court would not reform itself. Pressure for judiciary change further weakened on April 12, when the court found the National Labor Relations Act constitutional by a 5 to 4 decision.[20] The sudden reversal of the court's attitude toward New Deal legislation tore the heart out of Roosevelt's arguments, but the President distrusted a court in which one vote decided the constitutionality of state and federal laws.[21] On May 18, however, Roosevelt unexpectedly gained opportunity to name a liberal justice to the Supreme Court when Justice Van Devanter, one of the oldest and most conservative members, notified the President that he would retire.[22] On the same day, the Senate Judiciary Committee voted 10 to 8 against the Judiciary Reform Bill, declaring that "this bill is an invasion of the judicial power such as has never been attempted in this country. . . . Under the form of the Constitution it seeks to do that which is unconstitutional."[23]

The Supreme Court's reversal brought praise from many conservatives who under other circumstances would have deplored the exten-

17. Newton D. Baker to Bailey, March 25, 1937, *Bailey Papers*.
18. Interview with A. Hand James, Raleigh, N.C., November 1, 1961; A. Hand James to Hinton James, March 26, 1937, *Bailey Papers*.
19. See: *Virginia Railway* v. *Federation*, 300 U.S. 515; *Wright* v. *Vinton Branch*, 300 U.S. 440; *West Coast Hotel Co.* v. *Parrish*, 300 U.S. 379.
20. See: *Labor Board* v. *Jones & Laughlin*, 301 U.S. 1.
21. Roosevelt, *Public Papers and Addresses*, VI, 153–156.
22. Elliott Roosevelt, ed., *F.D.R.: His Personal Letters, 1928–1945* (New York, 1950), I, 681.
23. Alsop, *The 168 Days*, pp. 196–207.

sion of federal power.[24] Bailey noted that the court's recent decisions would likely be followed by two retirements, thus giving the President a court to his liking. He thought the court unwise, however, in making concessions with a view to softening the blows of the President. Nevertheless, the court's decisions encouraged moderate members of the Senate to seek a compromise court plan authorizing Roosevelt to appoint two additional judges instead of the original six. Had Roosevelt been willing to accept such a compromise in mid-April, Bailey judged that a majority of the senators would have approved.[25] The President did turn to compromise in mid-May, but his chances had greatly diminished because of growing bitterness among many liberal senators over the administration's high-pressure tactics. Postmaster General Farley's sardonic remark at a Cabinet meeting typified the administration's mismanagement. Farley observed that if a senator's conscience would not let him support the President's court proposal, it ought not to let him ask favors from the administration.[26] Bailey gleefully pointed out that Farley's statement alienated many wavering senators, for "Hatch, O'Mahoney and McCarran sat in with us in a conference yesterday. Men who have come to our side cannot go back now without more or less disgrace."[27]

The President foresaw the defeat of his original plan by early June, but hoped to secure a face-saving compromise. He relinquished command to Majority Leader Robinson, who had long been in line for a seat on the Supreme Court and who had backing from conservative and liberal senators alike. Throughout June, Robinson sought commitments for a compromise, but the absence of Vice President Garner made his task more difficult. Garner had expressed his displeasure with the administration's policy toward sit-down strikes and budgetary problems by departing in mid-June for a Texas vacation. Acting under Robinson's advice, Roosevelt arranged a three-day meeting on Jefferson Island to heal Democratic wounds and to conciliate potential opponents of the compromise, but the President had little to show for his last-minute efforts.[28] Although the Senate received the compromise

---

24. Roosevelt, *Public Papers and Addresses*, VI, 153–156.

25. Bailey to Robert Latham, April 15, 1937, *Bailey Papers*.

26. Harold L. Ickes, *The Secret Diary of Harold L. Ickes* (New York, 1953–54), II, 141.

27. Bailey to Julian Miller, May 18, 1937, *Bailey Papers*.

28. Alsop, *The 168 Days*, pp. 219–243; Ickes, *The Secret Diary*, II, 145, 153, 158–160; Roosevelt, *Public Papers and Addresses*, VI, 263.

bill on July 2, debate did not begin until four days later. In the interval Robinson and his lieutenants worked frantically to hold their forces and to persuade wavering members. The opposition counted approximately forty-two votes against the measure, but the filibuster constituted their chief defense. Under Senate rules, which Robinson promised to enforce to the letter, each senator could speak only twice on the bill itself, but could also speak twice on each amendment. At the final meeting of the opposition steering committee, each senator agreed to speak as often as the rules allowed and as long as his physical condition permitted. The committee instructed Senator Burke to prepare a vast number of amendments—a task which he turned over to a group of young lawyers supplied by the American Bar Association. After twenty-four hours the lawyers had drafted only fifteen amendments and turned in despair to Senator Bailey. When Bailey saw the results of their labors, he burst into laughter, and, requesting that one of the lawyers prepare for dictation, rattled off in less than two hours nearly fifty amendments covering the enacting clause to the last sentence. Versed now in the intricacies of legislative maneuvers, the official amendment writers quickly compiled a total of one hundred and twenty-five amendments, which they delivered to Burke.[29]

Robinson opened debate in the Senate on the compromise court plan shortly after noon on Tuesday, July 6. He warned that means would be found to meet the obstructionist filibuster. Throughout his speech he hammered at his opponents, but was constantly interrupted by questions from anti-court-plan Democrats.[30] Three other stalwart supporters of compromise, Senators Logan (Ky.), Hatch (N.M.), and Minton (Ind.), spoke on Wednesday and Thursday, but attention turned Friday to the opposition led by Senator Wheeler, who fervently denounced any plan whatsoever to tamper with the Supreme Court. The opposition continued the battle on Saturday through Senator McCarran, who rose from a sickbed to declare dramatically: "I think this cause is worthy of any man's life."[31] On Monday the Senate reassembled to hear Senator O'Mahoney's eloquent and effective criticism of the bill and Bailey's initial remarks in defense of the Judiciary. Continuing on Tuesday afternoon, Bailey surveyed the history

29. Alsop, *The 168 Days*, pp. 248–250.
30. *Congressional Record*, 75th Cong., 1st Sess., pp. 6787–6797.
31. *Ibid.*

Editors Bailey *(Biblical Recorder)* and Clarence Poe *(Progressive Farmer)*, 1904.

Senator Cameron Morrison welcomes Bailey to the U. S. Senate, 1931.

Berryman, Washington *Evening Star*

Berryman, Washington *Evening Star*

Conservative responses in 1937

Berryman, Washington *Evening Star*

Berryman, Washington *Evening Star*

and 1938 to Roosevelt's New Deal.

Wide World photo

Chairman Bailey interrogates witnesses during a 1937 hearing.

Wide World photo

Senators Bailey, Caraway, and Connally led a 1938 filibuster.

of judicial review, making repeated points against setting a precedent of political domination over the courts. The substitute bill was no compromise at all, since it still violated the principle of an independent Judiciary. For rows around Bailey every desk was filled, and the chamber was impressively still. "That rare thing, a successful and convincing argument, was being made on the Senate floor, and Robinson, tired and sick as he was, sensed it at once."[32] Leaving in the midst of Bailey's message, he telephoned a friend in the Justice Department to report that "Bailey's in there and he's making a great speech. . . . He's impressing a lot of people, and I tell you I'm worried."[33] The speech did influence several marginal senators. Bailey later recalled that "there were ten Senators before us who had not committed themselves. They were leaning a little the other way. The problem was to change them. We needed to change three and three were changed."[34] The three senators who joined forces with the opposition that afternoon were Prentiss M. Brown (Mich.), Edwin C. Johnson (Colo.), and Charles O. Andrews (Fla.).[35]

The following morning Senator Robinson was found in his apartment dead from a heart attack. Robinson's death left administration supporters leaderless and confused, while the opposition saw victory at hand. The President, however, elected to continue and released to the newspapers a letter to Senator Barkley, which read: "Since the untimely death of our Majority Leader, I had hoped with you that at least until his funeral services had been held a decent respect for his memory would have deferred discussion of political and legislative matters." He also stressed the desirability of continuing the court-reform plan and denounced rumors that he would abandon the bill. Roosevelt further complicated an already overheated atmosphere in the Senate by explaining that he was writing Barkley, "because you are the Acting Majority Leader in the Senate."[36] Many senators rightly construed this to mean that the President actively supported Barkley in the race developing between Barkley and Pat Harrison for Senate leadership. On July 16 Bailey dictated a statement for the press on the "My Dear Alben" letter, but apparently decided upon discretion, for he never released it. He declared in part: "We are in

---

32. Alsop, *The 168 Days*, pp. 261–262.   33. *Ibid.*
34. Bailey to Horace Williams, December 21, 1937, *Bailey Papers*.
35. Alsop, *The 168 Days*, p. 265.
36. Roosevelt, *Public Papers and Addresses*, VI, 306–308.

the midst of a tragedy of great magnitude—a great and beloved leader has fallen suddenly in the midst of conflict. . . . None of us are quite as capable of calm thinking as we may believe. . . . Indeed it is difficult to imagine what could have been said to the President that would have induced or justified his statement."[37]

Following Robinson's funeral, Vice President Garner informed Roosevelt that sufficient votes could not be secured. Roosevelt, at last willing to face facts, requested that Garner arrange the best compromise possible under the circumstances.[38] On July 21 Democratic members of the Senate caucused on whether Barkley or Harrison would become the new majority leader. When the ballots were counted, Barkley had won by a bare majority of one, a vote probably cast under White House pressure.[39] Immediately thereafter Garner notified Wheeler that the court-packing fight was over. Wheeler hurriedly located Bailey, and the two senators of such diverse political and economic philosophies sought out Garner to discover exactly what he had meant. Garner suggested several compromise plans, but Wheeler and Bailey, well aware that they held the winning hand, flatly rejected any measure affecting the Supreme Court in any way. Forced to capitulate, Garner consulted Senators Ashurst and Barkley on the best method to recommit the pending bill. Word of the conference spread quickly among anti-court-plan senators, twenty-seven of whom gathered in Wheeler's office to hear the news. The group decided that the court bill should be recommitted to the Judiciary Committee when the Senate convened on the next day, a decision Wheeler and Bailey promptly relayed to the new majority leader.[40] On Thursday, July 22, a motion to recommit Senate Bill 1392, to reorganize the judicial branch of the government, was duly made and approved by a vote of 70 to 20.[41]

The court fight ended, but antagonism between the President and influential members of Congress persisted. Congress convened in

37. Bailey press release, July 16, 1937 (not released), *Bailey Papers*.
38. Bascom N. Timmons, *Garner of Texas* (New York, 1948), pp. 222–223; Grace Tully, *F.D.R.: My Boss* (New York, 1947), pp. 224–225.
39. Alben W. Barkley, *That Reminds Me* (New York, 1954), pp. 155–156; James A. Farley, *Jim Farley's Story: The Roosevelt Years* (New York, 1948), pp. 91–93; Ickes, *The Secret Diary*, II, 170; Timmons, *Garner of Texas*, pp. 223–224. Farley and Ickes assert that F.D.R. pressured William H. Dieterich (D., Ill.) to change his vote from Harrison to Barkley.
40. Alsop, *The 168 Days*, pp. 283–291.
41. *Congressional Record*, 75th Cong., 1st Sess., p. 7381.

January with the greatest Democratic majority in the nation's history, but that majority splintered into factions under the impact of Roosevelt's court-packing proposal. Despite defeat of the bill in Congress, the President apparently achieved his main objective, a Supreme Court which would approve New Deal legislation. Whether a compliant court would be of greater value to Roosevelt's domestic program than a co-operative Congress remained to be seen.

A more immediate consequence of the court fight was postponement of legislative action on many reform measures advocated by Roosevelt in his annual message. Although greatly preoccupied with the court-packing proposal, Congress approved with Bailey's support legislation extending the Reconstruction Finance Corporation, the Civilian Conservation Corps, the Federal Housing Administration, the Home Owner's Loan Corporation, the Soil Conservation Act, the Agricultural Marketing Agreement Act, the Excise Tax Act, the Commodity Credit Corporation, and the Reciprocal Trade Agreements Act.[42] Congress overrode, however, two presidential vetoes, an extension of the Veterans' Insurance Act and a reduction of interest on Federal Land Bank Loans. Bailey upheld the first veto, but not the second. Congress also passed the Guffey-Vinson Bituminous Coal Bill providing for governmental and private co-operation in price control and trade practices. Bailey voted against this measure as an unwarranted attempt by the federal government to regulate prices, but favored an amendment, offered by James F. Byrnes (S.C.), declaring sit-down strikes by labor organizations illegal.[43] Although the Senate rejected the amendment 48 to 36, the vote reflected growing fear of the aggressive policies of the Congress of Industrial Organizations under John L. Lewis' leadership.[44] Bailey also approved the Neutrality Act of 1937, prohibiting export of arms, ammunition, and implements of war to belligerent countries and restricting travel by American citizens on belligerent vessels during war.[45] His record in support of the New Deal on these important, although secondary matters, was nearly perfect.

Two major New Deal programs, relief for tenant farmers and slum clearance, found Bailey upholding the first and opposing the second.

42. Bailey to W. H. Collins, September 25, 1937; Bailey to Charles A. Webb, June 26, 1937, *Bailey Papers.*
43. *Congressional Record,* 75th Cong., 1st Sess., pp. 5146, 7374.
44. *Ibid.,* pp. 3136, 3145; New York *Times,* June 30, 1937, p. 1.
45. *Congressional Record,* 75th Cong., 1st Sess., p. 1807.

Roosevelt had stated in a special message on farm tenancy that "while aggravated by the depression, the tenancy problem is the accumulated result of generations of unthinking exploitation of our agricultural resources, both land and people. We can no longer postpone action."[46] The Bankhead-Jones Farm Tenant Act passed Congress with Bailey's support, although he had sidetracked a similar measure in 1935.[47] The Farm Tenant Act established the Farm Security Administration and provided ten million dollars during the first year for loans to tenants who wished to purchase farms. The second major New Deal program securing approval was the Wagner-Steagall Housing Act to provide financial assistance to states in eliminating unsafe and unsanitary housing conditions and in building low-cost housing projects. Bailey apparently voted against the measure on the grounds that it would place the federal government in competition with private enterprise and might cripple building and loan associations.[48] The two votes undoubtedly reflected Bailey's concern for rural improvement and his lack of awareness of the problems of urban centers.

A third important measure, which passed the Senate but not the House, was the Fair Labor Standards Bill. Bailey contended that it would arrest industrial growth in the South where low labor costs attracted industry and that it would also raise the cost of agricultural labor.[49] A turbulent series of sit-down strikes during the first half of 1937 heightened Bailey's opposition. Not unsympathetic to labor's problems and strongly in favor of collective bargaining, Bailey disliked the CIO's aggressive efforts to recruit members and to force recognition from management. He regretted the action of Governor George H. Earle of Pennsylvania, who declared martial law in Johnstown and closed industrial plants affected by sit-downs. According to Bailey, the industries had been operating, and thousands of employees who did not wish to strike were working as usual, but the CIO brought in forty thousand men from other cities to aid the strikers. By shutting down the factories, the Governor effactually sided with the CIO, whereas Bailey claimed that "the proper course would have been to call out the militia for the purpose of protecting men in their

46. Roosevelt, *Public Papers and Addresses*, VI, 80–85.
47. Raleigh *News and Observer*, July 3, 1937, p. 2.
48. *Congressional Record*, 75th Cong., 1st Sess., p. 8373.
49. *Ibid.*, p. 7956.

right to work, not for the purpose of aiding those who were engaged in preventing men from working."[50] As chairman of the Senate Post Offices and Post Roads Committee, moreover, Bailey deplored several incidents in which strikers defied postal laws by blocking mail delivery.[51]

Before Congress adjourned on August 21, Roosevelt, bitter still over defeat on the court-packing plan, again irritated conservatives by appointing Senator Hugo L. Black (D., Ala.) to the Supreme Court position vacated by Justice Van Devanter. The President evidently nominated Black for personal and, perhaps, vengeful reasons. Black had consistently supported liberal New Deal measures, and his nomination would affront anti-court-plan Democrats, who would feel the pressure of senatorial courtesy to confirm the appointment. Ironically, the only objection raised to Black's confirmation was that he had been elected to the Senate with the backing of the Ku Klux Klan. The subject of the Klan was handled gingerly throughout the Senate debate, however, and on August 17 the Senate voted 63 to 16 to confirm Black's nomination. Only six of the conservative Democrats—Burke, Byrd, Glass, Copeland, Carey, and King—voted against confirmation.[52] Bailey, who might have joined them in opposition, rested at home in Raleigh, where he noted, "I think my whole trouble is I became entirely too intense in the struggle over the Court bill. It seemed to me that I was rather quiet, but I realize now that I was burning up inside."[53] For Roosevelt confirmation of Black was a pleasing victory. Returning from a conference with the President, Harold L. Ickes, the loquacious secretary of the interior, commented: "So Hugo Black becomes a member of the Supreme Court of the United States while the economic royalists fume and squirm and the President rolls his tongue around in his cheek."[54]

Roosevelt's sweet taste of victory soured several weeks later, when the Pittsburgh *Post Gazette* published proofs that Black held a lifetime membership in the Ku Klux Klan. He had apparently taken the

50. Raleigh *News and Observer*, June 23, 1937, p. 1.
51. Bailey news release, June 28, 1937; Bailey to H. B. Jennings, August 4, 1937, *Bailey Papers*.
52. For the Senate vote see *Congressional Record*, 75th Cong., 1st Sess., p. 9103. For Roosevelt's attitude and motives see: Farley, *Jim Farley's Story*, pp. 97–99; Ickes, *The Secret Diary*, II, 190–192.
53. Bailey to Peter G. Gerry, August 12, 1937, *Bailey Papers*.
54. Ickes, *The Secret Diary*, II, 196.

Klan oath in 1923, just a year before he won the Democratic nomination from anti-Klan Senator Oscar W. Underwood.[55] Again Ickes aptly summarized the situation: "There isn't any doubt that this incident is very bad for the President. . . . Here is a man who has always fought the Klan and stood against intolerance now put in a position of having apparently, either deliberately or carelessly, appointed as a member of the Supreme Court a man who was a member of the Ku Klux Klan."[56] In London when the scandal broke, Justice Black returned to Washington, and acting under Roosevelt's advice addressed the nation in an unprecedented radio speech. He admitted joining the Klan, but emphasized his resignation and denied the validity of the unsolicited life membership card. He further denounced intolerance and pointed to his record in support of civil liberties.[57] Shortly afterward, Bailey privately pointed out inconsistencies in the address:

> He confesses that he was a member of the Klan and admits that he stood silent when the impression was being made in the Senate . . . that he was not a member. He confesses that he joined the Klan, but he repudiates its principles. . . . He claims that he resigned, but . . . I have always understood . . . one gets out of the Klan only by banishment. . . . He does not deny that he made a speech thanking the Klan for its membership stating that he was in sympathy with the Klan.[58]

Nevertheless, Bailey considered Black a studious, hard-working man, who hopefully would "read the Constitution to find what it means, and not what he wishes it to mean or what he thinks the people may wish it to mean."[59]

The Roosevelt administration, which in January gave promise of amplifying and broadening its reform program, met defeat with the court-packing proposal, splintered the Democratic party into dissident factions, alienated the good will of many senators in the majority-leadership tussle, and now further embarrassed itself over Black's Ku

---

55. Farley, *Jim Farley's Story*, pp. 97–99; Burns, *Roosevelt: The Lion and the Fox*, pp. 312–313.
56. Ickes, *The Secret Diary*, II, 216.
57. Rauch, *History of the New Deal*, p. 285.
58. Bailey to Robert Gray Taylor, October 4, 1937; Bailey to Joseph P. Tumulty, October 4, 1937, *Bailey Papers*.
59. Bailey to John H. Bankhead, October 3, 1937, *Bailey Papers*.

Klux Klan relationship. Roosevelt had lost his best opportunity to secure social justice legislation. The mood of the country had undergone a great change. The President had operated during his first term under the psychology of depression and emergencies, but Bailey believed Roosevelt would now find it necessary to operate under the psychology of recovery and prosperity. In distress, the American people would approve any sort of reform measure, but they became conservative when fairly well off. Even granting need for new measures, Bailey observed that "there is a time for all things and the time for new measures has passed. It will come again, but they would do harm now, no matter how good they may be."[60]

60. Bailey to James F. Byrnes, May 7, 1937, *Bailey Papers*.

CHAPTER NINE

THE CONSERVATIVE MANIFESTO[1]

THE RECESSION that began in the late summer of 1937 crystallized growing opposition in Congress to administration policies. Behind the opposition was concern over past New Deal programs, but senators collaborating in formulation of a "Conservative Manifesto" in December, 1937, worried more about the future. America was being led dangerously close to collectivism, they believed, and the leader, wittingly or unwittingly, was Franklin D. Roosevelt. The senators who shared this fear belonged to both parties. They had come to think alike and sometimes act together in opposition to domestic measures of the administration. The clash of ideas in New Deal years had blurred or shifted lines between conservatives and liberals, yet by late 1937 a so-called coalition of Republicans and conservative Democrats was discernible in Congress. This group formulated the document which the press quickly tagged a "manifesto." The draftsman was Senator Josiah W. Bailey.

While the origin, nature, and even the existence of a formal coalition of conservative Democrats and Republicans during the New Deal have not been established to the general satisfaction of scholars, the increased frequency of southern Democrats' voting with the Republicans and against the majority of their own party on key roll calls after 1937 has often been remarked. Whether formal or informal, the beginnings of a conservative alliance in the United States Senate can probably be traced to the spring and early summer of 1937 when conservatives of both parties formed a tightly knit faction in opposition to White House efforts to "pack" the Supreme Court. The hard core of this alliance, forged in the heat of political conflict, did not dissolve after Roosevelt's court plans met defeat. Conservatives realized, however, the need to redefine their position and to devise a

1. This chapter was published in substantially this form in *Journal of Southern History*, XXXI (February, 1965), 21–39. ©1965 by the Southern Historical Association. Reprinted by permission of the Managing Editor.

general program around which they might unite. Bailey, believing that New Deal excesses could be stemmed only through bipartisan conservative action, set himself the task of formulating conservative policies. The rash of sit-down strikes conducted by organized labor in the summer, together with the economic recession, gave direction and purpose to his efforts.

Bailey suspected that Roosevelt intended to create a new party with assistance from John L. Lewis and organized labor, for Roosevelt "wants a party of his own, molded to his own conceptions and of course he intends to run for a third term."[2] Viewing the court bill, the wage-and-hour bill, the governmental reorganization bill, and others, Bailey concluded that they would irretrievably centralize the federal government and end representative government in the United States. "With a board here at Washington controlling hours and wages, and therefore industry, and a Court sooner or later compliant," on what, he asked, "can we base our hopes for the preservation of this Republic or this civilization?" Conservatives throughout the nation should unite in one last effort to block this subversion of representative govern-ment. Foreseeing conservative coalition against Roosevelt in 1940, he confided, "I have felt for many months now that the time would come when I would arise and say what is in my heart without reservation. . . . The element of timeliness has been a serious question in my mind, but has not the time come?"[3]

Bailey grew increasingly concerned early in August, however, about the split in the Democratic party and sought ways to restore harmony between Roosevelt and Congress. To a North Carolina Re-publican who suggested that Bailey lead a conservative coalition, he gently replied that "great issues create political parties, but the work of creation should come naturally from the people rather than from political leaders. . . . At the present moment the battle line is well drawn on the issues rather than parties. Let us stick to our issues."[4] The political tide had turned in the conservative direction, and he hoped that Roosevelt would follow. Manipulating the two wings in the body politic and the Democratic party had cost the President influence in the right wing, through his efforts to hold the left's allegiance, but he could still return to middle ground. In the future

2. Bailey to Julian Miller, May 18, 1937, *Bailey Papers.*
3. Bailey to Newton D. Baker, June 14, 1937, *Bailey Papers.*
4. Bailey to W. E. Ryon, August 2, 1937, *Bailey Papers.*

the political trend would be more liberal than it had been before the New Deal, but it must be liberal without being radical. For Bailey the word "liberal" had a distinctly eighteenth-century connotation which implied personal freedom for individuals under republican government. "I am a great liberal when it comes to the fundamental meaning of the word," he asserted, "but I am not a liberal when they interpret liberalism in terms of a return to the old reactionary system of centralized power and control of the individual with a view to limiting his activities."[5]

During September and October it became apparent that the nation had entered a recession of uncertain duration.[6] Remembering the failure of his programs in the previous congressional session, Roosevelt viewed the business decline as almost a conspiracy. He declared to his Cabinet on October 8, "I know that the present situation is the result of a concerted effort by big business and concentrated wealth to drive the market down just to create a situation unfavorable to me. . . . Everything will work out all right if we just sit tight and keep quiet. . . . The whole situation is being manufactured in Wall Street."[7] Ignoring the recession, Roosevelt sought legislation postponed by the court-packing fight. He issued a proclamation on October 12 calling Congress into special session in mid-November. In a fireside chat he told the American people that prosperity must be stabilized through legislation providing adequate pay for laborers and adequate returns for farmers, a balanced budget and a national economy that would regulate itself with as little government subsidy as possible, and a reorganized executive branch to eliminate uneconomical duplication.[8]

Bailey, anticipating the special session, had earlier alerted his conservative colleagues to the necessity of presenting a solid front on proposed legislation. Suspecting that Roosevelt would demand his own way, he described it as a way leading to "dictatorship, reelection, and, I deeply fear, revolution." Conservatives should pre-

5. Bailey to O. Max Gardner, August 2, 1937, *Bailey Papers.*
6. See Kenneth D. Roose, *The Economics of Recession and Revival: An Interpretation of 1937–1938* (New Haven, 1954). For an illuminating account of the recession by an intimate of Roosevelt, see John M. Blum, *From the Morgenthau Diaries: Years of Crisis, 1928–1938* (Boston, 1959), pp. 380–451.
7. Farley, *Jim Farley's Story,* p. 101. See also: Ickes, *The Secret Diary,* II, 223–224; Blum, *From the Morgenthau Diaries,* p. 395.
8. Roosevelt, *Public Papers and Addresses,* VI, 428–438.

serve the Democratic party against efforts to transform it into "the Roosevelt party" by framing and promoting conservative policy. "We must ascertain on whom we may rely—get them together and make our battle win or lose. . . . There is reaction, there will be more. It must be guided."[9] He saw little prospect for balancing the budget or for early increase in national income, nor did he expect conservatives to fare as well with general legislation as they had in the court fight. He did hope that they could organize a sound opposition. A farm bill providing some measure of surplus crop control could be accepted, if the bill also included special provisions for small farmers that would not restrict acreage below five acres for tobacco farmers or deprive cotton farmers of opportunity to produce six to ten bales without penalty. Conservatives could agree to reorganization of the Executive Branch in order to reduce expenses, but should be wary of a presidential power grab.[10]

Friends reported late in October that the recession appeared grave and that new business orders had dropped. Senator Gerry observed that lack of confidence in the administration's policies was the principle reason for the recession, but that the undistributed profits tax against which conservatives had fought in 1936, only to see it passed under White House pressure, had also greatly contributed. Although the administration opposed tax revision, he confided that conservative Democrats could gain sufficient support from western senators, influenced by mine operators opposing the tax, to pass limiting amendments.[11] Bailey promptly offered to co-operate on revision and to demand elimination of the undistributed profits tax as a principal objective. The depressing collapse of the stock market could not be explained easily. Men who owned stock saw little hope ahead for business and distrusted not only Roosevelt but government itself. And so did Bailey: "We do not have a Government at Washington. It is a gift enterprise and the gifts are at the expense of those who work and earn and save. Our President is not actuated by principle, but by fears. He will try to head off anything in order that he may stay at the head. I expect him to run for a third term, and if I am living, I expect to fight a good and last fight." In the meantime he suggested that

9. Bailey to Harry F. Byrd, September 25, 1937, *Bailey Papers*.
10. Bailey to Harry F. Byrd, October 11, 1937; Byrd to Bailey, October 14, 1937, *Bailey Papers*.
11. Peter G. Gerry to Bailey, October 19, 1937, *Bailey Papers*.

Gerry join him in New York City, where friends with similar views intended to organize "a well-planned concert of action, in which the objective will be to head off all this folly and restore our country to something like a normal course. . . . We must have a man of sound common sense and real courage for President no matter what party he belongs to."[12]

The business decline, dubbed the "Roosevelt Recession," reached such threatening proportions by early November that the President could no longer ignore it in the hope that it would conveniently vanish. At a cabinet meeting on November 5 he appeared greatly disturbed and uncertain about remedial action. He still argued that big money interests engaged in an "unconscious conspiracy" to force concessions from his administration.[13] Secretary of the Treasury Henry Morgenthau advised Roosevelt to issue a statement comparing business conditions in 1937 with those in 1933 and reassuring businessmen of his support, since many felt that taxes on capital gains and undistributed profits retarded recovery. Roosevelt, at first rejecting the proposal, declared again that business, particularly banking interests, schemed to force abandonment of his policies of restricting the power of wealth and of providing minimum wages, maximum hours, and favorable working conditions for labor.[14] Yet, just ten days later, the dark outlook so impressed the President that he exerted particular efforts to appease business.

In his message to Congress on November 15, Roosevelt urged that the immediate task in halting the recession was to increase investment of private capital in order to create employment and to advance business activity. He warned, however, that if private enterprise did not respond, the government must take up the slack. He admitted need for legislation that would encourage private investment and lighten tax burdens on small business. He tried to dispel fears that the nation's economy lacked stability by promising again to balance the

12. Bailey to Peter G. Gerry, October 25, 1937, *Bailey Papers*. No further reference to Bailey's conference in New York City was found, but a columnist reported in late December that several New York industrialists were sponsoring former budget director Lewis W. Douglas as a coalition candidate for the 1940 presidential nomination. See Charlotte *Observer*, December 23, 1937, p. 5.

13. Ickes, *The Secret Diary*, II, 242–243.

14. Farley, *Jim Farley's Story*, pp. 103–107; Blum, *From the Morgenthau Diaries*, pp. 391–393.

federal budget for the coming fiscal year. He also affirmed determination to continue a broad social program aimed at higher living standards and just income distribution. To attain the latter goals he demanded prompt congressional action on four important proposals. First, he recommended a new and permanent national farm act which would provide crop and surplus control, soil conservation, and stable prices. In a concession to conservative fears of governmental regimentation, he added that the American democratic way should be kept in mind and that the program should be planned and administered, as far as possible, by farmers themselves. Second, he again proposed wage-and-hour legislation intended not only to provide more uniformly adequate standards of living and purchasing power, but also to enable industries to adjust progressively to better living conditions. Third, he urged reorganization of the Executive Branch along lines of modern business practice to increase efficiency and to raise morale. Finally, he advocated regional planning for conservation and development of natural resources by dividing the country into seven administrative areas and by co-ordinating use of projects after completion.[15]

Roosevelt's message embodied a somewhat equivocal appeal. He placed responsibility for pulling the nation out of economic recession on business interests, while offering no real promise of governmental assistance. His proposals did not relate to the immediate problem of handling the recession, but were major New Deal reform measures left over from the abortive court-packing session. Placed on the defensive by a recession not attributable to Herbert Hoover's policies but demonstrating instead the failure of New Deal pump-priming efforts to achieve more than superficial recovery, Roosevelt appeared destitute of new ideas. Henry Morgenthau thought that the President "wanted to sit tight, as if he were in a poker game, to see who could last longer, the advocates of spending or the advocates of balancing the budget," but he also believed that Roosevelt "did not know where to put his strength to bring about recovery."[16] In view of Roosevelt's stated convictions that big business had engineered the recession to discredit him, his decision to give business the obligation of completing the nation's recovery had profound implications. Embittered by conservative reaction and failure of his program in Congress, Roose-

15. Roosevelt, *Public Papers and Addresses*, VI, 490–500.
16. Blum, *From the Morgenthau Diaries*, pp. 393–394.

velt seemed determined "to let Congress alone to find out whether or not it could run the Government without his help."[17]

The special session clearly demonstrated that, with an almost four-to-one Democratic majority in both Houses, Roosevelt had lost control of Congress. The recession stiffened attitudes of conservatively disposed congressmen, encouraging them to assert independence from the President. While administration supporters blamed business for the recession and urged unabated continuation of New Deal policies, they enjoyed little moral or political support from the President. Divisions in congressional membership crystallized into definite liberal and conservative camps that cut across party lines. Roosevelt's waverings between pro-business and anti-business positions and his appeals for economy and a balanced budget as well as for a renewed public works spending program thoroughly confused the situation.

On December 1 Senator Bailey publicly stated approval of the President's attitude toward the business economy as expressed in his message to Congress. Roosevelt had, he rejoiced, "manifestly undertaken to conduct our country through an inevitable period of transition, having postponed the time for this as far as was prudent." The nation could no longer employ people or keep money in circulation artificaly by borrowing funds for expenditure on non-profitable enterprise. The transition required sacrifices, but failure to remove government from its unnatural relationship to the business economy would precipitate a disastrous period of inordinate spending and uncontrolled inflation. He contended, perhaps with tongue in cheek, that "if the President is to undergo criticism in his effort to reduce public expenditure at any point whatsoever, I shall be happy to share the criticism with him."[18]

Several days later, Senator Byrd honored Lewis W. Douglas, former director of the budget and critic of New Deal finance, with a quail luncheon in a private dining room of the Capitol. The ten Democrats present were Byrd, Bailey, Gerry, Burke, Tydings, and Royal S. Copeland of New York. Also present were Arthur H. Vandenberg of Michigan, an outstanding prospect for the GOP presidential nomination in 1940, and John H. Townsend, Jr., of Delaware,

17. Ickes, *The Secret Diary*, II, 260.

18. "Statement of Senator Josiah W. Bailey," December 1, 1937, *Roosevelt Papers*; Charlotte *Observer*, December 2, 1937, p. 1.

who provided the quail and who was a prominent fund-raiser for the Republican party.[19] After listening to Douglas' informal statement of a conservative financial program,[20] the senators reportedly discussed an economic pro-business and anti-Roosevelt political alliance. Later they gathered informally with other sympathetic colleagues at private dinners sponsored by wealthy Peter Gerry to discuss their fears that continued economic relapse would impel an outburst of spending and radical legislation from Roosevelt, and to discover common grounds for agreement on objectives that would encourage recovery.[21] From these meetings arose a plan to draft a formal declaration of principles upon which all conservative members of Congress might unite. Nearly all of the inner circle of Democrats who had fought the court-packing proposal as well as several Republicans joined in preparation of the declaration. The actual writing was done chiefly by Bailey and Vandenberg in Bailey's office, but with suggestions for content and phrasing coming also from Warren R. Austin, a Vermont Republican, and from Burke, Byrd, Copeland, Gerry, Tydings, and others. Bailey himself acted as the "final editor."[22]

The declaration, entitled "An Address to the People of the United States," was designed to appeal to conservatives and traditionalist liberals. It expressed an anti-New Deal philosophy, but neither criticized the President nor overly attacked his past policies. In drafting the declaration, Bailey and Vandenberg quietly encourged suggestions and eventually submitted copies for their colleagues to circulate among other senators in order to receive criticism and support. Bailey planned to secure signatures from at least thirty to forty sympathetic senators before making the declaration public, but this plan quickly encountered such difficulties that signatures were abandoned in favor of simple "assents."[23] Many Democratic senators who may have

19. Charlotte *Observer*, December 10, 1937; New York *Times*, December 16, p. 1, and December 19, 1937, sec. 4, p. 3.

20. Douglas' remarks at the luncheon were not reported, but they probably differed little in content from his speech to the Economic Club of New York on December 7, 1937, attacking New Deal policies and urging co-operation among government, the Republican party, and business. See New York *Times*, December 8, 1937, p. 1.

21. Charlotte *Observer*, December 10, 1937, p. 2. See also *Newsweek*, December 27, 1937, p. 12.

22. New York *Times*, December 16, p. 1, and December 18, 1937, p. 1; Charlotte *Observer*, December 17, 1937, p. 1.

23. Charlotte *Observer*, December 17, 1937, p. 1. See also Arthur Krock on coalition failure, New York *Times*, December 19, 1937, sec. 4, p. 3.

approved the principles of the declaration refused to sign because the document had the appearance of a "coalition manifesto," while still others hesitated to participate in an open "declaration of congressional independence" which might aid and comfort the Republican party.[24] Republicans shied away after learning that Senate Minority Leader Charles L. McNary of Oregon had advised that "anyone who signs that thing is going to have a Liberty League tag put on him."[25] Many Republicans undoubtedly felt reluctant to sign because the executive committee of the Republican National Committee had just chosen Dr. Glenn Frank, former president of the University of Wisconsin, to lead the party's Committee on Program in drafting a declaration of party principles for 1940.[26] Other external events dissuaded moderates, who in any case may not have been in accord with every point of the ten-point program. The Far Eastern crisis created by Japanese bombing of the American gunboat *Panay* on December 12 encouraged senators to rally behind the President's handling of foreign affairs and temporarily overshadowed domestic differences.[27]

Confronted with the difficulty of securing sufficient commitments, Bailey and the other participants had reached an impasse when the matter was abruptly taken out of their hands. According to Bailey:

> Unfortunately, the statement fell into the hands of a Republican leader [Charles L. McNary] who thought that the utterance of it at this time would injure the Republican cause. He thought it would steal away a Republican opportunity. His party is preparing a policy and he did not wish any one else to prepare one. . . . We had thought that, in the effort to gain assents to the statement, there might be some premature publication, but we decided to go forward and take the chance on the ground that the idea would survive anything of that sort. We knew, of course, that there would be an effort to tag it and discredit it, but we believed that it was so necessary and so sound that it would overcome such an effort.[28]

The first public report was carried by syndicated columnists Joseph Alsop and Robert Kintner, who printed extracts in their column in the

24. New York *Times*, December 19, 1937, sec. 4, p. 3.
25. *Newsweek*, December 27, 1937, p. 12.
26. New York *Times*, December 17, 1937, p. 1.
27. *Ibid.*, December 19, 1937, sec. 4, p. 3.
28. Bailey to Julian Miller, December 20, 1937, *Bailey Papers*.

Washington *Post* on December 15; on the following day the New York *Times* published the full text.[29] Premature publication immediately brought embarrassment to the document's authors and denunciation and ridicule from administration leaders in Congress. New Dealers designated the declaration as an untoward act aimed at the President and as a treasonable attempt to form a Senate bloc in opposition to his program.[30] Plans for securing "assents" had to be dropped completely since unfavorable publicity frightened away potential recruits. The publicity even caught the originators of the "Address" off balance at first, with only Bailey acknowledging his part in the drafting.[31] The newspapers quickly identified the chief participants as Bailey, Byrd, Burke, Copeland, Gerry, Tydings, Vandenberg, Walter F. George, Carter Glass, William H. King, Ellison D. Smith, and Federick Van Nuys. Gerry "vigorously denied reports that he and Republican Senator Vandenberg did the phrasemaking." Vandenberg declined to comment except to say that he was "more than glad once more to indorse the view that like-minded Americans should work together in this emergency, and to subscribe without reservation to the general doctrine tentatively outlined."[32]

Following the Alsop-Kintner scoop, Bailey announced to reporters that he still hoped to obtain assents from a majority of the Senate and from the President himself, for, he contended:

> It is a statement of views and policies that anyone in America may espouse or reject. . . . It was not intended to form a Senate bloc, but to put forward an affirmative policy. . . . I have been working on it since President Roosevelt sent a message to Congress asserting that there was obvious need for investment of private funds in enterprise. It was not circulated to any special group. It is not a manifesto or a coalition plan. There is nothing partisan about it and no bloc involved.[33]

Despite Bailey's remarks, the press continued to speculate as to the authors and referred to the "Address" as an obvious attempt to form

29. New York *Times*, December 19, sec. 4, p. 3, and December 17, 1937, pp. 1, 4; *Newsweek*, December 27, 1937, p. 12.
30. Charlotte *Observer*, December 17, 1937, p. 1.
31. New York *Times*, December 16, 1937, p. 1.
32. *Ibid.*, December 19, 1937, sec. 4, p. 1; Charlotte *Observer*, December 18, 1937, p. 1.
33. New York *Times*, December 17, 1937, p. 18.

a conservative coalition against Roosevelt and the New Deal. The consensus was that the coalition effort had failed, but that the episode marked a new phase in Roosevelt's dealings with Congress. The New York *Times* columnist Arthur Krock summarized this view: "Secretly conceived, the dream-child was the unborn victim of premature publicity obstetrics. But no real harm was done, and perhaps some good was accomplished. The fact that coalition could be so formally proposed may impress the President with its future possibilities if the Administration should again make one of those sudden shifts which are responsible for much of the recession. Where signatures could not be obtained votes yet may be."[34]

Doubts concerning authorship were resolved in the Senate on December 20, when Burke requested unanimous consent to insert the "Address" into the *Congressional Record*, but met chiding demands from Majority Leader Barkley and such ardent New Dealers as Sherman Minton, Lewis B. Schwellenback, and Claude Pepper that the authors reveal themselves. While Burke hesitated, Bailey responded that he had drafted the program and willingly assumed responsibility; Vandenberg and Austin, both Republicans, rose to claim partial authorship. Taking the floor to defend the policy document and, incidentally, to read it into the record as part of his remarks, Bailey explained that the recovery program outlined in the "Address" had been inspired by President Roosevelt's message to Congress. After conferring with many senators who shared the President's views on encouraging private investment in business enterprise, Bailey acknowledged that he had prepared the statement. No effort had been made at secrecy, for the statement was intended for submission eventually to all for criticisms and suggestions and assents. In the course of circulation, however, the declaration had been made public and its purpose misconstrued. "I have said this," Bailey explained, "in order to disabuse the minds of Senators and the American people of all thoughts of anything like a political maneuver or anything like a secret matter, or anything like the formation of a bloc, or coalition, or anything like that damnable statement which was attached to the first publication, that it had come or might come from the Liberty League, or that someone might say that the Liberty League had something to do with it."[35]

34. *Ibid.*, December 19, 1937, sec. 4, p. 3.
35. *Congressional Record*, 75th Cong., 2nd Sess., pp. 1934–1937.

The ten-point program to encourage business and to restore prosperity called for: (1) immediate revision of taxes on capital gains and
undistributed profits in order to free investment funds; (2) reduced
expenditures to achieve a balanced budget and, thus, to still fears
deterring business expansion; (3) an end to coercion and violence in
relations between capital and labor; (4) opposition to "unnecessary"
government competition with private business; (5) recognition that
private investment and enterprise require a reasonable profit; (6)
safeguarding the collateral upon which credit rests; (7) reduction of
taxes or, if this proved impossible at the moment, firm assurance of no
further increases; (8) maintenance of state rights, home rule, and
local self-government, except where proved definitely inadequate; (9)
economical and non-political relief to unemployed with maximum
local responsibility; and (10) reliance upon the American form of
government and the American system of enterprise.[36]

Stripped to essentials, the ten-points hardly warranted classifica-
tion as anti-New Deal. Roosevelt in his November 15 message had
requested legislation to encourage private investment and to lighten
taxes on small businessmen and had promised to balance the budget.
Just relations between capital and labor were presumably the purpose
of the wage-and-hour bill he had demanded. Repeatedly throughout
the years the President in speeches had approved the profit motive and
the competitive system. References to "unnecessary" government
competition with business and to maintenance of state and local
control except where proven "inadequate" were not anti-New Deal
per se, although both were subject to interpretation and definition.
Few public officials could publicly oppose economical and non-
political distribution of relief funds. Why then had the "Address"
been immediately tagged as an anti-New Deal manifesto?

The answer lies partially in the anti-New Deal records of the
sponsors of the "Address" even though they had carefully refrained
in it from criticizing Roosevelt or his previous policies. The introduction to the ten-point program declared specifically: "We are concerned now only with our duty in view of the conditions that confront
us, in order that full activity of employment and commerce may be
had. To avoid controversy and make for unity, we may dispense with
appraisals of policies or arguments. The past is experience and is of
value only for its lessons. We propose no criticism, no politics."[37] The

36. *Ibid.*, pp. 1937–1938.   37. *Ibid.*, p. 1937.

major cause for denunciation of the "Address" sprang from the continuing battle between advocates of spending and advocates of budget-balancing—each group hoping to persuade the President to its view. The "Address" clearly stated the position against renewed spending to end the recession. "Public spending invoked in the recent emergency was recognized as a cushion rather than as substitute for the investment of savings by the people. . . . Without criticism of the public spending policy attendant upon the former emergency, we recognize that a repetition of 'that policy would not serve again, and, moreover, is out of the question. It ought to be borne in mind that private enterprise, properly fostered, carries the indispensable element of vigor."[38] The debate begun in 1933 between the spenders and the savers still waxed strong.

Despite its anti-New Deal label, the ten-point program revealed that Senate conservatives had accepted many of the economic and political objectives of the New Deal. On management-labor relations, for example, the "Address" declared that "enlightened capital must deal with labor in the light of a new conception of legitimate collective bargaining and the right to organize."[39] On unemployment relief, it asserted: "We propose that there shall be no suffering for food, fuel, clothing, and shelter; and that pending the contemplated revival of industry, useful work shall be provided to an extent consistent with the principles of this address." Regarding abuses of power by business, it avowed that "we can and will erect appropriate safeguards under the common-law principles of free men without surrendering in any degree the vital principles and self-reliant spirit on which we must depend."[40] The major burden of the program remained, however, encouragement of business through adoption of policies that would eliminate the fears that had deterred enterprise and the restraints that hampered investment and expansion.

After reading the declaration, Bailey delivered a short speech in which he rejoiced that no man in America had made stronger statements for balancing the budget than the President. He concluded with the exhortation: "If there is a thing wrong in that statement,

---

38. *Ibid.*
39. *Ibid.* The view expressed toward labor might have received more appreciation if it had not been followed immediately by the statement: "Enlightened labor must deal with capital in a due appreciation of mutual responsibilities for the success of enterprise indispensible to both."
40. *Ibid.*, p. 1938.

strike it out. If there is anything in it that offends you, condemn it. If you have a better paragraph, write it in. But, in God's name, do not do nothing while America drifts down to the inevitable gulf of collectivism. . . . Give enterprise a chance, and I will give you the guarantees of a happy and prosperous America."[41] At the beginning of his speech, Bailey's colleagues had rapidly congregated in the Senate chamber from offices and cloakrooms, for Bailey had long before established a reputation as one of the most gifted orators in the Senate. Vice President Garner left the rostrum to sit near the speaker, while George W. Norris of Nebraska, the elder statesman of Republican liberalism, crossed the aisle for the same purpose.[42] When Bailey had finished, Vandenberg shook his hand and Joseph C. O'Mahoney of Wyoming, Pat McCarran of Nevada, Rush D. Holt of West Virginia, Burton K. Wheeler of Montana, and Gerry of Rhode Island publicly congratulated him.[43]

Pleased with the attentive reception, Bailey reported to a personal friend that evening that the response throughout the country had already been tremendous and that *Business Week* was indorsing the statement in full on its editorial page. With respect to Roosevelt's course, he wrote hopefully:

> I may say to you that there are good evidences here that the President wishes to turn decidedly to the right. Mr. Wallace, the Secretary of Agriculture, said privately during the past week that this is the only thing the President can wisely do now. LaGuardia and John L. Lewis have left him and have openly broken with him. They can always move to the left faster than he can. . . . As for the President, he has repeatedly given utterance to statements indicating that he desires to turn to the right. He would prefer to do this gradually and, of course, he would like to have a great background of popular support in the turn.[44]

Almost at the same time that Bailey confided his optimistic views, a call from the White House brought stalwart New Deal Senators George W. Norris, Robert F. Wagner, Robert M. La Follette, Jr.,

41. *Ibid.*, p. 1940.
42. New York *Times*, December 21, 1937, p. 5.
43. Philadelphia *Inquirer*, December 21, 1937, pp. 1, 6 (clippings in *Bailey Papers*).
44. Bailey to Julian Miller, December 20, 1937, *Bailey Papers*.

Sherman Minton, Lewis B. Schwellenback, Theodore F. Green, Fred H. Brown, and Claude Pepper to the President's private study. "The main purpose of the meeting, as reported in informed circles," the New York *Times* recorded, "was to bring about a complete understanding between the President and the eight Senators, ardent supporters, as to purposes and to form the nucleus of a Liberal Senate organization to resist any inroads of the proposed conservative coalition upon the general plans of the New Deal."[45] The President obviously was responding to the challenge of Bailey and his colleagues, but during the next three months he continued to alternate between pro-business and anti-business statements.

Congress adjourned briefly for the Christmas holidays on the day following Bailey's speech, but already the work of the conservative senators had gained support outside Congress. The "Address" won indorsements from hundreds of chambers of commerce and citizens' organizations throughout the nation, while forty to fifty business and manufacturing associations reprinted it in lots up to 100,000.[46] By late February, 1938, Bailey estimated that almost two million copies had circulated, not counting newspaper printings. Senators and congressmen were reportedly deluged with petitions from every state in the union to uphold the policies stated in the declaration.[47] The "Conservative Manifesto" apparently reflected not only the antispending sentiments of many senators, but also the conservative temper of influential segments of the population. The charge that the document was the product of conspiracy was true only in that its authors did not publicly announce their intention to draft the declaration before doing so. The guiding intent was to create a broad foundation for conservatives to stand upon in dealing with New Deal proposals for ending the recession and encouraging business recovery. In this respect the "Conservative Manifesto" consolidated opposition to New Deal spending policies by crystallizing opinion among dissident groups and by providing a positive program for critics of the New Deal. This seems clearly to have been its purpose—to rally popular support for

45. New York *Times*, December 22, 1937, p. 6.
46. See, for example, George H. Barrows, Secretary of Chamber of Commerce, Rome, New York, to National Metal Trade Association, Chicago, January 11, 1938, *Bailey Papers*. (The Rome Chamber of Commerce published a full-page advertisement in the Rome *Daily Sentinel*, containing an outline of the ten points and a copy of a petition to Congress and the President. Similar groups throughout the country followed the same procedure.)
47. Bailey to Merwin K. Hart, February 22, 1938, *Bailey Papers*.

conservative financial practices and, thus, to influence the course of Roosevelt and Congress, rather than to form a "coalition" of conservative Democrats and Republicans in opposition to Roosevelt.

The assumption by the newspaper press that the "Conservative Manifesto" represented an abortive attempt to form an anti-New Deal coalition in the United States Senate overlooked the obvious fact that a formidable conservative voting bloc already existed. The most common explanation given by the press for the "failure" of the coalition effort was "political ineptitude" on the part of its leaders, but few of their contemporaries considered Bailey, Vandenberg, Burke, Tydings, or Byrd politically inept, either individually or collectively. The bloc composed of Republicans and conservative Democrats had functioned quite efficiently in wrecking Roosevelt's court-packing proposal and had come within a few votes of defeating the Fair Labor Standards Bill in the regular session of 1937. During the 1938 session the bipartisan conservative bloc, consisting of about thirty hard-core senators almost equally divided among Republicans and Democrats, maintained an essentially defensive posture, but managed nevertheless to repeal the undistributed profits tax, to reduce the capital gains tax, and to come within three votes of blocking the Executive Reorganization Bill. While the "Conservative Manifesto" did not initiate the bipartisan voting bloc, the ideas and principles enunciated in that document did reflect accurately the grounds upon which conservatives would attempt to restrain and later to dismantle many New Deal programs.

CHAPTER TEN

THE NEW DEAL PASSES

THE NEW YEAR—1938—brought no immediate change in the drift that had characterized Roosevelt's administration since early fall. Bailey hoped that the President would bolster business confidence by urging repeal of the pernicious undistributed profits and capital gains taxes in his annual message to Congress. Roosevelt, however, continued to vacillate between pro- and anti-business positions. He called again for a balanced budget and governmental economy, but not at the cost of letting the people down. Addressing Congress, he faced a front row of hostile Democratic senators in which Bailey, Glass, and Tydings stood out. Bailey applauded perfunctorily when the President was introduced, but throughout the forty-five minute speech these senators evidenced little interest, and as the President departed no applause was heard from them. Roosevelt had not encouraged congressional conciliation. He castigated men who proposed to conduct a national government after the practice of 1787, 1837, or 1887, and who refused to recognize the government's proper role in a society because of time-serving unwillingness to face facts.[1]

The congressional session did little to lighten the atmosphere of suspicion and bitterness left over from the Supreme Court fight and regenerated by the President's attitude toward the recession's causes. The first major legislative business in the Senate was the controversial Wagner Anti-lynching Bill, which, whatever its merits, aroused again the antagonism of southern Democrats. In the subsequent inevitable filibuster, the only relief offered was Bailey's humorous inquiry into the bathing habits of Secretary of the Interior Ickes. The mood of southern conservatives was well illustrated by Bailey's declaration that the South would not tolerate a Democratic party catering to the Negro vote. Affirming that no national administration could long survive without the southern Democrats, he warned that "we will

1. Roosevelt, *Public Papers and Addresses*, VII, 1–14. For description of senatorial reaction to Roosevelt's message, see Ickes, *The Secret Diary*, II, 287.

welcome these newcomers with the socialist trend. . . . [A]nd we will let them carry on with the zeal of renegades, but they must recognize that the old party is still here; and that the old type of man is still here, and they cannot get along without us."[2]

In mid-February the Senate approved the Second Agricultural Adjustment Bill, which had passed both the House and the Senate in special session, but which had been referred to conference committee to resolve differences. As reported from conference the bill assigned production quotas to producers of cotton, tobacco, rice, wheat, and corn and provided for artificial market control of surplus crops by the government at the option of two-thirds of the farmers. Bailey again opposed the measure as embodying the principle of compulsory control and described it as a perfect model of fascism. Although the Senate agreed to the conference report by a vote of 56 to 31, Bailey joined in opposition a hard core of twenty-five Democratic and Republican senators who had figured in the court-packing fight or in the conservative policy document.[3]

On less controversial matters of relief, few senators would risk their constituents' displeasure. The Relief Appropriations Bill, which passed the Senate on February 23 by a vote of 68 to 1, provided an additional $250,000,000 for the Works Progress Administration. Bailey opposed the additional appropriation as too large and as inconsistent with the capacity of the country to raise the money. He proposed an amendment requiring states, counties, and cities involved in any relief project to put up 20–25 per cent of the cost unless the President determined that the community could not afford assessment. The amendment was defeated 47 to 25, but again Bailey received support from most of the conservatives. Although he realized that the Relief Appropriations Bill would pass by a large vote and that public sentiment in North Carolina favored the measure, he refused to register disapproval by merely absenting himself from the roll call. When the bell rang for the vote, Bailey went down to the chamber slowly, letting the roll call pass by his name. As the clerk recalled the names of senators who had not answered and who were not paired, Bailey cast the only negative vote.[4]

2. *Congressional Record*, 75th Cong., 3rd Sess., p. 381.
3. *Ibid.*, pp. 1881, 1884. See also: Raleigh *News and Observer*, February 12, 1938, p. 1; Bailey to Julian Miller, May 9, 1938, *Bailey Papers*.
4. *Congressional Record*, 75th Cong., 3rd Sess., pp. 2337, 2344; Raleigh *News and Observer*, February 24, 1938, p. 1.

Secondary measures in the President's program, such as the bill to create a National Economic Committee to investigate monopoly and concentrations of economic power, passed Congress with little opposition. Major recommendations, such as reorganization of the Executive Branch, were either drastically weakened or defeated. The reorganization bill provided for expanding the White House staff; strengthening managerial agencies dealing with the budget, efficiency research, personnel, and planning; establishing civil service under a single administration; adding a cabinet department of social welfare; and placing the independent agencies within departments. Bailey, Byrd, and other conservatives argued that reorganization would increase the President's power over the bureauracy and, consequently, over patronage. Jealous of the rights of Congress, they contended that the bill involved abdication by Congress of its constitutional legislative functions. They also feared that the creation of a department of social welfare, handling all relief functions of the government, would lead to a partisan political instrument that could control elections.[5]

A barrage of sponsored and spontaneous telegrams to congressmen protesting that the bill would lead to dictatorship further heightened the issue. So serious were fears conjured up by this charge that Roosevelt publicly disclaimed any desire or intention to become a dictator.[6] The reorganization bill passed the Senate by an unexpectedly close vote of 48 to 43, but Bailey noted "that we could hold forty-three votes ought to be quite satisfactory, for a little analysis will show that Van Nuys was absent, and that Smith and Gillette, who are ordinarily with us, were not with us. These three would have made a tie."[7] In the House, where the so-called southern Democrat–Republican coalition had gotten an earlier start, the reorganization bill was recommitted by a vote of 204 to 196.[8] Congress was in open revolt.

The recession grew increasingly severe between September, 1937, and June, 1938, with a decline without parallel in the period of American economic history for which statistical data were available. "Industrial production declined 33%. Durable goods production de-

5. *Congressional Record*, 75th Cong., 3rd Sess., pp. 3364–3366.
6. Roosevelt, *Public Papers and Addresses*, VII, 179–192.
7. Bailey to Julian Miller, March 29, 1938, *Bailey Papers.*
8. Roosevelt, *Public Papers and Addresses*, VII, 192; Lindsay Roberts, "Reorganization: Post Mortem Notes," *Political Science Quarterly*, XIII (June, 1938), 161–172.

clined by more than 50%, national income by 13%, profits by 78%, payrolls by 35%, industrial averages by over 50% . . . and manufacturing employment by 23%. At the same time, although raw materials prices fell 21%, most prices and costs resisted the decline."[9] Addressing the American Academy of Political Science in New York on "The Essentials of Permanent Recovery," Bailey pointed out that cessation of the flow of capital into enterprise characterized the depression since 1930. The federal government had attempted to restore this flow by various means. Loans had been provided for industrial and commercial institutions. The banking structure had been rehabilitated. An immense gold reserve had been created. Mortgaged farms and homes had been refinanced. Foreign trade barriers had been destroyed in some cases. The unemployed had received assistance. Unsound financial practices had been suppressed. Still capital did not flow into enterprise.[10]

Bailey inquired whether, while accomplishing these excellent ends, the government did other things extinguishing private investment and initiative. The capital gains and undistributed surplus taxes curtailed the abilities of many people to invest. Even more detrimental to the flow of capital was popular suspicion concerning governmental policies. Public loans and work projects created the appearance of governmental competition with private enterprise. Men would not expose their savings to such ruinous rivalry. The twenty billion dollars increase in the national debt led to uncertainty concerning currency values, the entire price structure, present and future taxes, and all investments. Capital could not be expected to flow normally under such conditions, since it required a fair degree of stability. Of what value were relief and other public spending, asked Bailey, if they destroyed stability and repressed investment?[11]

He further stressed that industry had re-employed almost six million workers between 1936 and 1937, but that those years also featured a labor war of great magnitude. The National Labor Relations Act provided not only for desirable collective bargaining, but also for weapons of vicious warfare, creating antagonism between employer and employee. Strikers had taken possession of industrial

---

9. Roose, *The Economics of Recession and Revival*, pp. 237–238.
10. Josiah W. Bailey, "Essentials for Permanent Recovery," *Proceedings of the Academy of Political Science*, XVIII (May, 1938–January, 1940), 43–45.
11. *Ibid.*

plants, and the government had acquiesced. Collective bargaining should work both ways. "If owners may not exclude a worker on account of his organized affiliation, organized workers ought not to have power to exclude him because he chooses to have none." Capital would not flow into industries threatened with seizure by men who would neither work nor permit others to work. A just law between management and labor was, therefore, another essential of recovery.[12]

In agricultural matters, Bailey approved restriction of money crops in the interest of a sound farm economy and provision of soil conservation, flood control, and reforestation, but rejected the policy of reducing the production of annual wealth. "Let us not confuse money with wealth, or price with wealth," he argued, for "the time will never come when a government may so contrive that one bushel of wheat will contain more of wealth than two." Despite claims that artificial measures and drastic regulations were necessary because private incentive would not have operated, Bailey insisted that individual initiative had not been allowed a chance to work.[13]

President Roosevelt, who in Bailey's words was not "ready to stand the gaff," abandoned all pretext of balancing the budget and of relying on private enterprise and initiative on April 14, when he sent a series of pump-priming recommendations to Congress. To arrest the downward spiral of the nation's economy, he urged expending over two billion dollars for loans to the United States Housing Authority, the Farm Security Administration, and the Public Works Administration. The economic decline, he claimed, had resulted from overproduction by business and industry.[14] Bailey cynically observed that "the tune has changed and the President is now saying that business ran away with the ball. . . . Just a few months ago, he was saying that capital had gone on a strike. The whole idea is to put the blame on business . . . and any fool ought to know that business is not in control and cannot be responsible."[15] On May 21 Bailey charged over radio on the "National Grange Hour" that when Roosevelt began the borrowing-lending-spending program in 1933, he had promised permanent recovery and prosperity. After spending forty billion dollars in five years, however, the depression still existed. "One would think," he asserted, "that what has happened would be sufficient to

12. *Ibid.*   13. *Ibid.*
14. Roosevelt, *Public Papers and Addresses*, VII, 221–248.
15. Bailey to Thomas W. Lamont, May 11, 1938, *Bailey Papers.*

teach every teachable person that the borrowing-spending-lending policy is no remedy for depression."[16]

Roosevelt's pump-priming recommendations as embodied in the Relief and Work Relief Resolution received speedy approval from Congress, whose members felt great pressures from constituents to ease the recession. "It is much better under all the circumstances," Bailey himself reasoned, "for the Administration to be fully responsible than for the impression to be created that its plans have failed or will fail because of obstruction."[17] He admitted, however, that members of Congress could not easily resist demands for relief appropriations and that those who did resist were accused of not being friends of the people. "It has become the fashion in this country to make demands for money from the Congress. It has become a matter of local rivalry and civic pride to get Federal projects in towns and cities. . . . The benefit is for a few, but the burden is upon all."[18] Conservatives had probably done as much as they could for the present, he explained, since the President controlled the leadership and could sidetrack constructive conservative legislation.[19]

Bailey noted with approval the formation of the National Progressive party under the leadership of Governor Philip La Follette of Wisconsin in April. He believed this indicated the breaking up of the old parties and, perhaps, the repudiation of Roosevelt by the Progressives. He was pleased that the Progressives "are approving the position of the Conservatives in resisting the New Deal theory of reducing production. It is a big break for me and many others here."[20] Although he did not think that Roosevelt could or would return to the conservatives, the President would probably not go much farther in the radical direction. He did not care for changes made in the Democratic party under Roosevelt. He particularly feared that it would fall completely into the hands of men whose politics were distasteful to southern Democrats and whose support came from the Negro vote in New York, Pennsylvania, Chicago, and the cities of the Middle West. "They are common fellows of the baser sort," he declared, because

16. Josiah W. Bailey, "The Failure and Fallacy of Pump Priming," radio address on National Grange Hour, May 21, 1938, *Bailey Papers*.

17. Bailey to Earle Godbey, May 11, 1938, *Bailey Papers*.

18. Bailey, "Failure and Fallacy of Pump-Priming."

19. Bailey to Earle Godbey, May 11, 1938, *Bailey Papers*.

20. Bailey to Carl Goerch, May 2, 1938; Bailey to George Coffing Warner, April 30, 1938, *Bailey Papers*.

"they have no idea of political service. Their only thought is political patronage and power."[21]

Roosevelt also objected to the presence and prestige of certain men in the Democratic party, but his displeasure fell chiefly upon southern conservatives. He deeply resented the three major defeats dealt him by members of his own party—the Supreme Court reorganization plan, the wage-and-hour legislation, and the Executive reorganization plan. He undoubtedly feared also the growing power of the conservative "coalition" of Republicans and Democrats in both Houses, while hoping for constructive realignment of parties into conservative and liberal designations. His belief that, "at least since 1932, the Democratic party has been the liberal party, and the Republican party has been the conservative party," ignored, for political reasons, the obvious fact that both parties had radical, progressive, conservative, and reactionary elements. Resolving to purge the Democratic party of conservative congressmen, Roosevelt informed the nation in a fireside chat on June 24 that as head of the Democratic party he would speak out in party primaries in favor of liberal candidates and against reactionary and "yes, but" candidates. Roosevelt laid presidential blessings during the next three months on liberal candidates in Kentucky, Oklahoma, Texas, Colorado, Nevada, and California, while attacking conservatives, such as Senators Walter F. George, "Cotton Ed" Smith, and Millard Tydings, who campaigned for re-election.[22]

Roosevelt addressed the nation from Hyde Park on the eve of the November elections with a further appeal for liberal candidates: "New ideas cannot be administered successfully by men with old ideas, for the first essential of doing a job well is the wish to see the job done at all."[23] The President's efforts in the Democratic primaries, however, had been unavailing, for with the exception of Representative O'Connor's defeat in New York, every conservative candidate had been renominated, and in Texas the liberal incumbent, Representative Maury Maverick, had not secured renomination. Nor did Roosevelt's political fortunes fare better in the general election, which added eighty-two Republicans to the House and eight to the Senate. Roosevelt, making the best of the situation, later asserted that "the political struggle of 1938 had not been in vain. Liberalism in

21. Bailey to J. O. Carr, May 9, 1938, *Bailey Papers*.
22. Roosevelt, *Public Papers and Addresses*, VII, xxvi-xxxii, 463–371.
23. *Ibid.*, pp. 712–720.

Government was still triumphant."[24] A week after the elections, Bailey sarcastically related that everybody seemed satisfied with the results, including Roosevelt, Farley, Hoover, and Landon, and speculated that the next session would see more opposition to Roosevelt.[25]

The Democratic party still controlled the Congress in 1939, but the liberal bloc in the House had been halved. In the Senate the possibility of an alliance between disgruntled conservative Democrats and Republicans threatened further New Deal reform measures. Privately reviewing the situation for several conservative colleagues, Bailey observed that "perhaps we are getting on a little better than some of us suspect. The President appears to be inviting defeats and, if this is the case, we may look for some unusual developments. The Congress is no longer disposed to execute his wishes without question."[26] He saw tremendous reaction against the spending and borrowing program and interpreted the 1938 election as prophetic of what would happen in 1940. Conservative Democrats should not permit Roosevelt to place upon Congress responsibility for past policies. "We must restrain him in essential matters," Bailey advised, "but in non-essential matters, we may well afford to let him have his way, lest he go to the radio and tell the people their present condition is not due to the failure of his policies but to the obstruction tactics of the Senate and the House." Having had his way in economic matters and in public opinion for six years, Roosevelt "ought to accept the consequences for the next two."[27]

The New Deal, which for four years initiated reforms unparalleled in American history, had gradually lost momentum during Roosevelt's second term and by early 1939 came to a standstill. Samuel I. Rosenman later recalled about Roosevelt: "I do not know what course he would have taken in 1939 if events had not forced his major attention into international fields."[28] As Roosevelt delivered his State of the Union Message on January 4, 1939, an uneasy peace had been established in Europe only at the price of concessions to Hitler, but the policy of appeasement pursued by France and Great Britain provided a shaky barrier to the outbreak of war. Roosevelt warned that no nation could be safe so long as powerful nations refused to

24. *Ibid.*, p. xxxii.
25. Raleigh *News and Observer*, November 15, 1938, p. 1.
26. Bailey to John J. Raskob, February 8, 1939, *Bailey Papers*.
27. Bailey to Julian Miller, February 4, 1939, *Bailey Papers*.
28. Rosenman, *Working with Roosevelt*, p.181.

settle grievances at the council table. At the very least the United
States should avoid any action that would assist aggressor nations.
Dissatisfied with existing neutrality legislation, he asserted that "we
have learned that when we deliberately try to legislate neutrality, our
neutrality laws may operate unevenly and unfairly—may actually
give aid to an aggressor and deny it to the victims."[29] The arms
embargo provision prevented the United States from supplying material to victims of aggression, but Roosevelt was not yet ready to
demand repeal. Following a cautious course, which perhaps recognized isolationist sentiment in the country, Roosevelt called on Congress to approve only a half-billion dollars for national defense.

Attention concentrated increasingly upon European tensions, but
the shift of focus from domestic to foreign affairs was gradual. Bailey's chief concern was his new responsibilities as chairman of the
Senate Commerce Committee, a position of considerable power to
which he had been elevated by the death of Royal S. Copeland in the
summer of 1938. Bailey presided over hearings relative to confirmation of Harry L. Hopkins, former administrator of the Works Progress Administration, whom the President had appointed secretary of
commerce. Although newspapers indicated that Bailey had long
awaited opportunity to "blast" Hopkins, Bailey made every attempt
to be fair to Hopkins during the hearings. Questioning Hopkins at
length about political speeches made in his supposedly non-political
role as administrator of relief funds, Bailey appreciated Hopkins'
candor in admitting lack of discretion in some of his remarks. Hopkins replied to Bailey's questions: "I do not want to duck that question. I do not want to imply I withdraw the contents of these speeches,
but if I had the road to go again I would not have made them as Relief
Administrator."[30] Other members, particularly Hiram Johnson (R.,
Calif.), subjected Hopkins to hours of hair-splitting questioning. The
committee reported the nomination favorably to the Senate by a
divided vote in which Bailey refrained from voting at all. Disqualifing
himself, Bailey declared that he could consent to the appointment as a

    29. Roosevelt, *Public Papers and Addresses*, VIII, 1–12.
    30. Robert E. Sherwood, *The White House Papers of Harry L. Hopkins*
(London, 1948), I, 105–108. Interview with A. Hand James, clerk of the
Senate Commerce Committee between 1939 and 1945, Raleigh N.C., November
1, 1961. James disclosed that O. Max Gardner remarked privately that he and
several friends of Hopkins had conferred with the new secretary of commerce
almost all night convincing him that his best defense was to admit mistake.

courtesy to the President, but could not advise Roosevelt to make the appointment. He complained that Hopkins had not made sufficient effort to keep distribution of relief funds free from political influence and had admitted inability to prevent his assistants from organizing relief workers in primary campaigns.[31] On January 23, 1939, the Senate confirmed the appointment of Hopkins as secretary of commerce.

Hopkins was apparently being groomed by Roosevelt as a possible successor. If this was the case, Hopkins' steadily declining health made it unfeasible. When he resigned as secretary of commerce on August 22, 1940, he had, because of illness, intermittently spent no more than thirty days at his office.[32] Bailey, also in poor health, curtailed his activities on the Senate floor, but maintained heavy correspondence and worked industriously as committee chairman. During the greater part of Bailey's life he had suffered from migraine headaches which usually lasted about twenty-four hours. He had also been thoroughly exhausted by the 1937 Supreme Court fight and the bitter congressional session of 1938. He tired rapidly and rested frequently. He would get out of his car and walk a hundred yards to his office, close the door, and lie down. Unwilling to reveal his weakness, he sat at his desk when strangers visited, but received old friends lying down.[33] His letters and conduct of the Commerce Committee testified that his mental faculties were unimpaired, but his physical stamina had so greatly declined in his sixty-eighth year that he made few major speeches in the Senate during 1939 and 1940.

As chairman of the Commerce Committee Bailey had greater personal and political contact with Roosevelt, a relationship which he found agreeable. He remarked to Byrd that, having quit intoxicants on his doctor's orders, "I may go down to see the President and indulge myself a little in that sort of intoxication. He and I are on fairly good terms. He understands me and I understand him, and I really believe the man is inclined to lean away from the extreme left."[34] Bailey assured the President of his desire to broaden the

---

31. Josiah W. Bailey, "Individual Observations on the Nomination of Harry L. Hopkins to be Secretary of Commerce," *Senate Committee Print*, 76th Cong., 1st Sess., in *Bailey Papers*.
32. Sherwood, *The White House Papers of Hopkins*, I, 78–121.
33. Interviews with A. Hand James, Raleigh, N.C., November 1, 1961, James Hinton Pou Bailey, Raleigh N.C., November 2, 1961, and Mrs. Josiah William Bailey, Raleigh, N.C., February 7, 1962.
34. Bailey to Harry F. Byrd, December 12, 1939, *Bailey Papers*.

outlook and conception of the committee's functions. He explained that despite frequent newspaper reports that he opposed the administration and the New Deal, he was not himself aware of any sense of opposition. "I try to vote upon measures as they are presented upon their merits, and I begin always by giving the benefit of any doubt to your recommendations. I would much prefer to go along with you than to go against you."[35]

The Commerce Committee compiled an impressive record of business accomplishments, but Bailey found that his new role was not without hardships. The River and Harbor Bill of 1939, appropriating seventy-nine million dollars for one hundred small river and harbor projects, typified his difficulties. Senators with favorite projects for their own states maneuvered to include them. Addition of fifteen major flood control projects raised the total proposed appropriations to almost a half-billion dollars. According to Bailey's information, the President would veto the bill in its top-heavy condition, even if Majority Leader Barkley permitted Senate consideration. Bailey endeavored to eliminate the larger projects by insisting that any item authorizing as much as ten million dollars should be considered on its merits in a separate bill. Interested senators, including his good friend Walter George, frustrated his efforts. Bailey offered a substitute bill eliminating large flood control projects and providing for river and harbor projects requiring expenditure of only eighty-five million dollars, but the committee rejected the substitute. He reported the bill calling for a half-billion-dollar appropriation, but embraced the first opportunity to sidetrack it, notwithstanding its provision for twenty-four small projects in North Carolina. Although he wanted consideration of the major flood control projects on their own merits, he admitted that "the trouble is our North Carolina projects are hitched in with these big projects and this puts me in a very embarrassing position."[36]

Concerned with committee duties and in poor health, Bailey presented only one major speech outside the Senate during 1939, an address at Chapel Hill in defense of economic conditions in the South. In August, 1938, the President's National Emergency Council had released a report on the South, entitled "The Nation's No. 1 Economic Problem."[37] Bailey did not contend that the South had no problems and agreed that great and desirable advances were needed.

35. Bailey to Franklin D. Roosevelt, January 17, 1939, *Bailey Papers.*
36. Bailey to Thomas W. Davis, August 14, 1939, *Bailey Papers.*
37. Roosevelt, *Public Papers and Addresses,* VII, 421–426.

The report designated the region the prime economic problem on the basis of low industrial wages and low family consumer income as compared with other regions. Although correct, the figures cited in the report permitted several interpretations. On the problem of low industrial wages, Bailey observed that "all industrial workers in the South are paid within one point of the National average paid in wages of the value added by manufacture. The South's ratio is 37.9; the National ratio is 38.7." The average consumer family income in the South was $1,326, while the national average was $1,612 per year, but Bailey contended that lower taxes, short winters, abundant gardens, and lower rents offset the 17 per cent difference.[38]

A further significant factor in the difference between the national and the southern average family income, he asserted, was that the Works Progress Administration paid workers $600 per year in the North compared with $360 in the South and that sixteen billion dollars had been distributed on that basis since June, 1933. On relief, he asserted that "Pennsylvania with 9,000,000 population gets more money than eleven Southern states with 29,000,000 population. . . . Expenditures per family per State in eight States exceed $200 per year; but in no Southern State do relief expenditures amount to $100 per family."[39] He certified that every chart of trade and business between 1929 and 1939 showed that the South had withstood the long depression better than any other section, while receiving less federal aid. Although reasoned and documented from official government reports, the speech aroused criticism from North Carolina newspapers that Bailey ignored the very real problems of the South.[40] Ironically, on the same day that Bailey spoke at Chapel Hill, President Roosevelt declared at Auburn, Alabama: "I think that we have done more in those six years [1933–39] than in the previous sixty years all through these southern States to make them self-supporting and to give them a balanced economy that will spell a higher wage scale, a greater purchasing power and a more abundant life than they have had in all their history."[41]

Like other politicians in the summer of 1939, Bailey speculated on

38. For the full text of Bailey's speech, see *Congressional Record*, 76th Cong., 1st Sess., Appendix pp. 3903–3907.

39. *Ibid.* Bailey did not mention the sources for his statistics, but the following year he inserted in the *Record* a series of charts supplied by the Bureau of the Budget which supported his figures. See *Congressional Record*, 76th Cong., 3rd Sess., Appendix pp. 818–819.

40. See, for example, Charlotte *News*, March 31, 1939, p. 4.

41. Roosevelt, *Public Papers and Addresses*, VIII, 181–184.

the approaching presidential nomination and election of 1940. He concluded that Roosevelt did not plan to run for a third term, since "men who run for office usually try to unite their Party."[42] Insisting that only liberal candidates could win, Roosevelt declared, "If we nominate conservative candidates, or lip-service candidates, or a straddlebug platform, I personally . . . will find it impossible to have any active part in such an unfortunate suicide of the old Democratic Party."[43] Bailey realized that conservative Democrats could not wrest control of the party and the convention from the President, but hoped for a compromise candidate who would lean away from extreme radicals among labor groups. Although he would support John N. Garner, James A. Farley, Cordell Hull, or even former Governor Paul V. McNutt of Indiana for the Democratic nomination for president, he suspected that Roosevelt deliberately schemed to play the aspirations of each against the other.[44] Secretary of the Interior Ickes recorded in his diary a conversation with the President and Farley in which Roosevelt declared that if the old parties nominated reactionaries he would support a third ticket, probably the Labor party in New York. Roosevelt also told Ickes that he had not closed the door to a third term and that in the event of war in Europe "all bets will be off." Ickes thought that Roosevelt expected outbreak of war before the end of his term, and that he would surely seek re-election.[45]

Deeply concerned over the growing tension in Europe and anticipating a general war in the next few years, Bailey determined to oppose any intervention by the United States in European affairs. "I am not in favor of exposing one American to the bombs of any warfare save and except in defense of this country and in the neighborhood of our shores," he avowed.[46] Publicly, Roosevelt seemed equally determined to avoid war and to strengthen the nation's defense capacity, but he privately worried over the refusal of many people to perceive the threat of war in Europe. Expecting further aggressive acts by German and Italian leaders, he decided to press for revision of the 1937 Neutrality Act and especially for repeal of the arms embargo provisions.[47] Although Bailey did not commit himself

42. Bailey to O. Max Gardner, August 17, 1939; Bailey to James A. Farley, May 1, 1939, *Bailey Papers.*
43. Roosevelt, *Public Papers and Addresses*, VIII, 437.
44. Bailey to Peter G. Gerry, August 12, 1939, *Bailey Papers.*
45. Ickes, *The Secret Diary*, II, 691–692.
46. Bailey to J. H. McAden, April 13, 1939, *Bailey Papers.*
47. Roosevelt, *Public Papers and Addresses*, **VIII**, **xxxi.**

for or against repeal of the arms embargo, his letters indicated fear that Roosevelt would place the United States in an unneutral position leading to war.[48] In his judgment the existing Neutrality Act gave the President greater liberty in dealing with foreign nations than he would have under a new law. Despite war between China and Japan, the United States exported arms and ammunition to both nations and lent China twenty-five million dollars, since the President had not officially found a state of war existing. Would not Roosevelt have the same liberty with respect to possible warfare in Europe?[49]

The shadow of impending war hung heavily over Europe during the summer of 1939 and darkened perceptibly with the signing of a Russo-German non-aggression pact. At dawn on September 1 German armed forces invaded Poland. Two days later Great Britain and France declared war on Germany. The Second World War had begun. On the night of September 3 President Roosevelt expressed hope that the United States could avoid war and gave assurances that every effort of the government would be directed toward that end. "This nation will remain a neutral nation, but," he added, "I cannot ask that every American remain neutral in thought as well. Even a neutral has a right to take account of facts. Even a neutral cannot be asked to close his mind or his conscience."[50] Ten days later, he called Congress into extraordinary session to repeal the arms embargo provisions of the Neutrality Act.

Bailey entered the session with private fears that the United States would be maneuvered into the European war. He notified the President, however, that he had decided the new legislation would make more for peace and security than the existing neutrality law. "I have taken the side I have," he asserted, "because I have been driven to it by the most thorough-going consideration. . . . It seems to me that the logic of it is irresistible and the righteousness is not less irresistible than the logic."[51] To the people of North Carolina he declared on October 7 that the present policy unintentionally aided Germany by depriving England and France of their normal means of defense and sustenance based on control of the Atlantic and Mediterranean. He thought that the United States had made it plain that under no circumstances would this country lend money to England or France

48. Bailey to George Rountree, February 14, 1939, *Bailey Papers.*
49. Bailey to James A. Farley, July 7, 1939, *Bailey Papers.*
50. Roosevelt, *Public Papers and Addresses,* VIII, 460–464.
51. Bailey to Franklin D. Roosevelt, October 2, 1939, *Bailey Papers.*

or engage its sons in the war. "Since we are unwilling to aid England and France, surely," he insisted, "we must see to it that we do not assist Germany and her associates by following a policy recognized the world over as unnecessary to neutrality as defined by international law."[52] He had read official documents relevant to engagement of the United States in the First World War. He had also reviewed the process which had driven Woodrow Wilson to ask Congress to recognize that Germany made war upon this country. He had studied an essay by Newton D. Baker, former secretary of war under Wilson, entitled "Why America Went to War." Bailey found that both Wilson and Secretary of State Bryan had concluded that citizens of the United States should be permitted to manufacture and sell arms because manufacture of arms was a necessary process of national defense.[53]

With these considerations in mind, Bailey undertook to modify and liberalize shipping prohibitions in the pending neutrality bill. He particularly opposed the position taken by Senator Pittman that the United States should prohibit its ships from carrying munitions to ports of belligerents in the Pacific. Having committed himself to repeal of the arms embargo, Bailey pursued with inexorable logic the implications of the country's new course. He argued that not only would the prohibition be an unnecessary abandonment of the nation's rights, but also that it would inhibit growth of the nation's merchant marine. If the war should be prolonged, there would undoubtedly be a shortage of merchant ships due to airplane attacks on merchantmen. "If I am right, we should not foreclose our right to carry whatever we please in the Pacific and the adjacent water. . . . It may be necessary for us to supply Australia, Singapore and Hong Kong with airplanes and other means of warfare. One cannot say just what Japan may do. I think we can count always on the Oriental strategy of surprise."[54]

Bailey's efforts and State Department pressure induced Pittman to introduce several liberalizing amendments, which satisfied almost all objections raised by the State Department to the shipping provisions. On November 4 the President signed the bill, issuing at the same time

52. Bailey statement on neutrality legislation, October 7, 1939, *Roosevelt Papers*.
53. Bailey to Theodore Rondthaler, October 30, 1939, *Bailey Papers*.
54. Bailey to Franklin D. Roosevelt, October 14, 1939, *Bailey Papers*.

proclamations revoking arms embargoes and defining new combat areas created by the European war.[55] Several days later, Admiral Emory S. Land, chairman of the Maritime Commission, sought the State Department's opinion on the proposed transfer of nine of the merchant vessels of the United States Lines, controlled by the Maritime Commission, to the registry of the Republic of Panama. Secretary of State Hull, anxious to preserve the absolute integrity of the United States, opposed the transfer as a moral violation of neutrality.[56] Roosevelt at first indicated approval of the transfer, but eventually adopted Hull's viewpoint. Bailey argued that Congress had not obligated the nation to keep all ships out of war zones, but merely to remove ships under the United States flag. This was done not to placate any other nation, but because "the sinking of ships under our Flag and carrying our men would arouse our people and cause them to demand war. That is to say, we were fearful of provocation at home rather than abroad." The transfer would provide excellent opportunity to dispose of many old ships at good prices and to replace them with new ships built according to Maritime Commission specifications.[57]

Roosevelt also recognized the advantages of disposing of obsolete tonnage, but distinguished between outright sale of vessels to foreign interests with no retention of interest by United States citizens and transfers of title to foreign corporations, subsidiary to or affiliated with the present owners. He admitted that objections to the latter course on grounds that it violated the "spirit" of the Neutrality Act were invalid. He apparently did not think the Neutrality Act limited him in permitting either transfer of title or outright purchase of American vessels by foreign nations, including belligerents. He did fear that transfers of title involving other American republics might place those nations in an unneutral position.[58] Operating under these assumptions, the State Department approved sale of eight vessels of

55. Hull, *Memoirs*, I, 697; *Congressional Record*, 76th Cong., 2nd Sess., p. 1024; Roosevelt, *Public Papers and Addresses*, VIII, 524, 559–564.

56. Hull, *Memoirs*, I, 697.

57. Bailey to Franklin D. Roosevelt, November 10, 1939, *Bailey Papers*. Bailey had already begun in 1939 to strengthen the merchant marine. He introduced legislation, which Admiral Land described as "the greatest step in advance that we made during the past year." Bailey press release, September 27, 1939, *Bailey Papers*.

58. Franklin D. Roosevelt to Bailey, December 1, 1939, *Bailey Papers*. The draft of the letter was prepared by E. S. Land, chairman, Maritime Commission; see Land to Roosevelt, November 20, 1939, *Roosevelt Papers*.

the United States Lines to a private corporation in Belgium, as well as sale of privately owned American ships to the British and French, in the early months of 1940. The Neutrality Act of 1939 opened the arsenal of the United States to Great Britain and France, but not until May, 1940, did Britain place substantial orders.[59]

59. Hull, *Memoirs*, I, 699–700.

CHAPTER ELEVEN

CAUTIOUS INTERVENTIONIST

FIGHTING IN Europe came to a virtual standstill during the winter of 1939–40. American opinion quickly dubbed the hostilities as "the phony war." President Roosevelt warned of the folly and danger of isolationist thinking, however, and called for increased defense funds and extension of reciprocal trade agreements in his State of the Union Message on January 3, 1940.[1] Lulled by Germany's continued inactivity and concerned with approaching national conventions and general elections, Congress delayed action on expanded defense appropriations and approved continuation of the Trade Agreements Act only after a long fight. Secretary of State Hull industriously rallied votes in the Senate, but the outcome remained doubtful until the final vote on April 5. The Senate passed the measure with Bailey's support by a mere five-vote margin, with fifteen Democratic senators in opposition.[2] In the notably inactive first three months the most damaging indication of congressional indifference to the threat implied in a general European war was failure to increase funds for national defense speedily.

The "phony war" ended suddenly on April 9 with Hitler's massive invasion of Denmark and Norway. German conquest continued on May 10 as armored units supported by bomber and fighter planes spearheaded an assault on Belgium and Holland. The Blitzkrieg shook the complacency of many Americans, but did not overcome Bailey's innate reluctance to involve the United States. He wrote bitterly that newspaper accounts in the last six months had inflamed the minds of the American people.[3] By late May the Germans had conquered the Low Countries, and on June 5 attacked France, which

---

1. Roosevelt, *Public Papers and Addresses*, IX, 1–10.
2. *Congressional Record*, 76th Cong., 3rd Sess., p. 4105; Hull, *Memoirs*, I, 746–750.
3. Bailey to C. L. Shuping, May 11, 1940, *Bailey Papers*.

quickly collapsed before onrushing German armies. On May 16 Roosevelt averred that the threat of attack made it imperative that the United States immediately strengthen its defenses. Congress adopted in rapid succession five major defense appropriation bills, amounting to thirteen billion dollars.[4] In each case Bailey approved the President's recommendations, but not without considerable fear that pressures exerted by Great Britain would drag the United States into war. Nevertheless, he thoughtfully concluded that he could not back Roosevelt's policies one day and critics of those policies the next. Aware that he possessed neither scientific nor technical knowledge to cope with problems of total war and that the nation needed one strong leader, Bailey followed Roosevelt's lead in the war preparation.[5]

The European war by no means eclipsed domestic politics. The chief issue remained whether Roosevelt would seek a third term. Although unreconciled to a third term, Bailey did not actively oppose Roosevelt's renomination, for the Democratic party in North Carolina had instructed its delegates to vote for Roosevelt. He turned down a position as delegate to the Democratic National Convention, but observed, "I think we should, in any event, undertake to preserve the unity of our Party in North Carolina and in order that that unity be preserved, we should pursue a policy of real tolerance. All of us can afford to make concessions where no great principle is involved, and even where a great principle is involved, we may be patient." He refused to participate in the fight to halt Roosevelt's nomination and rejected all requests to join in formation of a third party.[6]

Assembling in Philadelphia in late June, the Republican party nominated on the sixth ballot Wendell L. Willkie of Indiana for president. An unexpectedly imaginative choice for Republicans, Willkie possessed great personal magnetism and indorsed a mild internationalism and many New Deal social reforms. In mid-July the Democratic National Convention in Chicago drafted Roosevelt for a third term on the first ballot, but fought bitterly over its choice of a

4. Roosevelt, *Public Papers and Addresses*, IX, 198–212; *Congressional Record*, 76th Cong., 3rd Sess., pp. 6685, 7935, 8934, 12352.

5. Interview with A. Hand James, Raleigh, N.C., November 1, 1961. See also Bailey to Loren C. MacKinney, October 3, 1940, *Bailey Papers*.

6. Bailey to C. L. Shuping, May 11, 1940, *Bailey Papers*. Also see: Bailey to James A. Reed, June 27, 1940, *Bailey Papers*; P. H. Appleby, "Roosevelt's Third-Term Decision," *American Political Science Review*, XLVI (September, 1952), 754–765.

vice presidential candidate, accepting Henry Wallace only after Roosevelt threatened to decline renomination.[7] Speaking to the convention of Young Democrats at Raleigh, Bailey supported Roosevelt's nomination. He initially prepared a speech not mentioning Roosevelt, but bowed to his better judgment and the advice of friends. He announced that he had been elected senator because of his loyalty to the party and that, consequently, he should be the last man to turn his back on the party. He opposed a third term on principle, but gave wholehearted support to Roosevelt as the choice of the Democratic party.[8] Except for the single speech, however, Bailey did not actively campaign for Roosevelt's re-election. His health remained poor and his congressional duties continued heavy throughout the summer and fall. Perhaps the most controversial of Roosevelt's national defense measures which Bailey upheld during this period was the Selective Service Bill, which authorized the first peacetime conscription in the history of the United States. Although vigorously opposed by isolationists, substantial majorities in both Houses approved the bill on September 7, 1940.[9]

Willkie stumped the country with considerable success, while Roosevelt struck a non-partisan posture and pleaded preoccupation with problems of national defense. The chief threat to Roosevelt's re-election came from isolationist groups, which accused him of reaching secret agreements with England, of warmongering, and of dissipating American military and naval strength. Between October 23 and November 2, Roosevelt responded to the isolationists' challenge. In five ringing speeches he refuted these "falsifications" with statistics on Republican voting records in Congress. His unequaled command of sarcasm and humor thoroughly disrupted the Republican campaign. Roosevelt received only 57 per cent of the total popular vote in the November election, but triumphed over the ancient prohibition of a third term and the accumulated public irritations of eight years. His re-election rested largely on his ability to convince the American people that his leadership would preserve the peace. "I have said this before," he assured, "but I shall say it again and again

7. Rosenman, *Working with Roosevelt*, pp. 205–221; Roosevelt, *Public Papers and Addresses*, IX, 292.
8. Interview with A. Hand James, Raleigh, N.C., November 1, 1961.
9. *Congressional Record*, 76th Cong., 3rd Sess., p. 11142; Raleigh *News and Observer*, September 3, 1940, p. 12.

and again: Your boys are not going to be sent into any foreign wars."[10] Following the election, United States aid to Great Britain and China rapidly increased. Bailey concluded that "we cannot avoid now the role of an interventionist in the war. This may be necessary to our own self-preservation." Nevertheless, he also confided: "I have gone to bed at night and arose in the morning thinking of what it means to commit our country to any war under existing conditions. Nothing less . . . than grim necessity would justify it."[11]

While the United States held its presidential campaign, Japanese troops invaded Indochina, Italy attacked Greece, and the Battle of Britain had been fought and won. Resistance to Nazi aggression had almost exhausted Britain's dollar reserves. Fearing British collapse without aid, Roosevelt sought to circumvent the "cash-and-carry" provisions of the Neutrality Act. The "lend-lease" program, he explained, would operate on the same principle as the man who lent his neighbor a garden hose to put out a fire without first demanding payment. In his annual message to Congress on January 6, 1941, Roosevelt requested authority and funds to manufacture additional munitions and war supplies for nations resisting Germany. At the end of the war the beneficiary nations would pay not in dollars but in goods and services.[12] Bailey fought diligently for passage of lend-lease, but noted privately, "I am hoping that whenever the settlement is made, we can so arrange that we will not have to defend England every few years."[13] He considered lend-lease a definite act of intervention which might justify a declaration of war from the totalitarian powers. He doubted that such a declaration would come from Germany or Italy, but did suspect that one might come from Japan.[14] The Senate began deliberations on lend-lease on February 17, but approved the measure only after three weeks of acrimonious debate. Senator Wheeler's reference to lend-lease as a program to "plow under every fourth American boy" characterized the extreme isolationists' position.[15] Challenged by Wheeler to explain his about-face from non-intervention to intervention, Bailey stated to a hushed, impressed Senate: "I have utterly changed my mind. . . . I am advocat-

10. Roosevelt, *Public Papers and Addresses*, IX, 514–524.
11. Bailey to Loren C. MacKinny, October 3, 1940, *Bailey Papers*.
12. Roosevelt, *Public Papers and Addresses*, IX, 604–615, 663–672.
13. Bailey to Oliver J. Sands, January 31, 1941, *Bailey Papers*.
14. Bailey to A. D. Beittel, January 27, 1941, *Bailey Papers*.
15. Rosenman, *Working with Roosevelt*, p. 273.

ing intervention with all its implications. I am not hedging. All my life I have looked a thing in the face and argued it as it is."[16]

Shortly thereafter, Senator Arthur H. Vandenberg, who fought the bill adamantly, wrote Bailey, "I particularly admire your candor in frankly embracing the logical sequence of war if it has to come as a result of this new policy. But I am still staggered by your willingness to let the Great White Father become 'number one power politician of the world.' "[17] Bailey responded that while the unusual powers given the President could have been further restricted, the President needed abundant power in the conduct of foreign relations. The United States might escape the ordeal of actual warfare, but if war came it would probably stem not from lend-lease but from Japanese movement in the Far East. "I think a great deal more depends upon Japan," he declared, "than depends upon the Congress or the President. It may develop upon the President to take steps to protect our interests in the Orient. Such steps may lead to an incident, the consequences of which will be that the President will call upon the Congress to recognize that Japan is challenging our rights and our sovereignty."[18] By no means a pacifist, despite his aversion to war, Bailey knew that men and nations must fight upon provocation. Although he disliked growing federal centralization, he knew that in wartime the President would vastly extend his influence, responsibility, and power. Bailey had deplored and often resisted authorization of enormous, "blank-check" appropriations for New Deal relief programs. He now unhesitatingly voted with the majority of the Senate for the Defense Aid Supplemental Appropriation Bill, which alloted seven billion dollars for lend-lease production and export—the largest single appropriation in time of peace in the history of the United States.[19]

Committed to underwriting a British victory and to strengthening home defenses, the United States embarked upon an intensive program of rearmament and economic mobilization. However, production for defense gained momentum only slowly, and shortages due to strikes in essential industries threatened. Bailey suggested that real danger existed that demands for increased wages and insistence upon the right to strike by labor organizations would seriously curtail

16. *Congressional Record*, 77th Cong., 1st Sess., pp. 1160–1162, 1589–1592.
17. Arthur H. Vandenberg to Bailey, February 20, 1941, *Bailey Papers*.
18. Bailey to Arthur H. Vandenberg, March 17, 1941, *Bailey Papers*.
19. *Congressional Record*, 77th Cong., 1st Sess., p. 2509.

defense production. He suspected that previously enacted wage-and-hour legislation would retard efforts to reach full productive capacity. Production could be greatly increased by the simple expedients of lengthening the hours and of working a six-day week. Roosevelt did not seem inclined to follow this course, but Bailey predicted that "he will change his course whenever he finds that social gains are being preserved at the cost of fully fortifying and defending our country."[20] Roosevelt was concerned with preserving the social and economic gains made by labor during the New Deal, but wished also to prevent the delays of labor-management disputes. The number of strikes and lockouts in defense industries rose from 147 in December, 1940, to 316 in March, 1941, while the man-days of idleness because of labor-management battles increased from 485,314 to 1,543,803. To provide more adequate procedures for resolution of industrial disputes, Roosevelt created by executive order on March 19 the National Defense Mediation Board, with representatives from labor, industry, and the public.[21]

Although Bailey approved establishment of the mediation board, he was not convinced that the more militant labor unions would abide by its decisions or that the board itself would pursue a strong policy in regard to strikes. He held that sit-down strikes violated the rights of private property and that pickets violated the right to work of non-union employees. He approved use of federal power to prevent abuses by business, but insisted that the government should also prevent abuses by labor unions. "We need now the work of every worker," he insisted, "and the right of any worker to work must be protected, and that without paying for the privilege. If there are grievances, let them be referred to Government arbitration, but in the meantime the work must go on."[22] Bailey's statement was prompted by the threatened strike of United Mine Workers, under John L. Lewis, in the Appalachian bituminous coal mines. Despite efforts by Roosevelt and the federal mediator, John Steelman, the 400,000 bituminous coal miners, producing 85 per cent of the nation's output, struck on April 2, 1941. After nearly a month the miners resumed work with their demand for an increase in wages satisfied and with another demand

20. Bailey to Loren C. MacKinney, February 13, 1941, *Bailey Papers*. Also see Bailey to Dorothy Thompson, March 1, 1941, *Bailey Papers*.
21. Roosevelt, *Public Papers and Addresses*, X, 76–79.
22. Bailey press release, March 27, 1941, *Bailey Papers*; New York *Times*, March 28, 1941, p. 17.

under examination by the National Defense Mediation Board, which on June 3 recommended elimination of the North-South differential in wages.[23]

The war in Europe drew steadily closer to the shores of the United States. Nazi submarine activity in the North Atlantic threatened to choke off lend-lease shipments of supplies to the British Isles and to interfere with America's neutral shipping. To combat the situation Roosevelt embarked on a series of piecemeal measures between March 25 and May 21. He authorized naval yards to repair British vessels, transferred ten Coast Guard cutters to Britain for antisubmarine operations, and requisitioned idle foreign ships in American ports. He extended the neutrality patrol into the mid-Atlantic to search out and report, but not attack, Nazi submarines.[24] Decidedly unneutral, the latter measure brought charges from isolationists in Congress that American vessels convoyed British ships in the patrol area. Bailey approved the patrol system, however, and advocated full-fledged convoying of British vessels, for the United States only postponed the moment when it would be forced to participate fully in the war. "I am thinking of this whole matter in terms of all out war," he stressed, "rather than all out aid because I see what is coming. . . . After the convoys comes naval warfare and with the naval warfare will come fighting by infantry."[25]

"We are I fear, on the ragged edge of war," Bailey suggested to Roosevelt on May 5, "and I think we should realize that when we take the ultimate step it will be ultimate and will call for everything we have in men, ships and material. Our difficulty so far has been that nothing we have done has been sufficient to relieve England of her manifest distress."[26] He also informed the President that considerable reaction to national policy had developed in North Carolina as war prospects grew darker. People had supported lend-lease and other measures on assurances that actual belligerency would be avoided. They now thought of the national policy in terms of war and suspected that British influence was too strong. The reaction stemmed partly from strikes. Many people questioned whether a successful outcome of war could be anticipated while labor asserted the right to

---

23. Roosevelt, *Public Papers and Addresses*, X, 122–123.
24. *Ibid.*, pp. 88–89, 132–138.
25. Bailey to Folger Townsend, May 5, 1941, *Bailey Papers*.
26. Bailey to Franklin D. Roosevelt, May 5, 1941, *Bailey Papers*.

strike against the national defense. The convoy question most troubled the people. "It confronts them for the first time with the realization that aid to Great Britain means war—as the isolationists have
contended."[27] Roosevelt responded that the reaction was not restricted
to North Carolina. A nationally known advertising man had written
him that "the constant reiteration by the Wheelers, Nyes, Lindbergs,
etc., that we are doing all this to save the British Empire, rather than
ourselves, has had much effect." Asserting that convoying was a
matter of military and naval strategy, he concluded, "Frankly, I do
not think that is much of a subject for laymen like you or I to waste
much time about in public."[28] Ironically, just two weeks later Roosevelt found it necessary to address the nation through a special radio
broadcast on the subject.

Shortly before Roosevelt spoke to the nation on May 27, Bailey
opined that the President would not only clarify the war situation, but
also take a firm stand on union activities. "It seems to me that it
would be the course of folly to get into the war," he advanced, "if we
are not going to control the industrial situation." He thought that
Roosevelt realized the seriousness of strikes, but confronted the fact
that many people in his administration, as well as his own wife,
considered the strikes not unpatriotic. Roosevelt's difficulties with
foreign affairs were heightened by his belief that the United States
ought to enter the war in order to save Great Britain, despite contrary
pledges.[29] Roosevelt made the clear-cut and uncompromising statement that Bailey anticipated; he declared that "a Nation-wide machinery for conciliation and mediation of industrial disputes has been set
up. That machinery must be used promptly—and without stoppage of
work. Collective bargaining will be retained, but the American people
expect that impartial recommendations of our Government conciliation and mediation services will be followed both by capital and by
labor." On the war and the sinking of an American freighter, the
Robin Moor, by a submarine on May 20, the President explained that
the neutrality patrol had been extended and stressed the importance of
increasing shipbuilding and reducing losses on the seas. To accomplish the latter objective, "our patrols are helping now to insure

27. Bailey to Franklin D. Roosevelt, May 10, 1941, *Bailey Papers*.
28. Franklin D. Roosevelt to Bailey, May 13, 1941, *F.D.R.: His Personal
Letters*, II, 1154–1155.
29. Bailey to R. M. Gantt, May 27, 1941, *Bailey Papers*.

delivery of the needed supplies to Britain. . . . All additional measures necessary to deliver the goods will be taken. . . . I say that this can be done; it must be done; and it will be done."[30]

Germany attacked the Soviet Union on June 22 and threw the war into a totally new phase. The attitude held in Washington was that Russia would not prevail, but would so damage the Germans that they would make no further progress against England during the present year. Bailey greatly feared that Japan might be emboldened by Russia's involvement in the war to resume expansion in the Pacific. He apparently knew little more about the futile negotiations between Japan and the United States than the general public, but surmised that the United States had put Japan to the point of making a decision. "If she presses on with her policy in Indo China, she will pay a fearful price, and it may be that she will find herself at war with us. . . . She has a great fleet and she can do much damage on the sea, but she cannot last, and certainly she cannot prevail unless Germany shall prevail. . . . The President has come to the end of his appeasement policy with Japan." Thoughtful men on Capitol Hill believed that if the United States became a belligerent, England would request an expeditionary force to Syria and North Africa, but that if Japan were fighting it would be difficult to send such a force. "The fact is," he observed, "I do not think we could do so in time, as we would have first to sink a large portion of the Japanese navy and bottle up her raiders. In this view, the coming in of Japan may expose England."[31]

Bailey presented a major address on September 20 to the Young Democrats' convention at Winston-Salem, which he entitled "We Defend Our Security." Reviewing steps bringing the United States to the brink of war, he pointed out four progressive phases: "Our policy of October 1939 was a policy of strict neutrality. Our policy of 1940 was strictly a home-defense preparation policy. Our policy of March 1941 was a policy of intervention for defense. Our policy of September 1941 is a policy of conditional action on our part as necessary to our defense, let the consequences be whatever the Axis Powers by action may determine." Pulling no punches, Bailey dealt with every major question concerning the course of the United States and its relations with Germany, Great Britain, and Russia. "We must sup-

---

30. Roosevelt, *Public Papers and Addresses*, X, 181–195.
31. Bailey to Julian Ruffin, July 25, 1941, *Bailey Papers*. See also Bailey to Franklin D. Roosevelt, July 1, 1941, *Bailey Papers*.

press the Communists in our land," he asserted, "but we have no concern as to the character of the Russian Government. When I see a Russian standing between me and a mad dog I raise no question as to his culture or his politics." He bluntly pointed out that war was not an engagement of limited liability and that American soldiers would have to pay the price of victory. To those who complained of the cost of the policy of preserving American security, he answered, "Security comes before prosperity." To those who argued that this policy meant war, he responded, "Security comes before peace." To others who suggested that too much power was given to the federal government, he replied, "It is better to give power to our own Republic than to yield to the power of a foreign nation and an alien dictator." To those who feared that the country was surrendering its liberties, he answered, "It is better to waive for a season our liberties to our own Government than to risk the permanent loss of them to foreign powers."[32]

Writing to Roosevelt on October 7, Bailey asserted that the nation's course should be calculated to avoid the role of aggressor or provocator. He recalled Prime Minister Chamberlain's speech on September 3, 1939, stating that Britain entered the war with a clear and easy conscience. If the United States must also fight, utmost pains should be taken to assure every American a perfect satisfaction about his duty. "Given time, the conduct of Hitler in this matter of our ships, will fully unite our people, but," he warned, "if we move too quickly, we may get in with a domestic controversy on our hands." Bailey declared his own intention to support administration policy: "If I should differ with you, I should consider it my duty first to discuss the matter with you rather than in the papers or on the floor of the Senate."[33]

Roosevelt asked Congress on October 9 to revise the Neutrality Act of 1939 to permit arming of American merchantmen and to allow American ships to enter belligerent ports.[34] To a critic of Roosevelt's proposals, Bailey replied that "the question is not one of avoiding war—war will come to us whether we will or not. . . . [T]he only possible means of preventing this is to aid those who are now resisting

32. Josiah W. Bailey, "We Defend Our Security," September 20, 1941, manuscript in *Bailey Papers*.

33. Bailey to Franklin D. Roosevelt, October 7, 1941, *Roosevelt Papers*.

34. Roosevelt, *Public Papers and Addresses*, X, 405–413.

the Axis powers."[35] Calling for drastic revision of the Neutrality Act, he asserted that the right of American ships to sail the seas must be protected "if it takes every battleship we have got to defend them."[36] While the Senate debated neutrality revision, a German submarine torpedoed the destroyer *Kearny*. This act did not arouse Congress, Bailey noted, since "we consider that our destroyers are convoying British ships and are thus exposed to attack. Very probably they are sinking German submarines." He assumed that the President wished the United States to suppress piracy on the seas rather than become a belligerent, but "his danger is that Japan may take steps which will necessitate a declaration."[37]

On December 8, 1941, President Roosevelt declared before a joint session of Congress: "Yesterday, December 7, 1941—a date which will live in infamy—the United States of America was suddenly and deliberately attacked by naval and air forces of the Empire of Japan."[38] The Senate unanimously and the House with but one exception resolved that a state of war existed between the United States and Japan. Three days later declarations of war from Germany and Italy against the United States brought similar responses from the President and Congress. The nation was committed to mobilization of its resources to meet the requirements of total war. Overnight the bitter debate between isolationists and interventionists vanished, but problems of economic conversion and control created new and controversial issues. In the following four years of war, Bailey upheld the President on all matters directly affecting the war itself and on almost all domestic measures except debatable New Deal programs. The Second World War provided a final testing of Bailey the man and Bailey the statesman.

Sixty-eight years old in December, 1941, Bailey had served North Carolina and the nation in the United States Senate since 1931. He had participated in the successive crises of the New Deal experiments in meeting the problems of the Great Depression. He had reflected deeply, written voluminously, and applied himself to restraining what he thought were the excesses of the New Deal. His reputation had suffered in some quarters from the uncompromising independence of

35. Bailey to A. D. Beittel, October 13, 1941, *Bailey Papers.*
36. Raleigh *News and Observer*, October 31, 1941, p. 1.
37. Bailey to Julian Ruffin, November 5, 1941, *Bailey Papers.* On November 7, 1941, the Senate approved revision of the Neutrality Act by vote of 50 to 37.
38. *Congressional Record*, 77th Cong., 1st Sess., pp. 9504–9505.

his nature, which scorned to buy a little popularity with a little discretion, and in other quarters from his seeming subordination of human needs to constitutional principles. His desire to solve the problems of the depression frequently conflicted with his dedication to traditions of individualism, hard work, self-help, sound money, a balanced budget, strong local government, and administrative efficiency. He believed that Roosevelt wanted to follow a moderate course, but had been diverted by radical advisers. Although Bailey applauded Roosevelt's bold efforts to throw the full power and resources of the nation against the economic disaster, he thought that Roosevelt was motivated not by principles but by fear that democracy itself might fall victim to depression hysteria. He criticized Roosevelt for going too fast and too far in his experimentalism, for espousing causes without having sufficiently tested them, and for failing to look beyond the fickle opinion of the hour to the welfare of future generations. Bailey's opposition votes rested upon his conviction that the measures under consideration gave special privileges to special interests, encouraged unsound financial and economic practices, violated trusted constitutional principles, involved unwise centralization of power, or tended toward collectivist regimentation.

Convinced that the people of the United States depended too heavily on their government for personal aid and special privilege, Bailey objected to the unashamed and unrestrained scramble for advantages that characterized individuals and narrow special interest groups. The fault lay not only in the people's lack of appreciation of the rightful function of government, but also in the weakness of public leaders in catering to special groups out of fear that they would be thrust from office by even more subservient successors. Ultimately the few might benefit, but the burden would be carried by all. He insisted that laws preventing coercion by one side should also prevent coercion from the other, lest unchecked efforts to rectify grievances create a new group of oppressors. He feared "bigness" in labor, business, and government, but he also believed that free enterprise constituted the keystone of the American economy—the source of jobs, wealth, and growth. While big business had been chastised by the crash and depression and its worst faults reformed by law, labor had taken advantage of the reaction against business to obtain not only long-needed recognition, but also special privileges providing unwarranted economic and political power. Bailey could no more sanction labor monopoly than industrial monopoly, since both endangered free government and free enterprise.

On economic and financial practices, Bailey often disagreed totally with New Deal efforts to end the depression. Deficit spending by the government, he contended, violated sound principles of business. While government might safely attempt to stimulate the economy artificially through public spending, he argued that if this expedient did not shortly prevail it should be discontinued. He knew that it might be popular to vote for public spending year after year, but he concluded that the people receiving the funds would never repay the money and that the debt would burden voiceless future generations. Nor did he believe that public works materially assisted economic recovery, since appropriations went into public buildings, highways, and other non-profit-making activities. Government spending competed with private enterprise, weakened individual initiative, and destroyed business confidence in the security of investments.

He consistently fought legislation that seemed to him calculated to undermine tested interpretations of the Constitution. Assuming that the gravity of the depression blinded the nation to the dangerous implications of many steps taken to ameliorate it, he suspected that the nation might discover too late that the Constitution had been abolished by an emergency not sufficiently different from other emergencies encountered successfully. In times of distress the people had always shown impatience with constitutional restraints, but he considered it his duty under his oath as a senator to uphold and protect the Constitution. Confident that the form of government set forth in the Constitution was the best yet devised, he hesitated to indorse departures from traditional interpretations for fear of disturbing the delicate balance of powers and liberties.

He regretted the continual transfer to the federal government of power that had previously belonged to the people, but he chiefly complained that the power came to rest not with the people's representatives in Congress but under the authority of a single man in the presidency. Fearful of possibilities for political abuse, he questioned whether Congress would long resist an Executive commanding an army of voters dependent on pensions, public works projects, and unemployment relief. In the depths of depression, relief had been necessary, but ultimately the function of government was order and justice. Once local and individual responsibility had been surrendered to the federal government it could not easily be reacquired, even in the unlikely event that individuals and communities were willing to resume their responsibilities. Objecting to measures that he deemed an unwise centralization of power, Bailey demonstrated his attachment to the federal principle and to division and balance of authority at all governmental levels.

Convinced that the individual must have the largest degree of liberty consistent with necessities of order and justice, Bailey rejected New Deal measures which he thought tended toward collectivist regimentation. Aggrandizement of government through removal of power from the people to boards and bureaus created a government of men in place of a government by law. He responded to various New Deal attempts to solve problems of agricultural surplus and low prices through acreage restrictions with the contention that the federal government had no authority to tell a farmer what he could plant or how much he could plant, or to penalize him for exceeding his quota. Defending the individual's liberty to fail as well as to succeed by his own efforts, Bailey emphasized co-operation rather than compulsion as a solution to agricultural problems. Yet paradoxically, this advocate of voluntary co-operation doubted the ability of the people to govern themselves without aid from wise public servants who looked beyond temporary self-interest to permanent benefits. He believed that the free enterprise system could not be compromised without confronting the alternative of the totalitarian state and that a planned economy inevitably required an authoritarian political system.

While there were ambiguities in his thinking and inconsistencies in his responses to New Deal programs, his opposition votes conformed remarkably to the positions outlined above. The advent of war in December, 1941, and the necessity of total mobilization of the United States provided severe tests of Bailey's conservatism. The crisis of the national emergency led to (1) special privileges for special interests and an inequality of sacrifice; (2) massive deficit spending and price and wage controls; (3) wartime restrictions at variance with peacetime constitutional principles; (4) vast centralization of power in the federal government and, specifically, in the Executive Branch; and (5) regimentation through the draft and economic controls. But old attitudes and responses, springing from a half-century of public, personal, and political responsibilities, could not and would not be thoroughly modified under the desperate circumstances of total war. A final test of Bailey the man and Bailey the statesman lies, therefore, in determining under what conditions and in response to what measures, he retained, altered, or rejected the grounds for opposition that characterized his position during the New Deal when challenged by the stresses of the Second World War.

CHAPTER TWELVE

WORK OR FIGHT

"WE ASK that you help to defend labors rights by preventing anti-strike hysteria from impairing labors defense efforts by dictatorial and prejudiced legislation," Ford Local Union 968 of Charlotte, North Carolina, telegraphed Bailey on December 6, 1941. Bailey replied that the general right to strike was not in question, for "it is the right of a group of men to provide a test of strength between themselves and their employers. The right to strike against the public safety has never been recognized."[1] House passage on December 3 of an extreme antistrike bill sponsored by Howard W. Smith (D., Va.) had stimulated the union request. The series of strikes called by United Mine Workers' President John L. Lewis in the fall of 1941 influenced Bailey's response. Incensed by Lewis' disregard of Roosevelt's pleas for settlement, Bailey did not sympathize with protests against antistrike legislation. He had himself proposed in October that work stoppages in defense industries be defined as sabotage and that heavy penalties be imposed.[2] He approved collective bargaining but abhorred strikes during the national emergency and feared the increasing power and influence exercised by labor leaders. "If the Government will pursue a policy allowing men to work who wish to work and putting the strikers in their proper place," Bailey argued, "all will be well." Since he saw no likelihood that Roosevelt would follow that policy, he insisted that "the unions ought to submit to a certain amount of Governmental control and supervision in order that the workers may have a fair protection as against those who would use the extraordinary powers of organized leadership in an adverse and prejudicial way."[3] Bailey's labor policy during the war sprang

1. Bailey to Ford Local Union 968, Charlotte, N.C., December 6, 1941, *Bailey Papers.*
2. Raleigh *News and Observer*, October 29, 1941, p. 1.
3. Bailey to R. M. Gantt, May 27, 1941, *Bailey Papers.*

from antagonism to strikes in defense areas, dissatisfaction over restrictions on the right to work, and fear of unprecedented and uncontrolled powers of ambitious labor leaders.

Shortly after Pearl Harbor, representatives of labor and management agreed on a "no-strike, no lock-out" pledge for the war's duration, but disagreed on recognition of extension of the union shop as a legitimate union objective. Labor leaders contended that without union shop security they could not maintain the no-strike pledge, since no means would be available to discipline workers who broke contracts and union rules. Representatives of management, fearing the increase in union strength and bargaining power afforded by union shops, argued that individual workers should decide for themselves whether or not to join a union. The War Labor Board's compromise provided for continuation of union shops and closed shops where they had existed previously and for "maintenance of membership" security clauses in other union contracts. Maintenance of membership required workers to continue union membership for the contract's duration or, if the worker dropped membership in the first fifteen days, to continue meeting financial obligations to the union. Thus, organized labor secured some recompense for loss of normal collective bargaining due to the no-strike pledge, while simultaneously protecting prior organizational gains. Bailey recognized that Roosevelt faced a delicate situation calling for great wisdom in efforts to satisfy war production demands and to co-ordinate activities of management and labor. He suspected that Roosevelt experienced more difficulty with labor than he wished to reveal, but that the President hesitated to undertake strong policies which might bring a severe and disastrous reaction. Noting the great difference between voluntary and compulsory labor, Bailey approved Roosevelt's attempts to discover solutions based on the voluntary principle, but regretted the lack of progress.[4]

The Fair Labor Standards Act of 1938, which Bailey had resisted, now complicated the labor controversy through its provisions for time-and-a-half pay for work over forty hours a week. "If we interfere with the forty-hour week," he pointed out in April, 1942, "it is just possible that we will run into a new series of strikes, slowdowns and sitdowns. If we do not interfere it is quite sure that our preparations

4. Bailey to A. J. Fletcher, March 20, 1942, *Bailey Papers*.

for war will cost us from four to seven billions more than it would otherwise."[5] The "maintenance of membership" provision for union security was distasteful on several counts: (1) labor union dues to be turned over to the union were deducted by the employer from the workers' pay, and (2) union members had to remain members or at least pay dues as long as they worked. While the policy induced labor organizations not to strike, the "consequence is that labor unions gain great advantage over the other groups in the population and they make demands upon the Government which work hardships upon all other classes. The farmers must accept parity but the labor unions accept only what they choose to accept."[6]

The policy of allowing continuation of closed and union shop contracts in industries where they existed before outbreak of war also aroused Bailey's ire. "It is quite clear," he protested, "that certain labor leaders are determined apparently at any cost to use the emergency to advance themselves, and monstrous things are going on. For example, the recent picket lines keeping workers out of a defense industry in order to collect dues from them."[7] The joint necessities of achieving full industrial mobilization and of drafting millions of able-bodied men produced labor shortages that could only be met by adding to the labor force men and women who had not previously been union members. Governmental approval of union shop contracts forced new workers to join the union and pay dues after receiving employment in certain defense industries. Heatedly corresponding with Paul V. McNutt, chairman of the War Manpower Commission, Bailey denounced these conditions. "Your letter," he retorted, "clearly implies that . . . your policy is to permit and encourage the imposition by labor organizations of conditions, terms, and fees upon men and women ready, willing and able to contribute to the war effort of our country; that you recognize their right to prevent men from working in the common defense unless they pay for this privilege." What reason could there be for a policy so contrary to standards of liberty? How could there be any justification for recognizing in labor unions a power superior to the country's need in the present dire emergency? What answer could be given to men in the armed forces who fought and died freely while labor unions at home exacted tribute

5. Bailey to H. G. Connor, Jr., April 3, 1942, *Bailey Papers.*
6. Bailey to Julian Miller, December 22, 1942, *Bailey Papers.*
7. Bailey to J. Harper Erwin, Jr., March 4, 1942, *Bailey Papers.*

from those who worked to support the soldiers? "Your remark that 'it would be unfair to condemn the labor movement because of occasional abuses' is without point and gratuitous," Bailey charged, for "no one is condemning the 'labor movement'; but millions are condemning the policy of labor organizations in standing between men and women ready to work for our country and taking toll of them as a condition of doing so."[8]

Antagonized by strike activities in 1942 in defiance of the "no-strike" pledge, Bailey grew more apprehensive in 1943 when work stoppages led to the loss of 13,501,000 man-days of labor, or three times the loss in 1942.[9] His angry determination to block union demands fell chiefly on John L. Lewis, whose striking miners had accumulated two-thirds of the idle man-days. The bituminous miners demanded a two-dollar-a-day increase and portal-to-portal pay, despite their previous receipt of full implementation of pay increases under the "Little Steel" formula of July, 1942, which permitted a 15 per cent wage increase to correspond with rising living costs. Roosevelt's apparent complacency about labor intransigence made more difficult Bailey's own stern policy toward demands from farm organizations.[10] Upholding Roosevelt's efforts to stabilize prices and wages, he spiritedly defended the veto of the inflationary Bankhead Bill to discount soil conservation payments to farmers in the computation of parity. James F. Brynes, director of the Office of Economic Stabilization, urged him to make a strong speech, for "if the President's veto should be over-ridden the President and the War Labor Board would have no means of resisting John Lewis and others who were leading strikes against the national defense."[11] In return Byrnes assured Bailey that should the motion be defeated Roosevelt would issue a "hold-the-line" order on prices and wages.

The "hold-the-line" order was issued on April 8, 1943, but strikes continued to spread in the coal industry. On May 1 the President seized the coal mines, and Lewis ordered the miners back to work until May 31. "It is the universal opinion," Bailey certified, "that the

8. Bailey to Paul V. McNutt, December 28, 1942, *Bailey Papers*; New York *Times*, December 30, 1942, p. 13.
9. Statistics on work stoppages during World War II are taken from Joel Seidman, *American Labor from Defense to Reconversion* (Chicago, 1953), p. 135.
10. Bailey to Louis R. Wilson, February 26, 1942, *Bailey Papers*.
11. Bailey to Arthur Krock, June 10, 1943, *Bailey Papers*.

responsible leader of the miners has taken a great advantage of our Government in the war emergency."[12] He insisted that Lewis deserved the unreserved condemnation of the nation for threatening the security of every citizen by his course. Lewis demonstrated to Bailey the terrible consequences of giving organized labor so much power. "Mr. Lewis is arrogant and, I think, stupid. Probably he will serve some purpose in convincing the American people that the time has come when this Government should enact legislation fully controlling labor organizations and labor leaders," declared Bailey.[13] Despite concessions by the War Labor Board, strikes resumed on June 1, but after a week the miners again returned to work following a strongly worded order from Roosevelt. Responding to a note from Bailey commending his action, Roosevelt wryly observed that "while my order to resume work on Monday has been obeyed, I am not at all certain that Mr. Lewis will in any way feel precluded from further action against the Government and the prosecution of the war."[14]

Meanwhile, Congress approved an extreme antistrike measure known as the War Labor Disputes Bill, which authorized seizure of striking war plants, set penalties for instigating strikes in government-operated defense industries, provided a thirty-day "cooling-off" period before taking a strike vote, and prohibited labor contributions to political campaigns. Ill and absent when the bill passed, Bailey would probably have voted for it despite his opinion that it was inadequate. The coal strike resumed in mid-June for the third time in two months, bringing a presidential threat to draft strikers into the Army for assignment to their customary civilian activities. Under this pressure Lewis ordered miners back to work until October 31, and with the crisis at least temporarily under control, Roosevelt vetoed the War Labor Disputes Bill. An angry and aroused Congress, however, overrode the veto. A fourth strike by soft coal miners occurred in November, again necessitating government seizure of the mines, but this time the miners' persistence won a complicated settlement giving them almost all their demands. The whole episode demonstrated for Bailey the inadequacy of governmental will and legislation in dealing with ambitious and recalcitrant labor leaders.[15]

Later in 1943 the railroad brotherhoods threatened to strike for

12. Bailey to R. Boyd Morris, May 11, 1943, *Bailey Papers.*
13. Bailey to Joel C. Pretlow, June 4, 1943, *Bailey Papers.*
14. Franklin D. Roosevelt to Bailey, June 8, 1943, *Roosevelt Papers.*
15. Bailey to R. L. Burleson, January 12, 1944, *Bailey Papers.*

wage increases. Fred M. Vinson, the new head of the Office of
Economic Stabilization, allowed an increase of only four cents an hour
instead of the eight cents demanded. Railroad brotherhood leaders
then requested Congress to raise wages through legislation and secured support from Senator Harry S. Truman (D., Mo.) in introduc-
ing an appropriate resolution.[16] Bailey contended that Congress would
set a dangerous precedent in attempting to legislate wages. He reminded labor organizations that if Congress could raise wages it
could also lower them. He chiefly objected that the resolution ignored
the President's stabilization policy and mocked established jurisdiction and responsibility of the OES. The Congress would be deliberately inviting "all discontented workers in America to abandon the
procedure which we provided for stabilization and to prevent inflation, and to appeal, one after another, to Congress to pass this bill or
that bill." Nevertheless, the Senate passed Truman's resolution by a
vote of 74 to 4, with only Bailey, Ellender of Louisiana, Ferguson and
Vandenberg of Michigan in opposition.[17] The House failed to act on
the resolution, and on December 27, 1943, Roosevelt authorized the
War Department to seize and operate the railroads. Not until mid-
night January 18, 1944, after a Special Emergency Board had settled
the dispute, were railroads returned to private control. James F.
Brynes, director of war mobilization, later recalled that "when the
bill was referred to the appropriate committee in the House of Representatives, Labor leaders came to recognize Bailey's wisdom in opposing the measure and they acquiesced in the defeat of the bill by the
House Committee."[18]

Bailey's influence on labor legislation was felt more heavily early in
1944. The revenue bill included a provision that labor unions, farm
co-operatives, and other non-profit organizations must file annual
financial reports, but Senator Bennett Champ Clark (D., Mo.) offered an amendment to strike out this provision. "Just before the
vote," reported the New York *Times*, "it appeared that the provision
might be stricken from the bill, but after Senator Bailey's speech,
twenty-one Democrats joined with twenty-two Republicans to kill the
Clark Amendment."[19] Bailey contended that Congress had given
labor unions means to secure power through collective bargaining and

16. James F. Byrnes, *All in One Lifetime* (New York, 1948), p. 198.
17. *Congressional Record*, 78th Cong., 1st Sess., pp. 10520–10526.
18. James F. Byrnes to John R. Moore, November 1, 1961.
19. New York *Times*, January 19, 1944, pp. 1, 13.

through maintenance of membership clauses in war contracts, but that this power would be abused unless subjected to supervision and regulation. Not only had Congress given unions power to tax workers directly through requirement of dues, but in many cases the government itself assumed responsibility for collecting the dues by the checkoff device. Citing stoppages of coal production and railroad transportation, Bailey proclaimed that the federal government stood in jeopardy from the excessive power of the unions. The government's clear duty was to get some information about the fiscal affairs of labor unions. Following his brief but persuasive speech, no senator attempted to reply and several clamored for the vote. Within minutes the Senate was recorded 34 in favor and 43 opposed to the Clark Amendment.[20]

Bailey believed that CIO leaders desired political and financial power rather than improvement of working conditions. The labor movement through the CIO's Committee for Political Action seemed bent on capturing the Democratic party and instituting class government. Roosevelt appeared to encourage labor's political aspirations and to depend on the unions to keep him in power. Bailey noted that when no one else could break the stabilization line, the unions could. "The President," he accused, "is just as loyal to Frank Hague and to the Kelly machine as he is to our Party. He is just as loyal to the American Federation of Labor and the CIO as he is to any Party and he is more loyal to these institutions than he is to what we call Southern Democracy which I think he despises."[21] Under the circumstances, it was hardly surprising that Bailey became more vehemently opposed to organized labor.

In his State of the Union Address on January 11, 1944, Roosevelt recommended that Congress adopt a "national service law—which, for the duration of the war, will prevent strikes, and, with certain appropriate exceptions, will make available for war production or for any other essential services every able-bodied adult in this Nation."[22] Although Senator Warren R. Austin (R., Vt.) and Representative James W. Wadsworth (R., N.Y.) had introduced in 1943 a War Service Bill providing for draft of labor for service in war industries, this bill met intense opposition from labor leaders and remained

20. *Congressional Record*, 78th Cong., 2nd Sess., pp. 320–323.
21. Bailey to C. L. Shuping, April 3, 1944, *Bailey Papers*.
22. Roosevelt, *Public Papers and Addresses*, XIII, 37.

bottled up in committee. Bailey and Owen Brewster (R., Me.) responded, therefore, to Roosevelt's request with a Work or Fight Bill (S. 36) providing for induction into special work units of an estimated one million 4-F draft registrants and men thirty-eight to forty-five years of age who had quit or failed to obtain essential war jobs. The Senate Military Affairs Committee in May, 1944, heard indorsements of the bill from Robert P. Patterson, under secretary of war, Ralph A. Bard, assistant secretary of the Navy, Maj. Gen. Lewis B. Hershey, director of the Selective Service System, James V. Forrestal, secretary of the Navy, and Donald M. Nelson, chairman of the War Production Board. These spokesmen agreed that the bill would decrease labor turnovers and obligate equally all men of service age to support the war effort. Organized labor, particularly the CIO, through its president Philip Murray and its general counsel Lee Pressman, countered that the manpower crisis could be solved without legal sanctions and that the bill would detrimentally transfer responsibilities of the Manpower Commission to the Selective Service System. Whatever the actual need for national service legislation, the Bailey-Brewster Work or Fight Bill was criticized on several counts. It ignored the fact that much of the industrial manpower of the country consisted of men and women over the age of forty-five, nor did it provide workable sanctions against citizens not supporting war production efforts. The bill would have drafted non-supporters into special work units at service pay and placed them on assembly lines beside regular civilian workers earning higher wages. The intention of the bill, however, was to discourage strikes by severe penalties, not to regiment labor unless no other feasible alternative appeared. Public opinion polls indicated that 56 per cent of the people favored passage, but the Senate Military Affairs Committee refused to report the measure.[23]

Although President Roosevelt had fought neither for the Austin-Wadsworth War Service Bill nor for the Bailey-Brewster Work or Fight Bill, he called again in his State of the Union Message on January 6, 1945, for national service legislation. His recommendation rested this time not on the need for prevention of strikes but on the necessities of assuring proper supply and distribution of workers, demonstrating to the armed services that the total effort of the nation supported them, and destroying the enemy's hopes that the nation had

23. New York *Times*, May 4–June 3, 1944.

become halfhearted about the war.[24] On the same day, Bailey and Representative Andrew J. May (D., Ky.), chairman of the House Military Affairs Committee, introduced identical bills to fulfil the President's request. Almost identical to the Bailey-Brewster bill of 1944, the May-Bailey National Service Bill required induction of 4-F's and other deferred draft registrants between eighteen and forty-five who failed to take or retain essential jobs into a special work corps under military supervision and pay rates. It placed responsibility for the labor draft under the Selective Service System. The military supervision provision was removed, however, after War Department officials testified that it would unduly burden them. The House Military Affairs Committee reported the May bill (H.R. 1752) favorably on January 24, and the House approved it on February 1 by a vote of 246 to 167. In the Senate Military Affairs Committee, however, the May bill encountered great opposition. A substitute bill sponsored by Joseph C. O'Mahoney (D., Wyo.), Harley M. Kilgore (D., W.Va.), Joseph H. Ball (R., Minn.), Homer Ferguson (R., Mich.), and Robert Wagner (D., N.Y.) had been prepared by the War Manpower Commission. The substitute gave statutory support to existing WMC regulations and delegated power to the Office of War Mobilization and Reconversion rather than the Selective Service System. The Senate committee reported the substitute favorably on February 22. The issue before the Senate, therefore, was between H.R. 1752, a draft bill drafting labor, and the substitute bill based on the voluntary principle with no provision for penalties on workers who violated the regulations.[25]

Bailey observed that supporters of the committee substitute argued that it would promote unity between industry and labor, but not that it would fulfil the stated needs of military leaders. "If we make a mistake here in our more or less commendable effort to appease capital and labor," he declared, "and fail to supply the fighting men with the arms by means of which they defend us, there will be very little for us to comfort ourselves about." To criticisms that the original May-Bailey bill affected only men between eighteen and forty-five, he retorted that those who complained that it did not draft everybody

24. Roosevelt, *Public Papers and Addresses*, XIII, 493–496.
25. New York *Times*, January 7–February 25, 1945. See also Roland Young, *Congressional Politics in the Second World War* (New York, 1956), pp. 80–81.

actually opposed any draft at all. "If I can get the vote of any Senator for something positive in this situation by changing the age from 18 to 95," Bailey asserted, "I will put it in." Critics also held that drafting citizens into the armed forces in order to defend the country was not analogous to drafting workers into essential war jobs, since the federal government employed the soldiers and private industry employed the workers. Scorning this argument, Bailey caustically asked "when did we get to the doctrine that the men who manufacture the munitions are not working for the United States?" He chiefly complained that the substitute provided no penalties for uncooperative workers either in fines and imprisonment or in special work units. The substitute was not a "work-or-fight" bill, but rather a "watch-and-wait" or "wait-and-see" measure. Without the element of compulsion, workers could not be effectively channeled into essential jobs or kept there. With considerable sarcasm Bailey observed that under the substitute, "if a worker is held to be necessary and indispensable, and is told where to work, and is given transportation, if he does not go, but chooses to stay at home, he must stay there and do nothing. That is terrible punishment, is it not?"[26]

Always cool to national service proposals, the Senate opposed compulsory or "work-or-fight" provisions. The committee measure itself bogged down in amendments and substitute proposals, of which the one offered by Chapman Revercomb (R., W.Va.) received greatest attention. The Revercomb substitute invoked the compulsory principle for those persons not engaged "in a lawful occupation"—presumably only loafers, gamblers, prostitutes, and a few others would have been affected. The issue of compulsion was tested on March 7 when the Senate rejected, 60 to 23, an amendment by Bailey to insert in lieu of the phrase "in a lawful occupation" the words "in an activity, profession, occupation, or industry essential to the war effort." Bailey declared that "there are those among us who believe in the compulsory principle. . . . That principle was invoked with respect to more than 10,000,000 American young men. . . . If the principle was fair with respect to them, it is fair with respect to those whose efforts are needed to produce war materials. . . . My whole case against the voluntary principle is that it will not do the work."[27] On March 8 the committee substitute passed 63 to 16, with

26. *Congressional Record*, 79th Cong., 1st Sess., pp. 1552–1558.
27. *Ibid.*, pp. 1776–1777.

Bailey voting "Nay." The conference committee later rejected the May bill for the Senate bill, but added provisions for "freezing" labor in essential war activities and for penalizing workers who voluntarily left such jobs without approval from the director of the Office of War Mobilization and Reconversion. The compromise bill was, therefore, too weak for supporters of "work-or-fight" legislation and too strong for advocates of the voluntary principle. Although the House narrowly accepted the conference report on March 27, by early April the apparent need for such legislation had passed because of successes of American and allied armies in Germany. The Senate rejected the conference report on April 3 by a vote of 46 to 29. Only twenty senators of the sixty that originally voted for the bill supported the conference report, but Bailey, considering the compromise better than nothing at all, voted for it. Thus ended efforts to secure national service legislation.[28]

Accumulated strains of the war period found release during the trying winter of 1945–46 in strikes by coal, auto, steel, and other workers. The number of idle man-days of labor increased each month until in January, 1946, over 3 per cent of available working time was lost. Labor leaders demanded price control without wage control, which Bailey thought would spell profit control and, indeed, no profits whatever for business. The key to successful reconversion was production, but "wage increases brought about by arresting production must be inflationary and really worthless."[29] Incessant strikes endangered President Truman's stabilization program and arrested the essential process of reconversion. "If I could give President Truman some advice," Bailey wrote in February, 1946, "I would tell him to stand up for the right and wise course, firmly and without compromise, let the consequences be what they may. I think the time has come when this must be the course or the consequences will be beyond description."[30] Work stoppages continued to increase, and the stabilization line collapsed in mid-February when steel unions received significant wage increases and the steel industry raised prices correspondingly. The coal and railroad unions, however, refused to settle for the steel wage-increase pattern, shutting down the mines on April 1 and beginning a nationwide railroad strike on May 23.

28. New York *Times*, March 8–April 12, 1945.
29. Bailey to Robert B. Woodwon, May 10, 1946, *Bailey Papers*.
30. Bailey to Robert M. Gantt, February 6, 1946, *Bailey Papers*.

Although Truman seized both industries, railroad employees continued to strike against the government. Truman requested on May 25 emergency powers to break strikes against the federal government in vital industries by subjecting strikers to induction into the Army. Two hours later the House overwhelmingly approved the President's recommendations. The Senate passed the Case Anti-Labor Bill, which watered down the National Labor Relations Act, brought unions under the Clayton Anti-Trust Act's ban on secondary boycotts, and repealed the Norris-LaGuardia Anti-Injunctions Act. Bailey, who was ill at the time, did not vote, but was announced in favor of the Case bill, as he was also on the President's labor bill, which the Senate approved with the draft-strikers clause removed on May 31, 1946.[31] Neither bill became law, but both clearly demonstrated that the temper of Congress had been inflamed by irresponsible activities of major labor organizations and presaged enactment of the Taft-Hartley Act in 1947.

The stresses of war aroused Bailey's deep abhorrence of abuse of power. He knew that labor generally had responded without reservation to war production needs, but he resented wartime strikes, the autocratic administration, the enforced maintenance of membership, the improper handling of dues, and the political activities of many unions. Organized labor had benefited from the National Labor Relations Act and the sympathetic attitude of Roosevelt's administration as demonstrated by the spread of collective bargaining throughout industry and by the 50 per cent increase in union membership between December, 1941, and August, 1945. Bailey approved these benefits, but not the methods by which they had been secured. "I think the consequence of the Wagner [National Labor Relations] Act," he asserted, "has been to bring Labor into disfavor and also to throw it into the hands of leaders who are making matters worse for it. The Act gave the leaders too much power, and they have abused it."[32] The federal government had gone far in providing for the workers, but labor leaders agitated for even more power and used that power with no thought whatever of the national interest. The only answer to abuses by labor leaders would be governmental regulation of unions analogous to New Deal regulation of business. Throughout

31. *Congressional Quarterly* (3rd quarter, 1946), pp. 611–613; *New Republic*, CXV (September 23, 1946), 372–374.
32. Bailey to M. L. Smith, March 9, 1946, *Bailey Papers*.

the war emergency Bailey unsuccessfully called for legislation to curtail strikes, stabilize wages, and control union activities. Presidents Roosevelt and Truman eventually recommended similar legislation, and Congress enacted such laws in postwar years. Bailey's record clearly testified to his pro-business bias and his lack of appreciation for militant labor. His position was contradictory, for he approved labor unions and collective bargaining, but disapproved strikes as a means of collective action when more peaceful means of bargaining failed.

Just as World War II led Bailey to approve regimentation of workers to meet defense mobilization demands, it eventually led him to accept greater governmental control over the economy. In prewar years he opposed anything that tended toward managed economy, yet when confronted with exigencies of total war he moved steadily closer to justification of government regulation of every phase of the economic process. As living costs rose during 1941 Roosevelt recommended price control legislation. Bailey remained unconvinced that price control was necessary to halt inflation, although he recognized the need to prevent hardship on consumers. Neither did he favor proposals to curtail purchasing power through heavy taxation. He believed that taxes should be imposed only to meet governmental necessities, not for economic control. Yet he noted that "probably for the first time we are meeting the situation in which farmers, workers, investors and consumers are so directly involved that each class must be considered and then all classes with a view to a national policy that will work out in a just way."[33] After Pearl Harbor, however, he became particularly receptive to administration proposals for converting the nation's economy to the war effort.

Bailey often went further than the administration on controls. For example, the Price Control Bill of 1942 provided for selective rather than overall price control, assuming that control of certain basic commodities would keep all other commodities in line. Bailey argued that price control should be comprehensive, that there was no assurance that some prices could be fixed and others not fixed, and that ultimately the dollar's value must be fixed. War production necessitated governmental expenditures of public money, which would be realized in enormously increased national income, but munitions and other implements of war represented waste not wealth. Consumer

33. Bailey to J. E. Baker, December 2, 1941, *Bailey Papers.*

demand would be vastly augmented while supplies of consumer goods decreased, creating intolerable pressures on price levels. For price control to be effectual, "we must go the whole way and fix the price of everything that is currently bought, and, more important than all else, we have to fix the price of the dollar, because if the dollar varies in value all other prices do."[34]

The Price Control Act of 1942 had several weaknesses. The price administrator's authority to establish ceilings on farm prices was curtailed by an amendment requiring approval of the secretary of agriculture. This amendment, sponsored by Senator Bankhead, passed the Senate by a vote of 48 to 37 with Bailey's support. A more damaging weakness was the provision permitting farm prices to rise to 110 per cent of parity. Although this provision was clearly inflationary, the bill passed the Senate by an overwhelming vote of 84 to 1.[35] In April, however, Roosevelt's "Seven Point Anti-Inflation Program" requested heavier taxation, general commodity price controls, wage stabilization, and credit controls. Subsequently the Office of Price Administration established the General Maximum Price Regulation, which set the highest price charged in March, 1942, as the ceiling on almost all consumer goods. In July the War Labor Board in the "Little Steel" decision declared that wage increases would be permitted only where they had not kept up with the 15 per cent rise in cost of living. Then in September the President requested revision of the Price Control Act to permit, among other things, the fixing of price ceilings on farm products at parity. Roosevelt assured congressmen, who were troubled by recurrent strikes by labor for higher wages, that "at the same time that farm prices are stabilized, wages can and will be stabilized also."[36]

Congress responded by reducing farm price ceilings from 110 to 100 per cent of parity in the Stabilization Act of 1942, but the Senate adopted an amendment that included farm labor costs in figuring parity. The "farm bloc" amendment passed 48 to 43, with thirty-one Democrats and fifteen Republicans in favor. Threatened by a Presidential veto, the Senate subsequently modified the amendment so that farm labor costs would merely be given "adequate weighting."[37]

34. *Congressional Record*, 77th Cong., 2nd Sess., pp. 51–53.
35. *Ibid.*, pp. 189, 242.
36. Roosevelt, *Public Papers and Addresses*, XI, 364.
37. *Congressional Record*, 77th Cong., 2nd Sess., pp. 7594, 7619.

Although Bailey voted both for the inflationary "farm bloc" amendment and for the weakening substitute, his declared intention was not to provide special favors for farmers but rather to cope with the serious problems of farm labor costs and shortages. He observed that "of course the farmers cannot pay the prices that are being paid in the Navy Yards and industries. They cannot pay the prices that the Government pays. At the same time food and clothing must be produced."[38] A partial solution was presented by Senator Tydings' amendment to the Selective Service Bill of 1942 providing for the deferment of farm workers "necessary to and regularly engaged" in farm work. Bailey voted for the amendment, which was approved 62 to 6.[39]

On September 7, 1942, President Roosevelt criticized the Congress for delay in passing the revenue bill. Bailey as a member of the Senate Finance Committee immediately issued a news release noting that the Treasury Department had in July asked the committee to raise two billion dollars more than the House bill provided and then in August called for another two billion dollars increase in taxes. The Finance Committee had held two weeks of public hearings in late July and subsequently had worked from 10 A.M. to 5 P.M. almost every day. "We are now proposing to transfer by taxation from the present war period between 4 and 5 billion dollars per year to the postwar period, in addition to taxes of $23,000,000,000.00," he asserted, but "how to do this without injustice to a great many people whose incomes have not been increased by the war effort is a very grave problem." Bailey declared willingness to call upon the people to pay taxes heroically. He resented suggestions by newspaper columnists that Congress did not want to pass a tax bill before the November elections. "The delay," he protested, "is due wholly to the fact that we are dealing with a problem of the gravest import, and the Treasury has made new plans every few weeks."[40]

The Revenue Act of October, 1942, actually provided for a $3.6 billion increase in taxes in 1943, less than half the amount requested by Roosevelt. During Senate debates, Bailey supported greater depletion allowances and opposed removal of tax-exempt status for city and

38. Bailey to W. H. Brumsey, October 16, 1942, *Bailey Papers.*
39. *Congressional Record*, 77th Cong., 2nd Sess., p. 8645.
40. Bailey news release, September 7, 1942, *Bailey Papers.*

state bonds. He voted increased depletion allowances for large oil, copper, or coal corporations in order to secure certain benefits for North Carolina farmers, whose properties contained small deposits of clay, potash, kaolin, feldspar, or rock asphalt. "The inducement of the war," he argued, "is to get him to mine it all in a year, under the ordinary procedure of our taxation, if there is no proper allowance for depletion, he loses his mine and derives no great profit, for 80 per cent of it all is taken." In preserving tax-exempt bonds, Bailey recognized that the well-to-do benefited directly, but he contended that states and municipalities could sell their bonds at low interest rates only because of the tax-exemption. If taxes were imposed on the income from bonds, then either the bonds would not be sold or the interest rate would have to be increased. "In either event," he pointed out, "the people of the city or State issuing the securities are required to pay higher taxes in order to pay the increased interest on the bonds or the difference on the principal if the bond is sold below par." Ultimately, therefore, the federal government would be placing an indirect tax on the city and state governments, a procedure not in accord with the American system of dual government.[41] While logical, Bailey's argument gave little evidence of his professed willingness to tax heroically in order to meet war costs.

Farm labor shortages and farm price ceilings irritated Congress throughout 1943. In March the Senate voted 40 to 24 to defer all farm laborers from military service and to prevent farm laborers from leaving their jobs without consent from the draft board. The bill (S. 729) made no distinction between essential and nonessential farm workers and consequently merited Bailey's rejection, despite his concern over the shortage and cost of farm labor. Joining Bailey in opposition, however, were only fourteen Democrats and nine Republicans. Of greater importance was the Parity Computation Bill or Bankhead bill (S. 660), which the Senate adopted overwhelmingly. The measure prohibited deduction of subsidies paid to farmers in the computation of parity prices. Roosevelt vetoed it on April 2 on the grounds that it would substantially increase farm prices and living costs. Bailey spoke strongly in favor of sustaining the veto. He won praise not only from James F. Byrnes, director of the Office of Economic Stabilization, who had requested him to make the speech,

41. Congressional Record, 77th Cong., 2nd Sess., pp. 7934, 8026.

but also from Majority Leader Barkley, who declared that "it was a great speech . . . marked by deep conviction as well as profound emotion and a high sense of duty which lifted me out of the bog and mire of little things, I hope onto a firmer foundation and understanding of our problems in this nation and in the Senate."[42] Nevertheless, rather than sustaining the veto, the Senate merely referred the Bankhead bill back to committee, where it died.

In refusing to override the veto, the Senate was influenced by knowledge that Roosevelt planned stronger antiinflation policies. On April 8 the President issued his famous "Hold-the-Line" Order on prices and wages, bringing all items affecting cost of living under controls. However, the coal strikes called by Lewis in the spring and summer raised congressional doubts concerning Roosevelt's ability to stabilize wages and encouraged farm supporters to demand higher farm incomes. Bankhead introduced an amendment to the Agricultural Appropriations Bill to eliminate soil conservation payments from the parity computation formula. Bailey again defended Roosevelt's stabilization program, observing that "if we yield to Mr. Lewis' demands, we can do precisely the same thing with respect to the farmers, and we can justify the demands of John Lewis by yielding to the demands—if there be demands—from the farmers. I am taking my position against the farmer demand and against the labor demand, and for a stable national policy."[43] On June 11 the test vote on Bankhead's amendment revealed again the strength of the "farm bloc" and the division of opinion in the Senate. The amendment was defeated by only one vote, with 36 in favor and 37 against. Curiously, only 18 of the 37 upholding the President were Democrats, while 27 Democrats voted for the Bankhead amendment.[44]

Determined to help Roosevelt "hold-the-line" on prices and wages, Bailey supported the consumer price subsidy program in 1943, although he questioned the policy's soundness. To prevent increased costs of living, the government through the Reconstruction Finance Corporation and the Commodity Credit Corporation purchased certain consumer goods and then resold them at less-than-purchase prices. Although reluctant to commit himself to the theory of the subsidy, Bailey asserted, "I would infinitely rather vote for subsidies

42. *Congressional Record*, 78th Cong., 1st Sess., p. 3031.
43. *Ibid.*, p. 5478.   44. *Ibid.*, p. 5718.

in order to keep the cost of living down and thereby justify me in voting to hold wages and prices where they are, than not vote for them and yield to John Lewis on the one hand and the farmers on the other."[45] Bailey joined thirty-one other Democrats and four Republicans on June 26 against an amendment to the Commodity Credit Corporation Extension Bill that would have prohibited payment of consumer subsidies after June 20. The Senate voted 39 to 37 for the amendment, but the President vetoed the bill.[46] Nevertheless, by February 1944, Bailey had reversed his position on subsidies, a switch probably due in part to his original doubts and in part to growing suspicion that Roosevelt would continue to yield to labor's demands for increased wages.

Bailey also remained divided on the issue of taxation, willing to vote for taxes necessary for financing the war, but unwilling to use the taxing power to create economic controls. In May, 1943, he opposed the popular Ruml "Current Tax Payment" Bill, which passed the Senate 49 to 30. This measure, which did not have Roosevelt's support, provided "forgiveness" of 1942 taxes due in 1943 and "pay-as-you-go" collection of 1943 taxes in 1943.[47] Exhausted by controversy over the Ruml bill, which did not increase tax revenue, Congress begrudgingly considered Treasury Department requests in October for $10.5 billion in new taxes. The revenue bill of 1943, however, raised only about $2 billion in additional taxes, bringing a recommendation from Roosevelt in his State of the Union Message on January 11, 1944, for "a realistic tax law which will tax all unreasonable profits, both individual and corporate, and reduce the ultimate cost of the war to our sons and daughters."[48] Bailey, opposing confiscatory taxation, believed that only the existence of large savings for investment in the postwar period would provide the production and employment necessary for successful reconversion. The revenue bill passed both the House and Senate without record votes, but was immediately vetoed by the President, who described it as "a tax relief bill providing relief not for the needy but for the greedy."[49] In the subsequent congressional revolt, Majority Leader Barkley denounced the veto and resigned his position but was quickly and

45. *Ibid.*, p. 5478.   46. *Ibid.*, p. 6558.   47. *Ibid.*, p. 4448.
48. Roosevelt, *Public Papers and Addresses*, XIII, 37.
49. *Ibid.*, p. 80.

unanimously re-elected. On February 25 Bailey supported the motion
to override the veto, which was adopted 72 to 14.[50] No further tax
increases were made during the war, although in 1945 a Tax Adjustment Act was adopted to rebate taxes and, thereby, to assist postwar
reconversion. Bailey's opposition to what he called "confiscatory taxation" often conflicted with his support for compulsory work-or-fight
legislation.

Bailey's response to Roosevelt's stabilization policies was not consistent. He began the war period advocating a general freeze of all
prices and wages to prevent inflation and undue hardship on consumers, but the Roosevelt administration did not take this position until a
year and half later when price and wage levels were getting out of
control. Bailey generally resisted efforts of farm groups to break the
stabilization line, despite the political repercussions his course might
have in agricultural North Carolina. However, he was never convinced that Roosevelt would firmly resist labor's demands for increased wages. The success of the coal miners under John L. Lewis
justified Bailey's doubts. He willingly voted taxes when revenue was
needed for war efforts, but not to impose economic controls. He
opposed war profiteering by greedy individuals and groups, but was
unable to cope with the problem of taxing these groups without
damaging taxpayers who had not profited from the war effort.

After V-J Day, Bailey believed that the nation had real opportunity
to end artificial stimulants and economic controls and to return to
normal operation of business, agriculture, and industry. He noted that
the American people had accumulated vast savings, but that there
were great shortages of durable consumer goods. He saw the situation
not as an invitation to inflation, but as a means to full production and
employment. He recognized that conversion from a war to peacetime
economy required some regulation and opposed crippling amendments to the Price Control Act. He did not want the Office of Price
Administration to become permanent, but would extend its operation
until mid-1947 when he believed any danger of inflation would have
passed. He asserted that the reforms and restraints instituted since
1933 would prevent repetition of the economic blunders of the
1920's, but he considered it unwise for the Democratic party to attempt major reforms in the near future. Having experienced twelve
full years of reform, he proposed, "Let us consolidate our progress

50. *Congressional Record*, 78th Cong., 2nd Sess., p. 2050.

but not try to reform every day of the year for an indefinite time. People get tired of reform even when it is a good thing. . . . The government may do well in restraints and guidance. It should continue to act as umpire but let the ball players do the pitching and the batting and the running."[51] Bailey's conservative philosophy of government remained essentially unchanged.

51. Bailey to George Killion, September 8, 1945, *Bailey Papers.*

CHAPTER THIRTEEN

POLITICAL CULMINATION

"THE YEARS have modified my views to a considerable extent," Bailey admitted following his renomination in the 1942 Democratic primary. Evaluating his twelve years in the United States Senate, he professed that he had always been more of a New Dealer than he had been credited with. He still maintained that the free enterprise system must be preserved, but recognized that preservation depended upon attainment by the federal government of improved conditions for workers and farmers. He had somewhat reconciled himself to an enlarged view of the Commerce and General Welfare clauses in the United States Constitution. "The social objective must be achieved and I hope we may achieve it without running into anything like socialism," he privately acknowledged, but "whatever may be the outcome we must maintain a policy looking to the social objective, that is the elevation of the great masses of men, improvement of their conditions, the education of their children, and all the means of well-being of their families. This may not have been the original objective of the Federal Government, but undoubtedly it is the objective now. All of it must be done in coordination with the States, and the States ought to be more inclined to do their part."[1] His statement represented not so much a change of heart or a modification of basic philosophy as reluctant acceptance of the changing role of government in an urban and industrial society. Although tacitly committed to the social objectives of the welfare state, Bailey could not overcome his deep-rooted suspicion of bureaucratic government, his essentially pessimistic concept of man's nature, or his southern Democratic heritage of white supremacy and states' rights.

Bailey easily triumphed over token Republican opposition in November, 1942, but Democrats across the nation lost heavily. Although the party out of the White House usually gains in off-year congressional elections, the strong conservative upsurge in 1942

1. Bailey to Santford Martin, June 12, 1942, *Bailey Papers.*

added forty-seven Republicans to the House and ten to the Senate. Bailey advised Roosevelt early in December, "I do not think the recent election was by any means a repudiation of yourself. It appears to me that our people are united on your foreign policy and on your war policy. Domestically they are enjoying better incomes and they are not disposed to call for treatment. A successful administration often defeats itself for the simple reason that when people are prosperous they cease to be progressive politically."[2] He feared that Republican victories would increase in the next election, but rejoiced that the more militant New Deal Democrats were disappearing. "It is a great pity," he observed, "that our Party has fallen into the hands of a faction of extremists most of whom never were Democrats, and it is a great pity also that it is the Democratic Party which has destroyed States' Rights and it is the Democratic Party which has erected certain labor leaders into the positions of tyrants. It is the Democratic Party that had intensified bureaucracy to such an extent that the people are in revolt."[3] All these things could and should have been avoided, he maintained, and if avoided, the Democratic party would have enjoyed repeated victories.

Democrats held a margin sufficient to retain nominal party control in both the House and Senate. However, the Seventy-eighth Congress, convening in January, 1943, was clearly dominated by a majority coalition of Republican and conservative southern Democrats. While the coalition aggressively supported Roosevelt on essential war measures, the conservative antibureaucratic temper of Congress manifested itself in the liquidation of several New Deal programs. First to go were vulnerable agencies created to provide jobs during the depression—the Works Progress Administration, the Civilian Conservation Corps, and the National Youth Administration. Bailey approved dissolution of these agencies, which had no function in a wartime economy. "I believe the people are 100 per cent behind the President in the war effort," he noted early in 1943, "but they have reacted against the New Deal program, having seen the handwriting on the wall. They know now that there is real danger that this country will become what I have so often warned against—a centralized National Socialism."[4] Bailey, nevertheless, assured the President

2. Bailey to Franklin D. Roosevelt, December 4, 1942, *Bailey Papers*.
3. Bailey to James A. Farley, December 5, 1942, *Bailey Papers*.
4. Bailey to C. L. Shuping, February 19, 1943, *Bailey Papers*.

that he realized how great were his burdens and that he would give him the benefit of every consideration. "This does not mean that I may not differ in some matters," he admitted, "but it does mean that I do not intend to take any action tending to handicap you in the mighty task which is imposed upon you, and on the other hand I shall wish at all times to be as helpful as possible."[5] He failed, however, to support Roosevelt's National Resources Planning Board, which was engaged in developing programs for the postwar period. The board had never been popular with Congress, and when in 1943 it submitted a full production and employment plan for peacetime, conservatives in the House not only killed the plan but also withheld appropriations for the agency. With the tide running strongly against the NRPB, the Senate defeated an amendment by Senator McKellar to provide even token funds by a 43 to 31 vote. Twenty-six Republicans and seventeen Democrats, including Bailey, united against the board.[6]

Early in the session sentiment developed in the Senate for submission to the states of a constitutional amendment limiting service in the presidency to eight years. After carefully canvassing the Senate, proponents of the resolution apparently secured pledges of support from approximately fifty-five senators. According to Arthur Krock of the New York *Times*, the canvassers reached three conclusions: (1) the Democratic majority would give little support to the resolution unless President Roosevelt was clearly exempted from its provisions; (2) the resolution would tend to accelerate efforts to assure Roosevelt's fourth-term nomination unless it was supported by a two-thirds majority, but such a majority would at least place a psychological barrier in way of a fourth term; and (3) the proposal should be made by a Democrat with a strong record of support for the President on foreign policy, "whose assertions of independence in Congress have been chiefly on radical New Deal economic and social legislation." The first problem was solved by providing that the incumbent at the time of ratification of the amendment would serve out his term, and by the physical impossibility of securing ratification by three-fourths of the states before the 1944 elections. The second problem regarding the political effect of the resolution made it necessary to defer presentation until sufficient pledges of support were in hand. The third

5. Bailey to Franklin D. Roosevelt, March 26, 1943, *Bailey Papers*.
6. *Congressional Record*, 78th Cong., 1st Sess., p. 4965.

conclusion concerning the qualification of the sponsor of the resolution pointed to Senator Bailey.[7]

Bailey opposed more than two terms for a President. He had been disturbed in 1940 when Roosevelt sought a third term and feared that the powerful federal machine might be used to continue a President in office for many terms. He wished to discourage a fourth-term nomination by the Democratic party in 1944, but was more concerned with preventing a repetition in the future by another President. Bailey drafted the resolution, but delayed its introduction until he thought it might secure the necessary two-thirds majority. Secrecy was impressed upon those senators and representatives inspecting the resolution for almost a month, but eventually one member leaked the secret to the newspapers. On May 20 Jay G. Hayden of the Detroit *News* reported the plans in the Washington *Evening Star*. Bailey, still not confident of sufficient support, did not introduce the resolution until June 3. "The result was," according to Arthur Krock, "that what was projected as a perfectly timed coup had become almost stale as news when Mr. Bailey finally introduced the resolution." Or, as an advocate of the resolution said, Bailey "failed so long to drop that other shoe that those who were tensely waiting either went to sleep or turned to other things."[8] The resolution received little public attention not only because it lacked surprise, but also because the coal strike attracted the country's attention. The resolution itself was referred to the Senate Judiciary Committee, where it died. On March 12, 1947, a similar resolution passed Congress, and on March 1, 1951, became the Twenty-second Amendment to the United States Constitution.

Politics dominated Congress throughout the winter of 1943–44. Most controversial was legislation introduced by Senators Scott W. Lucas (D., Ill.) and Theodore F. Green (D., R.I.) to provide a federal ballot to facilitate voting by soldiers in the armed forces for the national candidates. The Soldier's Voting Act of September, 1942, had passed so late that only 28,000 soldiers voted under its provisions in the November elections. While providing slight improvement over complicated procedures, the 1942 act involved a time lag which might prevent a voter from receiving the ballot in time to

7. New York *Times*, June 6, 1943, sec. 4, p. 3.
8. *Ibid.*

return it to be counted. The Soldier's Voting Act had passed Congress by substantial majorities, but by 1943–44 the various partisan blocs were aligned differently with both Republicans and southern Democrats favoring a state ballot. As a result, the Senate approved on December 3, 1943, the Eastland-McKellar-McClellan soldier's voting bill, which retained state authority over registration, residence, and poll-tax requirements and recommended to the states enactment of absentee voting legislation for soldiers. Bailey supported the states' rights bill because: "I do not think the Congress can modify or repeal State election laws or fix voters' qualifications, and if it could fix voters' qualifications I hold the view that it is not to the interests of the people of North Carolina to recognize that Congress should do this."[9] Roosevelt, however, charged that the proposed legislation was "a fraud on the soldiers and sailors and marines now training and fighting for us and for our sacred rights. It is a fraud on the American people."[10] Senator Guffey, who strongly backed the Green-Lucas bill, accused northern Republicans and southern Democrats of conspiring to deprive the armed services of the right to vote in the "most unpatriotic and unholy alliance that has occurred in the United States Senate since the League of Nations for peace of the world was defeated in 1919."[11] Guffey quickly found himself buried beneath a torrent of scorn from Byrd and Bailey. Bailey in an unusually bitter and scathing speech threatened secession of southern Democrats from the party and cuttingly observed that "Pennsylvania has produced some lofty men—Ben Franklin, William Penn—and then, it has produced some others—Thad Stevens, Boies Penrose, Mr. Vare, and the junior Senator from Pennsylvania."[12]

Acrimonious debate over the Soldier's Voting Bill resumed in February, 1944, after the House rejected an administration substitute and passed the states' rights bill, which had been denounced by the President. Confronted with the possibility of a veto, the Senate worked out a compromise measure permitting a federal ballot where state authorities certified it as valid under state election laws. The crucial vote came on a motion by John H. Overton (D., La.) to substitute the House bill for the compromise bill. The motion failed

9. Bailey news release, February 1, 1944, *Bailey Papers*.
10. Roosevelt, *Public Papers and Addresses*, XIII, 53–60.
11. Guffey quoted by Harry F. Byrd, *Congressional Record*, 78th Cong., 1st Sess., p. 10344.
12. *Congressional Record*, 78th Cong., 1st Sess., pp. 10345–10348.

Bailey and George stripped lending agencies from the Commerce Dept.

Henry A. Wallace before the Senate Commerce Committee, 1945.

Bailey and Fred Vinson, Director of War Mobilization and Reconversion.

Evolution of a Noble Idea

A view of the May-Bailey National Service Bill of 1945.

with a tie vote of 42 to 42 in which nineteen Democrats, including Bailey, and twenty-three Republicans supported the Overton motion, while thirty-five Democrats, six Republicans, and one Progressive opposed it.[13] The compromise bill, which still provided inadequately for soldiers' votes, passed on March 15 and became law without Roosevelt's signature. Bailey consistently opposed both the administration bill and the compromise bill, but not because he wished to deprive absentee members of the armed forces of the vote or because he particularly feared that the millions of soldiers votes would be cast for Roosevelt in 1944. He voted against each measure on the grounds that both raised the question of the power of Congress to repeal state laws and to determine voters' qualifications. He opposed this in principle and also feared that federal control would spell the end of what he called "southern Democracy"—a way of politics based on white supremacy and restriction of suffrage.

This fear intensified in April, 1944. The Supreme Court in *Smith* v. *Allwright* found Texas' "white primary" unconstitutional since the state itself was inextricably involved with the Democratic party which prevented Negroes from voting in primary elections.[14] This decision amplified and expanded the court's position in *United States* v. *Classic* (1941) that the power of the federal government over elections extended to party primaries in states in which the primaries were determining factors in the election of federal officers.[15] Taken together these decisions greatly improved the political position of the Negro, particularly in the South, but the implications were quite different for Bailey. "The Supreme Court decision is a very serious decision for our people. It practically gives the Federal Government control of our Party and our election machinery. . . . the Federal Government is in position to do all to us that was proposed to be done by the Republicans some years ago by means of a Force Bill."[16] The federal government, having asserted its power to control elections and primaries, would next through the Department of Justice send men into the states to see that Negroes were allowed freedom to vote in elections and primaries. With this in mind, Bailey wrote to Judge J. Ollie Edmunds of Jacksonville, Florida, to offer advice and encour-

13. *Congressional Record*, 78th Cong., 2nd Sess., p. 1267.
14. *Smith* v. *Allwright*, 321 U.S. 649 (1944).
15. *United States* v. *Classic*, 313 U.S. 299 (1941).
16. Bailey to H. G. Gulley, April 5, 1944, *Bailey Papers*.

agement in his Democratic primary struggle with Senator Claude Pepper. Pepper had stepped outside the characteristic southern Democratic mold to compile an impressive record in support of liberal reform legislation, but in Bailey's view, "he has always stood up for the extreme New Deal measures and he has run with that group of Senators from Northern States who have followed the demands of the Negro organizations in the Northern cities."[17]

Bailey saw definite threats to "southern Democracy" in expanding powers of the federal government, in militant demands of northern politicians receptive to wishes of Negro and labor organizations, and, perhaps most significantly, in signs that the "solid South" was crumbling as leaders like Pepper took liberal positions. These trends would continue under Roosevelt, but might be arrested under more conservative presidential leadership. Bailey came out strongly in April, 1944, for a Democratic ticket with Harry F. Byrd for president and James A. Farley for vice president. He questioned whether Roosevelt would seek a fourth term, although he recognized that the Democratic National Convention would surely place his name in nomination. He thoroughly disliked the idea that the Democratic party depended on one man for victory, particularly since he believed that Byrd had all the qualities of a president. Southern Democrats should refuse to take political orders from northern Democrats who paid more attention to the Negro vote in their states than they did to the white people in the South. "If we are to have any recognition in the South," he asserted, "we must let the Northern Democrats know what we want, and also let them know what we can do."[18] Indicative of Bailey's mood at this time was the verbal exchange reported between the Senator and Colonel Edwin Halsey, the secretary of the Senate. "The Colonel was in a joking mood, and turning to Josiah, he said, 'Well, do you think your man [Harry Byrd] will win?' A moment of icy silence ensued. Then Bailey whirled—one of his slow, stately, freezing whirls—and with iron in his soft Southern voice he said coldly, 'You say anything about my man and you'll hear from me!' "[19]

Normal Senate business ground to a halt in May as southerners filibustered against a bill to eliminate the poll tax as a voting qualifi-

17. Bailey to J. Ollie Edmunds, April 8, 1944, *Bailey Papers.*
18. Bailey to O. E. Finch, April 7, 1944, *Bailey Papers.* See also New York *Times*, April 6, 1944, p. 15.
19. Allen Drury, *A Senate Journal, 1943–1945* (New York, 1963), p. 144.

cation. Bailey thought that the anti-poll-tax bill stemmed directly from the political motivations of senators threatened by loss of Negro votes in northern and western states, where the Negro vote might hold the balance of power, and indirectly from pressures exerted by the Political Action Committee of the CIO. Speaking in his slow, academic, but powerful manner, Bailey correctly pointed out that the maintenance of membership policy established by the CIO with governmental support provided not only that a worker must pay union dues to vote in labor contests, but also that he must pay dues in order to work in an industry with a union or closed shop. Under CIO practices, what was at stake was not merely the right to vote, but the right to make a living. "Yet the same people are raising all sorts of riotous sentiment, assaulting the Constitution of the United States, and holding up the Senate in the supreme hours of conflict," declaimed Bailey, "not in protest against the States for depriving a man of his living for failing to pay a poll tax but for simply saying, 'If you have the money and are unwilling to pay it, we do not see why you should vote.' "[20] The same people protesting against the poll-tax requirements of eight states were themselves the chief proponents of the coercive collection of labor-union dues from workers. Not surprisingly, no liberal senator attempted to refute Bailey's contentions. The *New Republic* commented on May 22 that "the truth is that there was not one Senator sufficiently interested in the bill to make a fight of it."[21] On May 15 the Senate laid aside the anti-poll-tax bill, but liberals had made a timely gesture just before the national conventions and presidential election.

During the poll-tax filibuster, Bailey charged that the fight was Communist inspired and that it would be followed by efforts in the national conventions to subvert the Constitution. "I make no threats," he declared, "but I will say that when Sidney Hillman [chairman of PAC] and the Communist crew in the name of the C.I.O. come in the doors and windows of the party in which my father and I lived and served, I will go out."[22] Nor were Bailey's intemperate accusations just for public consumption, for he wrote to Senator Byrd, "What you and I have to consider is that the Communist Party and all the radicals are out front for Roosevelt and endorsing him for a fourth

20. *Congressional Record*, 78th Cong., 2nd Sess., pp. 4245–4250.
21. *New Republic*, CX (May 22, 1944), 709.
22. New York *Times*, May 10, 1944, p. 1.

term. . . . The Committee for Political Action is moving through the country and especially in the South. They will work to purge us and every other self-respecting and honest man who runs for office. . . . I do not intend to stand for it."[23] Bailey did have to stand for it, however, since PAC frightened its archenemy Martin Dies, chairman of the House Un-American Activities Committee, into withdrawing from the Democratic primary contest for renomination in his Texas district and since Sidney Hillman virtually vetoed as unacceptable to labor and northern Negroes the nomination of James F. Byrnes of South Carolina for the Democratic vice presidential nomination.[24] On July 19 the Democrats nominated Roosevelt for president and Senator Harry S. Truman of Missouri for vice president. Bailey accepted the result with what little grace he could muster. He would, of course, "stay in the Democratic party," but he would do what he could "to keep Hillman and his crowd out." Asked if this meant that he would vote for Roosevelt, he replied, "I am a Democrat"—thus reflecting again his deep-rooted belief that no matter how unwise Democratic policies might be they were still better than Republican policies.[25]

In the November general elections Democrats elected the Roosevelt-Truman ticket, regained twenty-five seats in the House, and held their own in the Senate. However, controversial partisan struggles quickly reappeared in the Seventy-ninth Congress, convening on January 3, 1945. Having replaced Henry Wallace with Harry Truman in the vice presidency, Roosevelt had to reward Wallace for "good sportsmanship" in campaigning for the Roosevelt-Truman ticket. While rumors spread that Wallace would be offered a Cabinet post, Bailey and Tom Connally (D., Tex.) conferred with Roosevelt on January 17 about appointing Wallace to the Department of Commerce and transferring incumbent Secretary of Commerce Jesse Jones to a position in which he would retain control of the Federal Loan Agency, which included the Reconstruction Finance Corporation and six other government lending agencies.[26] According to one reporter, "This would give Henry a job, save Jesse's face, and placate Senators who would never vote for Wallace for anything which involved the distribution of funds."[27] Apparently Roosevelt was com-

23. Bailey to Harry F. Byrd, May 22, 1944, *Bailey Papers.*
24. Matthew Josephson, *Sidney Hillman* (Garden City, 1952), pp. 610–635.
25. New York *Times,* September 24, 1944, p. 37.
26. *Congressional Record,* 79th Cong., 1st Sess., pp. 1897–1898.
27. Drury, *A Senate Journal,* p. 342.

mitted to giving Wallace all the powers and responsibilities held by Jones. Bailey recorded that "the President gave no assurances but he was very agreeable and really gracious. . . . It seemed clear that he had made promises to Mr. Wallace and that he could not modify the import of those promises without Mr. Wallace's permission—but he was very nice to us."[28] On Inauguration Day, January 20, 1945, the President notified Jones of his dismissal in favor of Wallace in a letter speaking bluntly of paying off political debts. "Henry Wallace deserves," Roosevelt certified, "almost any service which he believes he can satisfactorily perform. . . . He has told me that he thought he could do the greatest amount of good in the Department of Commerce. . . . It is for this reason I am asking you to relinquish this post for Henry. . . ."[29] The news of Jones's ouster first reached the nation through the Sunday night radio broadcasts. Immediately the Senate divided into liberal and conservative camps.

On February 22 President Roosevelt embarked for his meeting with Churchill and Stalin at Yalta. On the same day Senator George hastily introduced a compromise bill separating the lending agencies from the Department of Commerce. Both the George bill and the Wallace nomination were referred to Bailey's Senate Commerce Committee. The committee on January 23 voted to consider the George bill first, and Bailey announced that Jones and Wallace would testify at public hearings. Jesse Jones, a white-haired, seventy-one-year-old Texas millionaire and darling of the conservatives, appeared on January 24 to warn of the dangers of "amateur experimentation" and "visionary planning" in the administration of the vast lending authority with its resources of thirty-two billion dollars. Bailey came immediately to the point that most concerned him, asking: "Might the powers of the R.F.C. chairman be used to determine the economic direction of the country and affect its whole political and social structure?"[30] Jones's testimony clearly indicated that the concentrated financial power of the federal government's lending offices could be used to expand greatly federal policing of social and economic life. The loan administrator could lend any amount of money for any length of time and for any rate of interest to anybody he felt was entitled to a loan. The RFC owned outright 950 war plants, costing

28. Bailey to Don S. Elias, February 7, 1945, *Bailey Papers.*
29. Bascom N. Timmons, *Jesse H. Jones: The Man and the Statesman* (New York, 1956), p. 354.
30. *Time,* February 5, 1945, pp. 15–17.

six billion dollars, and owned parts of as many plants, which conceivably the government could continue to operate after the war.[31] Congress had unwisely permitted too much power to be concentrated in the hands of one man.

Henry Wallace, reading a seven-thousand-word statement, asserted that the real issue was whether the powers of the RFC would be used only to help big business or to carry out the President's plans for postwar expansion of job opportunities. Roosevelt had proclaimed eight points in his "Economic Bill of Rights," but Wallace proposed that the federal government should *guarantee* the rights to (1) a useful and remunerative job; (2) earnings to provide adequate food, clothing, and recreation; (3) a decent living for farmers; (4) freedom of business from monopoly; (5) a decent home for every family; (6) adequate medical care; (7) broader social security protection; and (8) a good education.[32] He argued for a government-managed economy before a committee the majority of whose members favored less governmental supervision. According to Wallace's biographer, however, "The remainder of the afternoon was on an unusually high plane. The Chairman, Josiah Bailey of North Carolina, a man of no mean mental caliber, engaged with the witness in an extended argument, conducted with mutual respect, on the soundness of governments going deeply into debt in wartime and during reconstruction periods afterwards."[33] Wallace insisted that the federal government must assume responsibility for full employment by planning mobilization of private and public enterprise during peacetime as well as in war. He stressed that the chief danger facing the United States was not budgetary deficit but labor unemployment. Bailey remained unconvinced, noting, "He disclosed not only a program but a method. There was nothing I could see but borrowing and lending money. I am against money spending, and I think this Government is in great danger from it. I am not going to put any man in charge of a department of this Government who is going to bring in the millennium by handing out money in all directions."[34]

The Commerce Committee voted 15 to 4 for the George bill and 14 to 5 against Wallace's nomination on January 26. The committee

31. New York *Times*, January 25, 1945, p. 14.
32. *Ibid.*, January 26, 1945, p. 13.
33. Russell Lord, *The Wallaces of Iowa* (Boston, 1947), p. 552.
34. New York *Times*, January 27, 1945, p. 1.

also added an amendment to the George bill forbidding the President from transferring the lending agencies back to the Department of Commerce. It soon became apparent that there would not be sufficient votes to confirm Wallace unless the Senate first passed the George bill. Supporters of Wallace led by Pepper found their position greatly improved after Wallace indicated willingness to accept the Commerce Department without the lending agencies. Opponents of Wallace, such as Byrd and McKellar, remained dead set against confirmation under any circumstances. Bailey, who was largely the key to the situation, moved on February 1 that the Senate consider Wallace's nomination before taking up the George bill, a move that would have ended almost all chances for confirmation of Wallace. Bailey's motion failed by a 42 to 42 tie, although the record would show a 43 to 41 vote against the motion, since Senator Robert Taft (R., Ohio) changed his vote at the last minute to make it parliamentarily possible for him to demand reconsideration. However, Vice President Truman chose to recognize Majority Leader Barkley, who immediately called up the George bill. Two hours later the Senate passed the George bill by a 74 to 12 vote and postponed further consideration of Wallace's nomination until March 1 in order to permit the House to approve the bill and the President to sign it.[35]

Throughout February Bailey engaged in a personal struggle over his proper course. He had no doubt that Wallace intended "to transfer this government from a government of law and order into a government devoted to full economic responsibility by way of borrowing and loaning money at risk of the government." Having read Wallace's book *Whose Constitution?*, he understood "why the CIO, Sidney Hillman, and the Socialists and Communists are so enthusiastic in his behalf. They intend through Mr. Wallace to capture the Democratic party."[36] The nation had undergone a revolution during the New Deal years, but Bailey believed that the country fast approached a period of revolutionary excesses. "Practically all the restraints upon Federal power have been removed," he complained, "and as matters stand the Congress assumes responsibility for the economic welfare of every group that demands it with sufficient votes. This is subversion itself and the consequences of it can hardly be foreseen. Certainly it means full regimentation of the entire popula-

35. *Ibid.*, February 2, 1945, p. 1.
36. Bailey to W. P. Horton, February 7, 1945, *Bailey Papers*.

tion. . . . This is what Mr. Wallace is driving at."[37] Nevertheless, on March 1 Bailey joined with forty-four other Democrats, ten Republicans, and one Progressive to confirm the nomination of Henry Wallace. The vote was 56 to 32 with five Democrats and twenty-seven Republicans unreconciled.[38] Bailey explained that while he disapproved of Wallace's views and the sources of Wallace's support for President, he gave great weight and respect to Roosevelt's appointments to his Cabinet, particularly since he had intimated in his conference with the President that he would support Wallace if the lending agencies were divorced from the Commerce Department.[39]

As chairman of the Senate Commerce Committee, Bailey was deluged throughout the war period with legislative requests from the Department of Commerce, the Maritime Commission, the War Shipping Administration, the Coast Guard, the Army Engineers, the Pure Food and Drug Administration, and Civil Aeronautics. He considered his responsibilities most seriously and expended his energies in the tedious process of examining proposed legislation with the Executive agencies. The chairmanship brought tremendous power over legislation, which Bailey used to stifle bills that he thought damaging to national interests, but he did not use the committee as a personal steppingstone to national recognition. Early in 1942 he revealed in an unguarded moment his great distaste for the activities of his fellow senators in winning reputations on the basis of congressional committee investigations. He recalled that early in his senatorial career Thomas J. Walsh (D., Mont.) offered him an opportunity to investigate alleged frauds in airmail activities, but had quickly withdrawn the offer in favor of Hugo Black (D., Ala.) after Bailey stated that he "would have a fair investigation . . . and would avoid anything like sensationalism." He expected many investigations during the war, but "as a rule the investigators feel that they must justify themselves and keep the investigation going. Therefore, they must have a mare's nest every few days." He noted that Senator La Follette investigated abridgment of civil liberties by employers, while ignoring similar abridgments by labor unions, and that Senator O'Mahoney produced seventeen unreadable volumes in order to arrive at his initial opinion

37. Bailey to Burton K. Wheeler, February 10, 1945, *Bailey Papers.*
38. *Congressional Record*, 79th Cong., 1st Sess., p. 1616.
39. Bailey to R. T. Holton, March 12, 1945, *Bailey Papers.* Also see *Congressional Record*, 79th Cong., 1st. Sess., p. 1898.

that a federal bureau should license and control corporations. Bailey himself headed a committee to investigate labor conditions in the merchant marine industry. "I inherited this responsibility from Senator Copeland upon his death," he recorded, "and at once put an end to public hearings because . . . only the most sensational matter is reported and therefore a totally false impression is gained."[40]

Bailey's most signal contribution to the war effort undoubtedly came from his co-operation with Rear Admiral Emory S. Land, chairman of the Maritime Commission and administrator of the War Shipping Administration. The Senate Commerce Committee dealt with such problems as buying and leasing foreign merchant vessels for national defense, deciding transportation priorities, providing marine insurance against war losses, refunding charges on frustrated voyages, determining seamen's re-employment rights, and, in the postwar period, selling government-owned merchant vessels. Land declared in a public letter on April 30, 1942, that "at a critical time like this, the nation is particularly fortunate in having at the helm of a committee which, in a great degree, controls the destinies of its maritime affairs, one who has such thorough understanding of the problems involved and the clarity of vision to make vital contribution toward the solution of these problems."[41] Bailey repeatedly defended Admiral Land against charges that the Maritime Commission paid exorbitantly high prices for old ships, insured old ships at excessive values, permitted waste and incompetence in shipyards, and allowed high profits to certain ship operators. He maintained that these charges should be directed against a system, not an administrator, and that they derived from transactions concerning only three or four out of the four thousand shipping companies dealt with by the commission.[42] Early in 1946 when the conference report on the Merchant Ship Sales Bill, which Bailey authored, came before the Senate, Bailey noted that the Maritime Commission had constructed and launched within five years over 5,700 ships averaging 10,000 deadweight tons each. Believing that this achievement set a standard for the nation, he declared that Admiral Land deserved the everlasting gratitude and honor of the country as an inspired public servant.[43]

40. Bailey to H. W. Kendall, February 4, 1942, *Bailey Papers*.
41. Charlotte *Observer*, May 1, 1942, p. 5.
42. New York *Times*, March 31, 1943, p. 10.
43. *Congressional Record*, 79th Cong., 2nd Sess., pp. 1424–1425.

The controversy over the nomination of Henry Wallace and the battle over Roosevelt's request for national service legislation occupied the Senate's attention throughout the first months of 1945, but more important matters soon appeared. On March 1 President Roosevelt, having just returned from his fateful Yalta meeting with Stalin and Churchill, addressed a joint session of Congress. Looking tired and speaking haltingly, the President discussed the two main purposes of the Yalta Conference—bringing about the speedy defeat of Germany and building world peace through the United Nations organization. Urging Senate ratification of the United Nations Charter, Roosevelt declared: "There can be no middle ground here. We shall have to take the responsibility for world collaboration, or we shall have to bear the responsibility for another world conflict."[44] Six weeks later, on April 12, 1945, the President was fatally stricken with a massive cerebral hemorrhage at his favorite retreat at Warm Springs. After thirteen years as architect of recovery from depression and of victory in war, Franklin D. Roosevelt was dead.

No less for Bailey than for the rest of the nation, Roosevelt's death brought shock and a distressing sense of loss. Bailey had often opposed Roosevelt's domestic programs and suspected his political motivations, but he admired and respected Roosevelt's dynamic leadership and courage. Five weeks after the President's tragic passing, Bailey declared,

> President Roosevelt has already taken a place amongst the great men of the ages. He was endowed with the attributes of greatness. He had a will and energy and grasp which set him apart from his fellowmen. He employed these three unusual gifts in the service of the United States and of mankind. It is my judgment that he willingly laid down his life for his country and for all men, and so he added to the three attributes which I have mentioned the attribute of self-denial and of living sacrifice.[45]

Although he had never been an intimate of Harry S. Truman, Bailey noted that Truman had started out well and that the Congress would almost certainly get along better with him than it had with Roosevelt. He characterized Truman as a very thoughtful and careful man who

44. Roosevelt, *Public Papers and Addresses*, XIII, 570–586.
45. Bailey to Cyril Clemens, May 19, 1945, *Bailey Papers*.

did the intelligent thing in a tactful way. Nevertheless, he predicted that Truman as the Democratic presidential nominee in 1948 would face a difficult battle for election, despite the fact that Henry Wallace's political prospects had declined and that Sidney Hillman was about to resign as chairman of PAC.[46]

Senators focused on the United Nations Charter between late April and late July, but there was no doubt about Bailey's position. In May, 1942, he had observed in reference to the First World War that "our soldiers and sailors won that war, but our politicians proved unworthy of their valor and did not finish the task when the power to do so had been placed in their hands, and a prophetic leader—Woodrow Wilson—had pointed the way."[47] He had no intention of proving himself unworthy when confronted with a second opportunity. He considered the Second World War to be the consequence of human folly, for "we were stupid in 1918, 1919, 1920, and 1921—terribly stupid, I might say criminally stupid. We had the world in our hands in 1918, and we had peace only for the asking. We could have avoided all this which we are now of necessity enduring."[48] In November, 1943, Bailey voted for the Connally Resolution indorsing Article Four of the Moscow Declaration to establish at the earliest practical date a general international organization. In February, 1944, he supported a bill authorizing appropriation of over one billion dollars for the United Nations Relief and Rehabilitation Administration. On January 24, 1945, he wrote: "I am thoroughly committed to a world peace organization with force and authority to repress aggressors and to that extent to repress war."[49] Early in July, 1945, Bailey informed the people of North Carolina that he supported ratification of the United Nations Charter earnestly and without reservation. He warned, however, that the future security and peace of the United States depended on the people themselves and their determination to maintain the military strength of the country, rather than on treaties. He recognized that there would be well-meant propaganda for disarmament and for pacifism, but he predicted that "if war shall ever come again we will not have two years in which to prepare. I think we

46. Bailey to C. L. Shuping, April 27, 1945, *Bailey Papers*.
47. Address to Carolina Political Union, May 12, 1942, in *Congressional Record*, 77th Cong., 2nd Sess., Appendix pp. 1678–1680.
48. Bailey to Santford Martin, June 12, 1942, *Bailey Papers*.
49. Bailey to Francis F. Bradshaw, January 24, 1945, *Bailey Papers*.

will have less than six months. . . . We must be ready from the outset."[50] The Senate ratified the Charter on July 28 by a vote of 89 to 2. Bailey, who was ill and absent, was announced "Yea."[51]

The formidable energies Bailey had brought to the Senate in 1931 were exhausted by the summer of 1945. Illness drove him from the Senate floor during July and August, and although he returned briefly in September and October, he also missed the last two months of the session. Attending Congress during the first three months of 1946, he appeared to have recovered, but by April illness and age had again taken their toll. On May 15, 1946, Bailey's office issued a statement that the Senator did not intend to resign but would return to his place in the Senate as soon as his health permitted. Bailey did not return. On December 15, 1946, at the age of seventy-three, he suffered a cerebral hemorrhage and died. During the long months of illness preceding his death, he decided not to seek re-election in 1948, suspecting that he would not live that long. He prepared an address to the people of North Carolina which reviewed the present state of the Union and presented his expectations for the future. This last will and testament on public questions read in part:

> I shall always be grateful to the people of North Carolina for the great honor they gave me and the trust they reposed in me. It seemed to me from the outset that the least I could do by way of appreciation was to be honest with them. This I have done.

The Labor Situation

> I could not support a considerable number of measures put forward by President Roosevelt. . . . I voted against the Wagner Act, for example. . . . We now see its consequences. Purporting to avoid strikes, it is an inducement to strike. Proposing to free the working men, it has placed them under the power of labor bosses. . . . The working men ought to be free. They ought to be free to join a union or not to join one. Employers ought also to be free. The labor unions can be made to do bargaining and prevented from dictating. . . . Any individual has a right to work at any given task, but no group of people has a right to injure and punish others in order to dictate terms to their employer. . . . There is no moral right for a group of men

50. Raleigh *News and Observer*, July 4, 1945, p. 3.
51. *Congressional Record*, 79th Cong., 1st Sess., p. 8190.

to strike and hold up the people of this country, preventing others from working and inflicting untold injury upon millions.

Solution to Labor Problems

A government that will not put an end to this sort of thing is not worthy to be called a government. . . . The working men ought to bear in mind that they have the sympathetic good will of their fellow men, and that they lose it only when they permit unwise leaders to put them in the position of ignoring the public interest. . . . We can apply our antitrust laws to monopolistic practices in labor relations just as we can apply them to any other relations affecting commerce among the States—and we should do it. We ought to restore the remedy of injunction to prevent irreparable injury. . . . If collective bargaining shall be preserved, the labor unions must be required to perform their contracts or be held liable in damages. Controversies ought to be settled in our courts of justice, and not by boards, commissioners, or panels.

Political Intentions of CIO

The CIO and the PAC are now invading the Southern States and in particular they are invading the Democratic primaries. . . . The CIO and PAC are political parties and they are united in the American Labor Party—confessedly a radical class party.

The American people will be well advised to realize that the professional Communist proceeds by way of deceit. . . . He intends that the American Labor Party shall take our party over. . . . Amongst other things they propose to overthrow white supremacy in the South, and vote great masses of the ignorant for their foul purposes. If this movement by the CIO-PAC shall succeed there is grave danger that the Democratic Party will go the way of the Liberal Party in England—that is, be absorbed by the Labor Party.

Russian and International Relations

I have been greatly disturbed by the international situation. So far Russia has made a policy of dissent and obstruction. . . . She means to dominate Europe and Asia, and then the whole world. There is evidence that Russia is operating in this country now by way of propaganda and infiltration. . . . If the United

Nations Organization falls, this does not necessarily mean war. It does mean that it will be necessary for us to get along in a world not fully organized for peace, which will be most difficult. We must avoid war, engaging therein only when the independence of this country and the security of our people are plainly at stake. Isolation is obsolete. But internationalism does not predicate that our country must have a hand in every controversy or that we should assume responsibility everywhere. Let us press in all events for a world organization to preserve peace throughout the earth.

Preparedness

This country can get along in the existing circumstances only by way of being armed to the teeth. . . . We must not run the risk of being attacked again. We must avoid war and establish our peace. And in order that we may, we must be so strong that every nation will know that we have the power to crush and to destroy any who rise against us. This is hard doctrine, but it is necessary. We may hope for a time when the nations disarm in the interests of peace, but we must not be the first to disarm. We must not disarm until we know that every other nation is disarming. This is why I am for the selective service and compulsory military training. . . .

Foreign Policy

I do not think we should tie ourselves up with the destiny of the United Kingdom of Great Britian. We should be as friendly as possible with every nation, but should act only in our own self-interest. . . . We must have our own foreign policy—the policy of being strong, firm, and peaceful, and of getting into no controversy except in clear defense of our own country. . . . I shall not support a direct loan for Russia nor for France nor for any other country. It is not wise policy. . . . Other nations will depend upon us and call upon us again and again as long as they find we can be persuaded to borrow money and send it to them. . . . I do not think we should be involved in the small quarrels of the little nations of Europe and other portions of the earth. . . . It is no concern of ours what sort of government Spain may have, or whether Russia is communistic or not, or whether

France is communistic or not. Let them have such a government as they please. Let us preserve the American Republic as received from our fathers and proved by experience.

A Follower of Woodrow Wilson

When I took the oath of Senator I was resolved to preserve this Republic in the true character in which it has served our people so well for 150 years. I was more a follower of Woodrow Wilson than of any other person. It seemed to me he understood the character of our Government and was determined to preserve it. I read all of his works in the interim between my nomination and the time I took my oath as Senator. I do not regret the fight I made, but I do not think it was won. I did my best. We will never know what was averted. I do not think the fight has been lost, although I realize our Republic has been changed to a great degree and very much to its injury. Much may be retrieved that now seems lost.

The Economy

Let me conclude with one remark: Before the war our country had run a deficit of about $3,000,000,000 every year since 1932. No country has ever spent the earnings and the substance of its people as this country has without ruining itself and its inhabitants. The war expenditures were necessary, but there is absolutely no excuse for the extravagant civilian expenditure during the period in which I have been Senator. We must have an end of it and without further delay. We must stabilize our currrency and our economy at the earliest moment possible if we are to avoid disaster and chaos. . . .

It seems to me to be appropriate that at this time I should lay this statement before our people. These are my views, honestly expressed, and I express them in part discharge of the great debt I owe the people of our State.[52]

Early in Bailey's senatorial career, he observed that the Declaration of Independence and the Constitution of the United States were radical expressions only in the sense that they were part of a revolutionary movement, for they were founded upon human experience and

52. Raleigh *News and Observer*, February 17, 1947, p. 5; *Congressional Record*, 80th Cong., 2nd Sess., Appendix pp. 602–603.

produced by men with due appreciation of the past. The true liberal would not disregard the past or the great landmarks of the Founding Fathers, nor would he be guided absolutely by these landmarks. Bailey could assert that he had been a lifelong liberal, for by his definition the true liberal did not believe in the aggrandizement of government at the individual's expense. The liberal worked on the premise that the individual must have the largest degree of liberty consistent with the necessities of order and justice, which were primary purposes of government. The liberal undertook improvement in government and society, but related that improvement to the experience of the nation and to fundamental concepts giving the individual as much freedom as possible. Bailey believed that democracy was inevitably liberal and that in preserving American institutions he in fact preserved the liberal institutions of the Founding Fathers.

Bailey also considered himself a conservative, but conservatism in the United States is bound up in the liberal tradition. He argued that the American Revolution was conservative in that its purpose was not to upset the status quo, but rather to preserve the independence already won in the colonies against the reactionary interference of George III. This interpretation found expression in Bailey's assertions that certain New Deal policies tending toward regimentation were reactionary, since they restored the European conditions from which Americans had revolted. He considered transferal of ultimate power from the people to boards and bureaus reactionary because it created a government of men embodying centralized power and control of the individual to limit his activities.

Bailey's conservatism derived from the writings of Edmund Burke, John Adams, Adam Smith, and Woodrow Wilson. He read Burke's *Reflections on the Revolution in France*, which fortified both his reliance on tradition and his belief that although change was inevitable, it should be directed not to utopian abstractions but to the preservation, renewal, or enlargement of benefits of the past. Adams' *A Defense of the Constitutions of Government of the United States of America* stimulated Bailey's concept of liberty under law and his conviction that true liberty was appreciated only by the few, not by the mass of men who in their unenlightened selfishness responded to appeals for temporarly panaceas to the detriment of their hard-won heritage. Also from Adams probably came much of Bailey's insistence on balance of powers in government and his fear of mass democracy. Bailey studied Smith's *Wealth of Nations*, but his correspondence gives little indication of Smith's influence except for the concept of the liberal economic society in which the market rather than the state regulated economic life through competition and free enterprise. Bailey equated free enterprise with democracy and, consequently, often applied his political beliefs to the economic sphere.

Bailey probably owed his greatest debt to Woodrow Wilson. Wilson's influence is extremely difficult to define, despite the probability that Bailey consciously modeled himself after Wilson. He deliberately studied Wilson's writings, and asserted that he had read all the works by and about Wilson. His correspondence includes specific references to Wilson's *A History of the American People* and *Constitutional Government in the United States*, as well as to presidential messages, but nowhere did Bailey acknowledge the precise nature of his indebtedness. Bailey did admit that he had followed Woodrow Wilson more than any other person, but only certain broad points of similarity can be indicated. Both Wilson and Bailey shared a reasoned philosophy of government, of statesmanship, of economics, and of social change and reform.

For Wilson and Bailey government should impartially mediate between extremes for the common interest, but do nothing for the people that they could do better for themselves through individual, community, or state activities. The role of a constitutional statesman was one of stewardship—a preserving of traditions and institutions in the public interest and avoidance of concern for narrow special interests. Pessimistic about the ability of the people to govern themselves, both men respected the representative system of government as the only means of providing that unhurried marshaling of thought and study necessary for passage of constructive legislation. Although each accepted conventional laissez faire and disliked governmental interference in business or social affairs, they nevertheless appreciated the government's responsibility in relieving the suffering of its people and in regulating destructive business and labor activities which endangered the general welfare. Both found rapid experimentation and unnecessary change repugnant, but each saw need for continual growth and reform of institutions and laws in order to preserve the democratic character of the American system. Recognized as outstanding orators, neither possessed warm and magnetic personalities that won friends or personal popularity. Facing United States intervention in foreign conflicts, each initially pursued courses of hopeful neutrality, although convinced that England and France must be saved from German aggression. After United States entry into war, both men set aside for the emergency's duration many of their most heartfelt convictions and accepted an authoritarianism that would have been unthinkable in peacetime. Had Bailey served in the United States Senate during Wilson's administration, he might have been considered a liberal. Under Roosevelt and in reference to New Deal domestic programs he was properly designed a conservative.

He was not unequivocally opposed to the New Deal, despite the legend nurtured by friend and foe as each viewed Bailey's course through partisan eyes. The fierceness of political struggles during the New Deal obscured Bailey's real record. In the first two years of the New Deal the extremity of the depression encouraged the attitude that the only fatal thing was not to try something radical as compared with previous policies. Many people gave unrestrained loyalty to Roosevelt and looked upon anyone who differed with the President as reactionary or obstructionist. The nation subsequently divided into those persons who considered Roosevelt as the savior of the country and those who viewed him as a radical visionary determined to mold society in the fires of revolution. Bailey's opposition to many key New Deal measures appeared to some a deliberate attempt to sabotage the President's efforts to lead the country from depression into wholesome prosperity and to others a valiant, last-ditch stand against the encroachments of socialism. Neither view was accurate.

Bailey saw himself in the great tradition of statesmanship in a struggle against political expediency. The citizen should value as the highest possible service from his representative a complete dedication of intelligence and character to independent consideration of public problems and hold in low esteem concessions made by politicians to temporary and uninformed public opinion. Bailey fulfilled in considerable measure his own definition of leadership and statesmanship. Yet he was limited in his approach to innovation by an ideology that defined democracy in political and legal terms and largely excluded government from the economic and social needs of citizens. At subsequent stages in his half-century of political service, he was called a dangerous radical, a progressive liberal, a constitutional conservative, and a reactionary obstructionist. His views throughout had not changed, only matured. He accepted the New Deal revolution with difficulty and incompletely. Always a spokesman of the past, he looked nevertheless to the future. More often than not, he correctly envisioned the centralizing trend of New Deal programs, while his critics viewed them only in relation to immediate self-interest. Bailey's perspective was one-sided, for he expected the worst from change rather than the best. His faith centered upon tested laws and traditions, rather than upon men. This faith was both his greatest strength and his great weakness. Yet during a period of intense national turmoil, of rapid change and experimentalism, which saw the rise of demagogues on both the Left and the Right, Bailey's moderate and thoughtful consideration of issues served his state and his nation well.

Selected Bibliography

I. Primary Sources

A. *Manuscripts*

Josiah William Bailey Papers. Manuscript Department, Duke University, Durham, N.C. This collection comprises over one-half million pieces, of which about one-fifth represents Bailey's correspondence between 1900 and 1930, and of which the remainder represents his correspondence during his senatorial career. Bailey apparently kept copies of almost every letter he wrote. Since his idea of a letter was several pages of typed analysis and explanation, the Bailey Papers provide an invaluable commentary on his life and times. Most valuable is the extensive correspondence between Bailey and Franklin D. Roosevelt, James A. Farley, O. Max Gardner, Newton D. Baker, Josephus Daniels, and Senators Harry F. Byrd, Peter G. Gerry, Walter F. George, Millard G. Tydings, Arthur H. Vandenberg, and Burton K. Wheeler.

The Bailey Papers have been neither edited nor catalogued, but remain in the same general "order" imposed by Bailey's secretaries. There are approximately 40 standard filing cases with four drawers each arranged in the following order: Personal and Political, 1900–1930 (32 drawers); Agricultural, 1930–46 (8 drawers); Banking 1931–46 (2 drawers); Civil Service, 1931–46 (2 drawers); Communism and Fascism (1 drawer); Economy, 1931–46 (1 drawer); Education, 1930–45 (1 drawer); Food and Drugs (1 drawer); Foreign Policy, 1930–40 (2 drawers); General, 1931–46 (15 drawers); Housing Industry, 1936–46 (1 drawer); Interior, 1931–40 (1 drawer); Interior, 1941, Jews, Justice, 1931–35 (1 drawer); Justice, 1936–46, (2 drawers); Labor Management, 1931–46 (5 drawers); Legislation, Bills and Speeches, 1929–46 (4 drawers); Lend-Lease, 1939–46 (2 drawers); Medical, (1 drawer); National Defense, 1936–46 (4 drawers); Navy and Marines, 1930–46 (3 drawers); Patronage, 1930–46 (23 drawers); Political and Miscellaneous, undated (2 drawers); Post Office, 1930–46 (4 drawers); Prohibition, 1930–46 (1 drawer); Railroads, 1925–46 (1 drawer); Relief, 1930–46 (4 drawers); State Department, 1930–46 (2 drawers); Supreme Court,

1937–46 (2 drawers); Tax and Tariff, 1930–46 (5 drawers); TVA, 1932–36 (1 drawer); Trade and Commerce, 1930–46 (7 drawers); Treasury Department, 1930–46 (1 drawer); Veterans, 1930–46 (6 drawers); War Department, 1931–46 (6 drawers); Newspaper Clippings, undated (3 drawers); Typed materials, undated (3 drawers).

William E. Borah Papers. Manuscript Division, Library of Congress, Washington, D.C. This extensive collection was particularly valuable for Republican reaction to the Supreme Court Reorganization Bill in 1937.

Tom Connally Papers. Manuscript Division, Library of Congress, Washington, D.C. The legislative file by subject offered a running commentary of the 71st to 78th Congress, but apparently has been severely edited.

Constitutional Democracy Association Papers. Manuscript Division, Library of Congress, Washington, D.C. The CDA was organized to fight the Supreme Court Reorganization Bill. Papers contain week-to-week counts on senators opposing the bill.

Josephus Daniels Papers. Manuscript Division, Library of Congress, Washington, D.C. These papers most clearly reveal the liberal opposition to Bailey among North Carolinians, as well as Daniels' senatorial prospects in 1936.

Robert L. Doughton Papers. Southern Historical Collection, University of North Carolina, Chapel Hill, N.C. Doughton, chairman of the House Committee on Ways and Means, was undoubtedly the most influential North Carolina congressman during the New Deal and World War II.

Governors' Papers. State Department of Archives and History, Raleigh, N.C. These papers are most valuable for New Deal activities in the state, particularly those of O. Max Gardner, J. B. Ehringhaus, and Clyde Hoey.

Clyde R. Hoey Papers. Duke University Library, Durham, N.C. Hoey, elected Senator in 1944, served with Bailey until 1946. There is little correspondence between the two senators, but the papers reveal attitudes of Congress in that difficult transition period.

Santford Martin Papers. Duke University Library, Durham, N.C. Martin, editor of the Winston-Salem *Journal*, frequently corresponded with Bailey, but their friendship gradually cooled during the New Deal period.

North Carolina Collection. University of North Carolina, Chapel Hill, N.C. This collection of political pamphlets and broadsides provides an invaluable record of the bitterly fought primary and election campaigns.

The White House Papers of Franklin D. Roosevelt. Franklin D. Roosevelt Library, Hyde Park, N.Y. These were particularly helpful for the period between 1939 and 1945, when Bailey's activities as chairman of the Senate Commerce Committee brought frequent contact with Roosevelt.

Furnifold M. Simmons Papers. Duke University Library, Durham, N.C. These papers were most rewarding for the North Carolina political situation between 1927 and 1930.

Lindsay Carter Warren Papers. Southern Historical Collection, University of North Carolina, Chapel Hill, N.C. As a United States Representative between 1924 and 1954, Warren worked closely with Bailey on many North Carolina projects.

B. *Government documents*

Ashton v. Cameron County District, 298 U.S. 513.

Biographical Directory of the American Congress, 1774–1949. Washington: Government Printing Office, 1950.

Carter v. Carter Coal Co., 298 U.S. 238.

Congressional Record. 72nd Congress, 1st Session—79th Congress, 2nd Session. Washington: Government Printing Office, 1931–46.

Labor Board v. Jones & Laughlin, 301 U.S. 1.

Morehead v. Tipaldo, 298 U.S. 587.

Railroad Retirement Board v. Alton Railroad Company, 295 U.S. 330.

Smith v. Allwright, 321 U.S. 649.

United States v. A.L.A. Schecter Poultry Corporation, 295 U.S. 495.

United States v. Classic, 313 U.S. 299.

U.S. Bureau of the Census, *Historical Statistics of the United States, Colonial Times to 1957.* Washington: Government Printing Office, 1960.

Virginian Railway v. Federation, 300 U.S. 515.

West Coast Hotel Co. v. Parrish, 300 U.S. 379.

Wright v. Vinton Branch, 300 U.S. 440.

C. *Bailey's speeches, articles, and political pamphlets*

Announcement of the Candidacy of J. W. Bailey for the Nomination for Governor. Raleigh: Bynum Printing Company, 1924.

"Argument for legislation in Bailey-Walter Bill," *Congressional Digest,* XXIII (October, 1944), 243 ff.

"Beware of Political Control," *Christian Science Monitor Weekly Magazine,* (February 16, 1938).

Biblical Recorder, 1895–1907.

"The Call of the Cardinal," *Progressive Farmer,* LXII (March, 1947).

"The Case for the South," *Forum* (April, 1901), pp. 226–230.

"Condition of the Farmers in North Carolina." Raleigh, 1921.

"The Democratic Process," *Vital Speeches of the Day,* IV (July 1, 1938), 550–553.

"Essentials for Permanent Recovery," *Proceedings of the Academy of Political Science,* XVIII (May, 1938–January, 1940), 43–45.

Four Services of Progress. Raleigh, 1922.

Governor Smith and National Prohibition. Raleigh, 1928.

The Grounds of Democratic Hope. Raleigh, 1909.

"May the Democratic Party Look to the South for National Restoration?" *Reviewer* (October, 1925), pp. 43–49.

The Issues of the Campaign. Raleigh: Allied Printing Company, 1924.

Needed Changes in Our Tax System: The Only Way to Relieve Land of the Ever-Increasing Burden. Raleigh: Allied Printing Company, 1924.

On Religious Liberty. Raleigh, 1928.

"Our Republic: It Must Be Preserved," *Vital Speeches of the Day,* VII (August 1, 1941), 633–637.

"The Political Treatment of the Drink Evil," *South Atlantic Quarterly,* V (April, 1907), 109–124.

"Popular Education and the Race Problem in North Carolina," *Outlook,* LXVIII (May 11, 1901), 114–116.

The Popularity of Governor Alfred E. Smith. Raleigh, 1928.

Proposed Constitutional Amendment on Taxation. Raleigh, 1920.

The Republican Failure and the Democratic Program. Raleigh, 1932.

The Revaluation Act, Its Effect upon Taxation. Raleigh, 1920.

"Senator Josiah W. Bailey Reviews the Work of Congress," *Biblical Recorder* (September 4, 1935).

"A Senator's Opinion," *Vital Speeches of the Day,* VII (March 1, 1941), 211–214.

"Shall Wages Be Regulated?" *Christian Science Monitor Magazine* (February 16, 1938), pp. 1–2.

"Some Thoughts on Lynching," *South Atlantic Quarterly,* V (October, 1906), 349–354.

"Speech in the Senate," *Vital Speeches of the Day,* III (August 1, 1937), 618–621.

Simmons—Organizer of Victory. Raleigh, 1912.

"The Supreme Court, the Constitution, and the People," *Vital Speeches of the Day,* III (March 1, 1937), 290–295.

A Valuable Message to the Farmers of North Carolina. Raleigh, 1927.

"Vested Interest in Public Spending," *Saturday Evening Post* (February 2, 1935), pp. 5–7.

The Way to Progress in North Carolina. Raleigh: H. S. Storr Co., 1924.

"Why Not Plan for Recovery," *Review of Reviews,* XCI (March, 1935), 29–30.

Why the Democrats Should Nominate Governor Smith for President. Raleigh, 1928.

D. *Collected sources, papers and memoirs*

Barkley, Alben W. *That Reminds Me.* New York: Doubleday & Company, 1954.

Brooks, A. L., and Lefler, H. T. (eds.). *The Papers of Walter Clark.* Chapel Hill: University of North Carolina Press, 1950.

Byrnes, James F. *All in One Lifetime.* New York: Harper & Brothers, 1958.

Connally, Tom, as told to Alfred Steinberg, *My Name Is Tom Connally.* New York: Thomas Y. Crowell, 1954.

Corbitt, David Leroy (ed.). *Addresses, Letters, and Papers of John Christoph Blucher Ehringhaus.* Raleigh: Council of State, State of North Carolina, 1950.

————. *Public Papers and Letters of Angus Wilton McLean, Governor of North Carolina, 1925–1929.* Raleigh: Council of State, State of North Carolina, 1931.

Daniels, Josephus. *Editor in Politics.* Chapel Hill: University of North Carolina Press, 1941.

Drury, Allen. *A Senate Journal, 1943–1945.* New York: McGraw-Hill, 1963.

Farley, James A. *Behind the Ballots.* New York: Harcourt, Brace, 1938.

————. *Jim Farley's Story: The Roosevelt Years.* New York: McGraw-Hill, 1948.

Flynn, Edward J. *You're the Boss.* New York: Viking Press, 1947.

Gill, Edwin (comp.), and Corbitt, David Leroy (ed.). *Public Papers and Letters of Oliver Max Gardner, 1929–1933.* Raleigh: Council of State, State of North Carolina, 1937.

Hoover, Herbert. *Addresses upon the American Road, 1933–1938.* New York: Charles Scribner's Sons, 1938.

————. *The Memoirs of Herbert Hoover.* 3 vols. New York: Macmillan, 1951–52.

Hull, Cordell. *The Memoirs of Cordell Hull.* 2 vols. New York: Macmillan, 1948.

Ickes, Harold L. *The Secret Diary of Harold L. Ickes.* 3 vols. New York: Simon and Schuster, 1953–54.

Kilpatrick, Carroll (ed.). *Roosevelt and Daniels.* Chapel Hill: University of North Carolina Press, 1952.

Lefler, Hugh T. (ed.). *North Carolina History Told by Contemporaries.* Chapel Hill: University of North Carolina Press, 1933.

Moley, Raymond. *After Seven Years.* New York: Harper & Brothers, 1939.

Myers, William Starr (ed.). *The State Papers and Other Public Writings of Herbert Hoover.* 2 vols. New York: Doubleday, Doran, 1934.

Poe, Clarence. *My First Eighty Years.* Chapel Hill: University of North Carolina Press, 1963.

Richardson, William H. (comp.), and Corbitt, D. L. (ed.). *Public Papers and Letters of Cameron Morrison, Governor of North Carolina, 1921–1925.* Raleigh: Edwards & Broughton, 1927.

Rippy, J. Fred (ed.). *F. M. Simmons: Statesman of the New South, Memoirs and Addresses.* Durham: Duke University Press, 1936.

Roosevelt, Elliott (ed.). *F. D. R.: His Personal Letters, 1928–1945.* 2 vols. New York: Duell, Sloan, and Pearce, 1950.

Rosenman, Samuel I. (ed.). *The Public Papers and Addresses of Franklin D. Roosevelt.* 13 vols. New York: Random House, 1938–50.

————. *Working with Roosevelt.* New York: Harper & Brothers, 1952.

Stimson, Henry L., and Bundy, McGeorge. *On Active Service in Peace and War.* New York: Harper & Brothers, 1947.

Tully, Grace. *F. D. R.: My Boss.* New York: Charles Scribner's Sons, 1947.

Vandenberg, Arthur H., Jr. *The Private Papers of Senator Vandenberg.* Boston: Houghton Mifflin, 1952.

Watson, Richard L., Jr. (ed.). *Bishop Cannon's Own Story: Life as I Have Seen It.* Durham: Duke University Press, 1955.

Zevin, B. D. (ed.). *Nothing to Fear: The Selected Addresses of Franklin Delano Roosevelt, 1932–1945.* Boston: Houghton Mifflin, 1946.

E. *Political pamphlets and broadsides*

Al Smith–Raskob–Bailey: Idea of Happiness. 1930.

Alexander, H. Q. *Some Facts that the People Generally, and Especially the Farmers, Should Read and Consider.* 1924.

An Attempted Fraud and Fake Intended to Deceive the Labor Vote of North Carolina. Raleigh: Allied Printing Trades, 1930.

Bailey Advocated Higher Taxes for Farmer/Senator Simmons the Farmers' Friend. Raleigh, 1930.

Broughton, J. M. *Bailey's Record on Liquor and the Liquor Traffic. Farms and Small Homes: Reply to an Anonymous Circular.* 1930. Raleigh, 1930.

Bailey's Great Record as a Democrat and as an Opponent of Taxation of

Bunn, J. W. *Simmons Raises Negro Racket: Eleventh Hour Desperation.* Raleigh: Allied Printing Trades, 1930.

The Candidacy of Josiah W. Bailey for United States Senator Endorsed by Democratic Women in Town and Country Throughout North Carolina. 1930.

The Case Against Senator Simmons. Raleigh, 1930.

Dalton, William R. *The Deadly Parallel.* 1930.

Dickens, O. W. *The Labor Vote Be Hanged.* 1930.

Grantham, G. K. *When Did Bailey Become the Friend of the Farmer?* Dunn, N.C., 1924.

Gulley, N.Y. *Josiah W. Bailey: A Brief Sketch.* Raleigh, 1924.

Hampton, Frank A. *For the Senate—Furnifold M. Simmons—Farmer, Lawyer, Statesman—Plain Statement of a Great Record.* Washington, N.C., 1930.

Hines, Charles A. *Let Us Reason Together: Shall We Stone the Prophet?* 1930.

Josiah W. Bailey Battling for Certain Great Causes. Raleigh: Allied Printing Co., 1924.

Land, E. M. *Why Defeat Simmons?* Raleigh, 1930.

Langston, John D. *Can North Carolina Afford to Pay the Price?* 1930.

———. *The Issue Clearly Defined: The Fight on Simmons Is a Liquor Fight.* 1930.

Let Us Have an End of Cut Throat Politics in the Democratic Party. Raleigh, 1930.

McLendon, L. P. *For U.S. Senator: Josiah W. Bailey.* Raleigh, 1930.

Noell, J. W. *Women under a Double Obligation.* Raleigh, 1930.

Party Loyalty and Simmons. Raleigh, 1930.

Ray, T. J. *Bailey Stands by the Party, But Not the Democratic Party.* 1930.

Simmons, F. M. *Exposure and Denunciation of the Tammany–Smith– Rascob Coalition for Destruction of Prohibition, Restricted Immigration and Jeffersonian Principles.* Charlotte, 1928.

Simons Talks to First Voters. Raleigh, 1930.

Tammany and North Carolina Negroes Would Defeat Simmons. 1930.

Taylor, J. A. *Political Irregularity and Precedent.* 1930.

A Tree is Known by the Fruit: Being an Answer to Attacks of Bailey and His Campaign Managers on Senator Simmons. 1930.

The Truth about 'Hog and Ham.' Raleigh: Allied Printing Company, 1924.

When the Farmers Needed a Friend. 1924.

Why Defeat Simmons? The Answer to a Question Propounded by Mr. Ed. M. Land. Raleigh: Allied Printing Trades, 1930.

II. SECONDARY SOURCES

A. *Newspapers and periodicals*

Asheville *Citizen*, selected copies.

Biblical Recorder, selected copies.

Business Week, selected copies.

Charlotte *Observer*, 1920–46.

Chicago *Tribune*, selected copies.

Commercial and Financial Chronicle, selected copies.

Congressional Digest, 1931–46.

Congressional Quarterly, 1945–46.

Current Biography, selected copies.

Durham *Herald*, 1926–46.

Elizabeth City *Independent*, selected copies.

Fortune, selected copies.

Fayetteville *Peoples Advocate*, selected copies.
Greensboro *Daily News*, 1920–46.
New Republic, 1931–46.
New York *Times*, 1928–46.
Newsweek, selected copies.
Outlook, selected copies.
Philadelphia *Inquirer*, selected copies.
Raleigh *News and Observer*, 1916–1946.
State (Raleigh), selected copies.
Time, selected copies.
Washington *Star*, selected copies.
Winston-Salem *Journal*, selected copies.

B. *Books*

Alsop, Joseph, and Catledge, Turner. *The 168 Days*. New York: Doubleday, Doran, 1938.

Bernstein, Irving. *The New Deal Collective Bargaining Policy*. Berkeley: University of California Press, 1950.

Brooks, Aubrey L. *Walter Clark, Fighting Judge*. Chapel Hill: University of North Carolina Press, 1944.

Blum, John M. *From the Morgenthau Diaries: Years of Crisis, 1928–39*. Boston: Houghton Mifflin, 1959.

Burns, James M. *Congress on Trial*. New York: Harper & Brothers, 1946.

———. *Roosevelt: The Lion and the Fox*. New York: Harcourt, Brace, 1956.

Cash, Wilbur J. *The Mind of the South*. New York: Doubleday (Anchor), 1941.

Cronon, Edmund David. *Josephus Daniels in Mexico*. Madison: University of Wisconsin Press, 1960.

Davidson, Elizabeth H. *Child Labor Legislation in the Southern Textile States*. Chapel Hill: University of North Carolina Press, 1939.

Democratic National Committee. *Democratic National Convention, Official Report of the Proceedings, 1928*. Indianapolis: Bookwalter-Ball-Greathouse, 1928.

———. *Official Report of the Proceedings of the Democratic National Convention, June 23–27, 1936*. Philadelphia, 1936.

Edmonds, Helen G. *The Negro and Fusion Politics in North Carolina, 1894–1901*. Chapel Hill: University of North Carolina Press, 1951.

Encyclopedia of Southern Baptists. Vol. I. Nashville: Broadman Press, 1958.

Flynn, John T. *The Roosevelt Myth*. Rev. ed. New York: Devin-Adair, 1956.

Freidel, Frank. *Franklin D. Roosevelt: The Triumph*. Boston: Little, Brown, 1956.

Garber, Paul N. *John Carlisle Kilgo.* Durham: Duke University Press, 1937.

Gatewood, Willard B. *Eugene Clyde Brooks: Educator and Public Servant.* Durham: Duke University Press, 1960.

Hacker, Louis M. *A Short History of the New Deal.* New York: F. S. Crofts, 1934.

Hartz, Louis. *The Liberal Tradition in America.* New York: Harcourt, Brace, 1955.

Haynes, George H. *The Senate of the United States.* 2 vols. Boston: Houghton Mifflin, 1938.

Holder, Rose H. *McIver of North Carolina.* Chapel Hill: University of North Carolina Press, 1957.

Jackson, Robert H. *The Struggle for Judicial Supremacy.* New York: Alfred A. Knopf, 1941.

Josephson, Matthew. *Sidney Hillman.* Garden City: Doubleday, 1952.

Key, V. O., Jr. *Southern Politics in State and Nation.* New York: Alfred A. Knopf, 1949.

Kirk, Russell. *The Conservative Mind.* Chicago: Henry Regnery, 1953.

Knight, Edgar Wallace. *Public School Education in North Carolina.* Boston: Houghton Mifflin, 1916.

Lefler, Hugh T. *History of North Carolina: Family and Personal History.* 4 vols. New York: Lewis, 1956.

Lindley, Ernest K. *Half Way with Roosevelt.* Rev. ed. New York: Viking Press, 1937.

Lord, Russell. *The Wallaces of Iowa.* Boston: Houghton Mifflin, 1947.

McCoy, Donald R. *Angry Voices: Left-of-Center Politics in the New Deal Era.* Lawrence: University of Kansas Press, 1958.

McKenna, Marian. *Borah.* Ann Arbor: University of Michigan Press, 1961.

Malone, Dumas. *Edwin A. Alderman.* New York: Doubleday, Doran, 1940.

Michie, Allan A., and Ryhlick, Frank. *Dixie Demagogues.* New York: Vanguard Press, 1939.

Mitchell, Broadus. *Depression Decade.* New York: Rinehart, 1947.

Morrison, Joseph L. *Josephus Daniels Says. . . .* Chapel Hill: University of North Carolina Press, 1962.

The National Cyclopedia of American Biography. New York: James T. White, 1934.

Nicolson, Harold. *Dwight Morrow.* New York: Harcourt, Brace, 1935.

Orr, Oliver H., Jr. *Charles Brantley Aycock.* Chapel Hill: University of North Carolina, 1951.

Paschal, J. Francis. *Mr. Justice Sutherland: A Man Against the State.* Princeton: Princeton University Press, 1951.

Peel, Roy V., and Donnelly, Thomas C. *The 1928 Campaign.* New York: R. R. Smith, 1931.

————. *The 1932 Campaign.* New York: Farrar & Rinehart, 1935.

Perkins, Dexter. *The New Age of Franklin Roosevelt, 1932–45.* Chicago: University Press, 1957.

Puryear, Elmer L. *Democratic Party Dissension in North Carolina, 1928–1936.* Chapel Hill: University of North Carolina Press, 1962.

Rauch, Basil. *The History of the New Deal, 1933–1938.* New York: Creative Age Press, 1944.

Republican National Committee. *Text Book of the Republican Party, 1936.* Chicago: 1936.

Robinson, Edgar E. *The Presidential Vote, 1896–1932.* Stanford: Stanford University Press, 1934.

———. *The Roosevelt Leadership, 1933–1945.* Philadelphia: J. B. Lippincott, 1955.

Roose, Kenneth D. *The Economics of Recession and Revival: An Interpretation of 1937–1938.* New Haven: Yale University Press, 1954.

Roseboom, Eugene H. *A History of Presidential Elections.* New York: Macmillan, 1957.

Rossiter, Clinton. *Conservatism in America.* New York: Alfred A. Knopf, 1956.

Satterfield, Frances G. *Charles Duncan McIver.* Atlanta: Ruralist Press, 1942.

Scammon, Richard M. *America Votes: A Handbook of Contemporary American Election Statistics.* New York: Macmillan, 1956.

Schlesinger, Arthur M., Jr. *The Age of Roosevelt.* 3 vols. Boston: Houghton Mifflin, 1957–60.

Seidman, Joel. *American Labor from Defense to Reconversion.* Chicago: University of Chicago Press, 1953.

Sherwood, Robert E. *The White House Papers of Harry L. Hopkins.* 2 vols. London: Eyre & Spottiswoode, 1949.

Timmons, Bascom N. *Jesse H. Jones: The Man and the Statesman.* New York: Henry Holt, 1956.

———. *Garner of Texas: A Personal History.* New York: Harper & Brothers, 1948.

Tugwell, Rexford G. *The Democratic Roosevelt.* New York: Doubleday, 1957.

Vandenberg, Arthur H., Jr. *The Private Papers of Senator Vandenberg.* Boston: Houghton Mifflin, 1952.

Wayman, Dorothy G. *David I. Walsh: Citizen-Patriot.* Milwaukee: Bruce, 1952.

Wecter, Dixon. *The Age of the Great Depression, 1929–1941.* New York: Macmillan, 1948.

White, William S. *Citadel: The Story of the U.S. Senate.* New York: Harper & Brothers, 1956.

Whitener, Daniel Jay. *Prohibition in North Carolina, 1715–1945.* Chapel Hill: University of North Carolina Press, 1945.

Wolfskill, George. *The Revolt of the Conservatives.* Boston: Houghton Mifflin, 1962.

Young, Roland. *Congressional Politics in the Second World War.* New York: Columbia University Press, 1956.

C. *Articles*

Altman, O. R. "Second and Third Sessions of the Seventy-fifth Congress." *American Political Science Review,* XXXII (December, 1938), 1099–1123.

———. "Second Session of the Seventy-fourth Congress," *American Political Science Review,* XXX (December, 1936), 1086–1107.

Appleby, P. H. "Roosevelt's Third-Term Decision," *American Political Science Review,* XLVI (September, 1952), 754–765.

Herring, E. Pendleton. "First Session of the Seventy-fourth Congress," *American Political Science Review,* XXIX (December, 1935), 985–1005.

———. "Second Session of the Seventy-second Congress," *American Political Science Review,* XXVII (June, 1933), 404–422.

Jones, Weimar. "North Carolina's New Senators," *Nation,* CXXXII (January 7, 1931), 11.

Nash, Gerald D. "Herbert Hoover and the Origins of the Reconstruction Finance Corporation," *Mississippi Valley Historical Review,* XLVI (December, 1959), 455–468.

Patterson, James T. "The Failure of the Party Realignment in the South, 1937–1939," *Journal of Politics,* XXVII (August, 1965), 602–617.

Riddick, Floyd M. "First Session of the Seventy-sixth Congress," *American Political Science Review,* XXXIII (December, 1939), 1022–1043.

Rogers, Lindsay. "Reorganization: Post Mortem Notes," *Political Science Quarterly,* LIII (June, 1938), 161–172.

Rudolph, Frederick. "The American Liberty League, 1934–1940," *American Historical Review,* LVI (October, 1950), 19–33.

Stern, Robert L. "The Commerce Clause and the National Economy, 1933–1946," 2 parts, *Harvard Law Review,* LIX (May, 1946), 645–693 (July, 1946), 883–947.

Tugwell, Rexford G. "The Compromising Roosevelt," *Western Political Quarterly,* VI (June, 1953), 320–341.

Watson, Richard L., Jr. "A Political Leader Bolts—F. M. Simmons in the Presidential Election of 1928," *North Carolina Historical Review,* XXXVII (October, 1960), 516–543.

———. "A Southern Democratic Primary: Simmons *vs.* Bailey in 1930," *North Carolina Historical Review,* XLI (Winter, 1965), 21–46.

White, John Ellington. "When the Tide Began to Turn for Popular Education in North Carolina, 1890–1900," *Proceedings of the State Literary and Historical Association of North Carolina* (1922), pp. 33–44.

Wilcox, Francis O. "The Neutrality Fight in Congress: 1939," *American Political Science Review*, XXXIII (October, 1939), 811–825.

D. *Unpublished*

Carter, Edward Jennings. "The Educational Awakening in the South." Doctoral dissertation, University of North Carolina, 1943.

Connelly, Owen S. "Amending the North Carolina Constitution, 1868–1948." Master's thesis, Wake Forest College, 1949.

Deskins, S. C. "The Presidential Election of 1928 in North Carolina." Doctoral dissertation, University of North Carolina, 1944.

Donovan, Clement Harold. "The Readjustment of State and Local Fiscal Relations in North Carolina." Doctoral dissertation, University of North Carolina, 1940.

Doughton, Josephine Lane. "Passage of the Sales Tax Law in North Carolina, 1931–1933." Master's thesis, University of North Carolina, 1949.

Steelman, Joseph Flake. "The Progressive Era in North Carolina, 1884–1917." Doctoral dissertation, University of North Carolina, 1955.

Swain, Herbert Lee. "Editorial Views of the Religious Press on Education in North Carolina." Master's thesis, University of North Carolina, 1942.

Thompson, Samuel Hunter. "The Legislative Development of Public School Support in North Carolina." Doctoral dissertation, University of North Carolina, 1936.

Index